AGITPROP

SUNY Series in American Labor History
Robert Asher, Editor

AGITPROP

The Life of an American Working-Class Radical

The Autobiography of Eugene V. Dennett

Eugene V. Dennett

With a Preface by
Jeremy R. Egolf

State University of New York Press

Published by
State University of New York Press, Albany

© 1990 State University of New York

For information, address State University of New York Press, State University Plaza, Albany, NY 12246

Library of Congress Cataloging-in-Publication Data

Dennett, Eugene V., 1908–1989
    Agitprop : the life of an American working-class radical : The autobiography of Eugene V. Dennett / Eugene V. Dennett.
        p.   cm. — (SUNY series in American labor history)
    Includes index.
    ISBN 0–7914–0078–6 — ISBN 0–7914–0079–4 (pbk.)
    1. Dennett, Eugene V., 1908–1989. 2. Trade-unions—United States—Officials and employees—Biography. 3. Trade-unions and communism—United States—History. 4. Trade-unions—Northwest, Pacific—Organizing—History. 5. Communists—United States—Biography.
    I. Title. II. Series.
    HD6509.D46A3   1990
    331.88'092'4—dc19
    [B]   88–31668
                                                                            CIP

To
VALERIE

CONTENTS

ACKNOWLEDGMENTS

Jeremy Egolf approached me as a stranger to ask if I would contribute to labor history because he had been finding my name frequently when he was doing research about the Northwest labor movement.

I was not aware that anybody thought my knowledge of Northwest labor politics had any importance. I had been participating in a seniors' writing class for over three years during which time I had been relating some of my experiences. My senior friends urged me to do a complete story. Egolf also urged me to make full use of my voluminous records, saved over fifty years.

That effort led to a point where I had to take a serious look at the possibilities. Egolf had several communications with Bob Asher who encouraged us to get my manuscript complete. Asher had the manuscript evaluated by some professional readers. Jeremy Egolf assisted me with the difficult job of revising the manuscript in accordance with the suggestions of Dr. Asher and the other readers.

It became clear that the job of revising and editing the manuscript would be easier if it was entered into the memory of a word processor. I had no knowledge about word processors so I asked some friends, who introduced me to Richard Keller, a retired communications expert. He willingly took me in tow to get equipped with a word processor, and spent endless hours teaching me how to use it to prepare this manuscript.

The original writing extended over a five-year period. The editing by Egolf, and my rewriting, has taken three more years; it has truly been a labor of love. I have rejoiced in reliving this exciting past. Egolf has given endless amounts of time editing, correcting my errors, and insisting on cohesive sequences and grammatical corrections.

Without the professional services of Egolf, Keller, and Asher, I wouldn't have been able to complete this project. I owe so much to each of them that I hereby acknowledge their guidance and contributions with grateful thanks.

Eugene V. Dennett
Seattle, Washington
June 27, 1988

PREFACE

Eugene V. Dennett's autobiography is one of the very few we have from regional left-wing Congress of Industrial Organizations (CIO) leaders who possessed their own mass bases.[1] Dennett was barely thirty years old in 1938, when he was elected the founding executive secretary of the Washington State CIO Council. His candid personal history of Pacific Northwest labor and left-wing organizing is full of the texture, immediacy and complexity of the grass-roots working-class left found in the comparable memoirs of other regional activists such as Wyndham Mortimer, Hosea Hudson, Al Richmond and Steve Nelson.[2] Dennett died in February, 1989, as this book was being prepared for publication. It is unlikely that we will see many more full-length memoirs by radical workers offering a comparable first-hand perspective on the early CIO.

Dennett's years of active involvement in the working-class movement (1931–56) spanned CIO's prehistory and history as an independent labor federation. Dennett shared in the Pacific Northwest labor and left movements' victories and defeats alike. He fought for a constructive resolution of the Great Depression's shattering of workers' lives, swept to victory with the massive organizing drives of the mid- and late-1930s, and experienced repression in 1940 and again in the 1950s by conservative labor leaders who would restrain or crush the left-wing militants who did so much to build the industrial unions.

This book is valuable as a primary source for the northwestern left and early CIO, providing first hand accounts of the Skid Road activism and hunger marches of the early 1930s, organization building and factional conflict, on-the-job grievances in the maritime and steel industries, political coalition building, and the regional resonances of national and international issues. Compared with the mines and steel mills of Pennsylvania and the Midwest, Michigan's auto plants, New York's garment shops, or the San Francisco docks, the Northwest might appear to be a minor backwater in the history of the CIO. Numerically, Washington State members accounted for only a few tens of thousands of the CIO's millions. Nevertheless, it

merits interest as the site of some of the hardest fought fights between workers and employers, American Federation of Labor (AFL)
and CIO, and pro- and anti-popular front union factions.

Partial perspectives on Washington State labor in the 1930s have
been provided by other writers: Lembcke and Tattam on the Woodworkers, Ames and Simpson on the 1936 Seattle *Post-Intelligencer* (P-
I) strike, Acena on the Washington Commonwealth Federation.[3] But
Dennett's book details his involvement on multiple fronts of battle,
elucidating the manner in which these movements and experiences
could be complexly joined in the daily activities of a single individual as they actually were for the left-labor movement as a whole.
Though Dennett's range of critical involvements was somewhat unusual, there were scores of others like him in the AFL, CIO, and
left-wing political organizations. His autobiography reflects the syn-
ergistic effects of the fortunes of various organizational components
on the left and labor reform movements as a whole. Had Gene Dennett and others like him not existed to tell their stories, a novelist
might be required to create a comparable composite character to em-
body the glory and the tragedy of the mid-twentieth century American working class on the march and at bay.

Dennett's life experience intimately involved several key issues
in labor and left life in the United States: the interrelation of democratic and socialist ideals; reformist vs. revolutionary strategies and
tactics on the left; the position of radicals and others regarding the
Soviet Union; flexibility, creativity, and pragmatism vs. discipline in
the Communist party and the trade union movement; and the
unions' very goals and purposes. These problems have attracted
and continue to attract the attention of academic historians and
working-class scholars. Dennett's autobiography contributes to the
literature as the record of an independent worker-thinker's reflec-
tions on his experiences and organizational policies as a guide to his
next steps. Though this book is not a work of formal scholarship, it
is a rare, thoughtful and generally non-polemical rendering of a
worker's public and historically significant acts.

Dennett was an idealist who sought to unify theoretical principle, policy, and practice. The book succeeds as an account of his
effort to live a good and ethical public life guided by his dedication
to the working class and his evolving interpretation and application
of the Marxist or socialist principles with which he had been raised.
There is also a strong thematic undercurrent of his and other workers' conscious efforts to extend formal democratic political ideals to

local as well as general democratic control of economic activity. Dennett's persistence and proclivity for asking questions and speaking his mind, courageously or rashly as the case may be, but always refusing to compromise his understanding of the world, thrust him into a life of nearly constant conflict with the forces that repress the intellectual, social, political, and economic vitality of the working class.

The Communist party's (CP) relationships with Dennett and with northwestern labor struggles runs as a red thread through the story. Dennett was a Party member for most of the period 1931–47, the years of the CP's greatest influence in the United States.[4] This book offers evidence that actions of the regional Party leadership and members alike were the product of a shifting balance among theoretical principle, pragmatism, personality habits and conflicts, high level policy decision, and the objective situation. As with humanity generally, Party members functioned as only one set of actors in a complex world, attempting more or less consciously to shape the world to come.

Dennett's story makes clear that, during the early 1930s period of the "United Front from Below", the more flexible popular front era and even into the 1940s, party activists enjoyed some degree of discretion—whose bounds were admittedly ill defined and all too often erratic—for interpreting and implementing overall Party policies as well as direct orders from the leadership. Furthermore, de facto lines of command and communication could be quite weak, allowing room for both individual initiative and errors in applying Party policy. In Dennett's experience, the Party was a multi-layered organization wherein use of one's judgment against the leadership's advice in a given situation could, but did not necessarily, lead to punishment. It appears that flexibility in applying the Party policies was tolerated more than was overtly expressing disagreement with the Party line or the leadership. It is not at all clear how typical Dennett's experience was; the relative balance between grass roots creativity and discipline in Party life (as in American life as a whole) remains an issue that objective scholars have not yet resolved. But the cold war image of the Party as a monolithic instrument carrying out Comintern orders certainly merits the revision which has begun to emerge from careful local and regional studies such as that of Mark Naison on Harlem in the 1930s.[5]

A genuine native radical, Dennett was born to militant Irish-American working-class socialist parents in Revere, Massachusetts, in 1908. They named him for their hero and the banner carrier of the Socialist party, Eugene Victor Debs. As a child, he witnessed the brutal realities of industrial class conflict in the shoe-manufacturing dominated city of Lynn, Massachusetts.[6] Dennett briefly recounts his family's search for cultural dignity in the midst of class struggle. Following his teenage years, spent on a small Oregon farm, Dennett attended the Oregon Normal School in the 1920s and thereafter taught briefly in rural elementary schools.

Driven by the whip of the Great Depression, Gene Dennett joined the Communist party late in 1931. A few months later, he left his formal teaching career forever to take the post of agitprop (agitation and propaganda director) with the Northwestern Party District Buro in Seattle. He almost immediately came into conflict with the district organizer, was exiled to the northern Puget Sound mill and port town of Bellingham as Party section organizer, and subsequently took a very active role in the movement of the unemployed. He drifted away from the Party as a result of further political disagreements with the district leadership. In 1934, he signed up with the federal government's Civilian Conservation Corps (CCC) and edited a CCC camp newsletter, but he was discharged from the CCC in July, 1935, as a result of his radical pro-labor leanings. (While in the CCC, he was tangentially involved in the 1934 Longshoremen's strike but missed altogether another one of the key moments in the prehistory of the Northwestern CIO, especially its left-wing—the 1935 timber strike.)

Shanghaied on the Seattle waterfront, Dennett unintentionally became a Puget Sound maritime worker and played central roles in the 1935 and 1936 Ferryboatmen's strikes. His prominence led to his being recruited back into the Party and ultimately being co-opted back into the Party's district leadership. His socialist upbringing, formal education, exposure to Marxist class-struggle thinking, and personal experience with hard labor, were conjoined with simply being in the right place at the right time, to make him a pivotal regional facilitator of the growing mass working-class upsurge's coalescence into left-wing AFL and CIO unions.[7]

The Communist party's mid- and late-1930s popular front strategy of uniting with other socialist and liberal forces against fascist tendencies at home and abroad had one of its high points in the Washington Commonwealth Federation (WCF).[8] Dennett was active in the WCF from 1936 onward. He managed the successful 1937 Seattle city council campaign of Hugh DeLacy, the marine fireman, laborer and University of Washington teaching assistant who was subsequently elected to Congress during World War II and was closely associated with the Communist party. Dennett served as a WCF vice-president in the latter 1930s while he was also a member of the state CIO Political Welfare Committee and the Party Buro.

Dennett was a strong supporter of industrial unionism in general and the AFL's Committee for Industrial Organization in particular. As the CIO was propelled into an independent existence (1936–37), Dennett's activism in the Maritime Federation of the Pacific and the Seattle Central Labor Council led to his election as the first executive secretary of the Washington Industrial Union Council (WIUC-CIO). He served in this capacity for two years, during which the state CIO's effectiveness was limited by employer and AFL attacks, the ongoing economic crisis, and a strong factional drive by anti-Communist elements allied with the CIO's national office.

Directly relevant to the Washington State CIO factionalism was the "institutional conservatism" that Lorin Cary describes as coexisting with militance in the early CIO.[9] Cary's case study of Adolph Germer argues that key staff positions in the early national CIO were occupied by older, experienced unionists who, like John L. Lewis himself, were deeply committed to the trade unions but had come to accept or even advocate a modus vivendi with capitalism, rather than seeking to make the unions part of a vibrant socialist movement. These bureaucratically oriented figures tended to emphasize the concentration of power in the leadership of stable unions, the suppression of internal conflict, and the winning of enforceable collective bargaining contracts that brought specific quantifiable gains in workers' consuming power. This business industrial unionist grouping stood in contrast to those who agreed with the position, advocated by the Communist party and others, that the unions were potentially the central element—but not the only element—of a powerful social movement that would ultimately overthrow capitalism. This latter grouping could be broadly characterized as the popular front in action and was represented in Washington State by the left CIO-WCF coalition. Germer played a key role in strengthening "stable," centrist elements in the Michigan and New York Industrial Union Councils, 1938–40. As has been previously described by Lembcke and Tattam, and is highlighted by Dennett's account, in 1940 the national CIO dispatched Germer to the Northwest, where he directly intervened against the left in the Woodworkers and WIUC faction fights.

Levenstein's work and other careful regional and local studies of
faction fighting among communists, social democrats, and business
unionists tend to demonstrate the factionalists had but minor differences on concrete issues of wages, hours and working conditions,
or on specific legislation being considered by the state houses. The
popular front unionists, it must be emphasized, were not simply
political visionaries, but also fought hard for contractual gains for
the membership. Similarly, even the more conservative anti-
communist "business" unionists in the CIO favored old age pensions and unemployment insurance, and social democrats like the
Reuthers and Sidney Hillman were vigorous anti-fascists and anti-
racists. The Washington State faction fights were generally based on
political, strategic and personal power struggles rather than questions of competence in narrowly defined trade union issues.

Gene Dennett was centrally involved in this northwestern conflict between the popular front and business industrial unionists.
When John L. Lewis sternly warned the CIO executive board at the
1939 national convention that "any Communists expecting to make
a career out of taking over the CIO had best forget it," he was looking Dennett straight in the eye. (Dennett's verbatim notes on this
fateful meeting are appended to this memoir and may be the only
full account of Lewis' speech in existence.) The Party in Washington
evidently ignored this portent of impending attack. Dennett and
several other left-wingers comprising the majority of the Washington Industrial Union Council executive board were removed from
their posts late in 1940 at Lewis' orders, following direct intervention by Germer and other Mine Workers who held appointed posts
in the regional and national CIO hierarchies.

Dennett desired to remain ashore after his removal from State
CIO office; he found work at Bethlehem Steel's Seattle plant and
became active in the local Steel Workers Organizing Committee.
Dennett, with his wife Harriette, led a large Party unit in a
working-class Seattle neighborhood, emphasizing black and ethnic
civil rights in the early years of World War II.[10] Late in 1942, Party
General Secretary Earl Browder published *Victory and After*, which
argued that workers should protect their interests by participating
in government agencies and submitting all disputes to arbitration
rather than engaging in independent political organizing and waging militant strikes. Once again, Dennett came into conflict with
northwestern Party leaders when he contended that Browder's pol-

icies represented tactical expedients for the war against fascism rather than a new theoretical, programmatic and strategic direction. He was dropped from the Party Buro.

In 1943, Dennett was drafted into the United States Army. After the defeat of fascism, he returned to Bethlehem Steel. Dennett found the Party had changed during his absence, and that he no longer "fit in".[11] He describes his evolving disagreements with the CP's changing emphases regarding civil rights and other organizing efforts, his doubts that Party policy was rooted firmly in reasoning based on the principles of class analysis, and his growing alienation from the Party leadership. The Party expelled Dennett and his wife in 1947 on charges which included the less than convincing one of being FBI agents who acted against the Party's interests.

Following his Party expulsion, Dennett remained active in his Steelworkers local, serving as recording secretary and grievance committeeman. He functioned as a rank and file militant in the pursuit of safe working conditions, justice on the job, enforcement of black fellow workers' seniority and the highest possible wages for his shopmates under the union contract. He reminds us that rank-and-file working-class activism was beleaguered but not dead in the early 1950s. Dennett's activities represented a fight for a moral order at the point of production, codified in contractual rules and procedures which could serve as a shield—but also as a trap. His conflicts with both the union hierarchy and Bethlehem Steel's management over contract negotiation and administration is part of the prehistory of the national Steelworkers reform movement that began to coalesce late in the 1950s.[12]

Though he maintained good relations with most of the local leadership and his shopmates, Dennett's militance and continued loyalty to his independent socialist world perspective led in 1954 to what appears to have been a blatantly framed-up expulsion from the Steelworkers. The expulsion was promoted by management and the national and district steel union hierarchies. The contrast between the enthusiastic bottom-up organizing of the 1930s labor crusade and the bureaucratic stifling of local workers' initiative is instructive. A subsequent lawsuit seeking to restore Dennett's union membership failed, but he remained on the job.

Dennett's union expulsion was abetted by the cold-war hysteria of anti-Communist witch hunting.[13] At the request of both the United Steelworkers and Bethlehem Steel, he was subpoenaed in

1955 by the House Un-American Activities Committee (HUAC). Despite his Party expulsion and not being subject himself to prosecution as a Party member, he initially took refuge in the Constitution's Fifth Amendment to avoid naming names. Politically isolated and under tremendous pressure at the steel mill, however, his resistance broke down. Dennett ultimately testified "freely and fully" before HUAC regarding his past associations with the Party. The ensuing enmity of many of his one-time comrades has lasted to this day.

Dennett's expulsion from the Steelworkers ended his trade union activity, but be continued working at the steel plant until 1966. A vitriolic confrontation with the bosses and a health breakdown induced him to retire early from mill work. He worked several years as a longshoremen's cargo checker on the Seattle docks. A complete physical collapse forced his total retirement in 1972.

Dennett endorses many familiar observations regarding the Party experience in the middle third of the twentieth century. "Defend the Soviet Union" was one of the most constant and distinguishing refrains in the CP's repertoire of slogans; at times, this emphasis seemed to supersede the domestic fight against reaction and for socialism. In the Northwest as elsewhere, Communists defending the Soviet Union and its policies engendered confusion among workers and estranged potential allies who could not accept as pro-working class phenomena the Moscow trials of Stalin's opponents, the expedient 1939 Hitler-Stalin non-aggression pact, or the emergence of a Soviet bureaucracy. Yet the emphasis of Dennett's own Party activity was on improving the lot of his fellow workers in the Northwest, where the Soviet Union had little non-symbolic significance. Struggling with local and regional problems was the daily experience and prime commitment of rank-and-file activists during the 1930s, although northwestern unionists who volunteered to fight in the Spanish Civil War did make abstract international solidarity against fascism a living reality.

The Communists' Popular Front and World War II experiences may have helped to "Americanize" the Party and its members in a manner similar to the CIO's Americanization of ethnic workers.[14] Communists' whole-hearted commitment to the World War II U.S.-Soviet alliance against the fascist powers seems to have deepened Dennett's and others' belief that socialism was compatible with patriotism and American constitutional democratic ideals so that Communism did appear to be, in Browder's phrase, "Twentieth Century

Americanism''. This made all the more painful the confusing shifts of domestic Party policy in the 1940s and the bitter factionalism regarding post-war direction, which contributed to the sense of disorientation among returning Communist veterans described by George Charney's and Junius Scales' memoirs as well as by the present book. The mass defections of nearly lifelong activists from the Party in 1956 and 1957 following the Soviet intervention in Hungary and Khruschev's revelations of the Stalin era's frameups and executions lend credence to the notion that for many American Communists, the Soviet Union was essentially an abstract symbol of hope for their efforts to extend democracy from a periodic ballot-box ritual to the day-to-day operations of the economy.

Dennett contends that the Party ought to have used HUAC's and the Washington State legislature's Canwell Committee hearings as opportunities to publicize and explain its vision and policies. Since the hearings were intended to expose Party members and friends and to frighten liberal reformers, a policy of open disclosure would probably have been self-destructive. Still, this raises an important question that James Prickett and James Weinstein have considered in detail: would the CP and the left generally have been more viable, could they have gained the broad support they needed to survive and, indeed, to win, had they been more willing to "show the face of the Party" and to propagandize openly for socialism rather than, from the mid-30s on, pursuing a militant social reformist role within the unions and the Democratic Party?[15]

This is not the place to consider the evidence in detail. This writer's studies of popular front unionism in Washington, however, support the argument that although CP union officers did have rank and file support as militant industrial unionists and social reform advocates, it is not at all evident that their popularity could be translated into support for an explicitly socialist agenda. 1938 was the pre-war high tide for the CP in Washington state, with some 3000 registered Party members, several Communists elected (as Democrats) to the state legislature and great successes in winning old age pensions, establishing public utility districts and defeating legislation limiting the right to strike. Even then, the left-Democrat alliance was able to win a bare electoral majority in one strongly working-class jurisdiction, Pacific County, where most Woodworkers union officers were Communists and a Communist logger was elected to the state Senate.[16] In 1939, as noted above, John L. Lewis announced that the Communists' days in the CIO were numbered;

by 1941, they had been contained or even eliminated as a significant, effective independent force in the Washington CIO.

Radicals' efforts to build the CIO, most of whose top leadership was committed not to socialism but to ameliorating workers' conditions under capitalism, had a "tar-baby" effect. The CIO integrated workers and their communities, through their own struggles, into national institutions while softening some of the most immediately painful aspects of working-class life. A more openly socialist stance in the 1930s might conceivably have planted a few seeds for the rebirth of a stronger left in later decades. However, to flourish, the seeds needed to germinate in the environment of a working class prepared to act against capitalism as such. The limited constituency for even reform legislation, the local as well as national divisions in the union movement, and the willingness of many workers even in the CIO's militant heyday to give heed to redbaiters discourage speculation that organizing openly as Communists for an explicitly socialist agenda would have won a socialist America by the mid-20th century or even a more secure position for the labor left during the Taft-Hartley-McCarthy era. The Popular Front strategy of building mass organizations, demanding social reforms attainable under capitalism, and opposing fascism appealed to the hearts, minds and souls of many rank-and-file Communists. It was a viable American pro-working class strategy in a period when the mass of workers were not prepared to commit themselves to an anti-capitalist movement.

One final point in this regard. Dennett expresses well his and thousands of other grass-roots radical workers' ultimate sense of the tragic futility of their efforts to effect a deep rooted social and economic transformation. He notes the state's role in crushing the American left, and suggests that President Franklin Roosevelt had a direct interest in forming the CIO as a means to contain the radical working class. The interrelations of intentionality, social setting and historical outcomes of human actions are always complex. Although historians rightly find conspiracy theories unappealing, our increasing knowledge of government surveillance and use of agents provacateurs in undermining reformers and radicals of all varieties during this century warns us not to dismiss out of hand the effects of covert government intervention as well as outright repression in the fate of the left. To investigate this problem, Dennett considered using the Freedom of Information Act's provisions to secure a copy of his FBI file. This was rejected as a resource for his autobiography because, given the usually total censorship of substantively valuable material from FBI records provided to other radical autobiographers such as Steve Nelson and Junius Scales, Dennett did not believe the results for the present purposes would justify the charge against his slim resources.[17]

When writing his memoirs, Gene Dennett was aided by a plethora of primary documentation—leaflets, correspondence, organizational minutes, rare newspapers and pamphlets—preserved in his personal files. Several key items appended to the body of the narrative are available nowhere else and should be of great interest to serious scholars.

My role in aiding the production of this book was fourfold: making stylistic and organizational suggestions; stimulating Dennett's memory through conversations; urging him to fill in gaps and clarify ambiguous points; and checking his recollections against newspapers and manuscripts outside of his possession. In this latter task, I was aided by my own previous research on the Washington State unemployed movement, the state CIO and the WCF, in all of which Dennett had been prominent. There are perhaps one or two points in the narrative regarding which we disagreed on chronology by a matter of two or three months, but scholars using this memoir as a guide to the still largely unpublished story of Washington state labor and the left in the CIO period should find it generally quite reliable. The decisions on style, organization, argument and subject matter (including appendices) were Gene Dennett's.

Dennett's life story is not simply a rich primary source for Northwestern left and labor history. His autobiographical perspective brings into sharp relief the potential tensions between the individual's conscience and the broader movements for social justice, and the ongoing process of resolving the disputes that do arise. Dennett's concluding remarks do not resolve with satisfying rigor the philosophical issues raised by his public life, but seem to lean toward a syndicalist vision of individual freedom in a society free of class repression. He addresses the conundrums of theoretically informed principle vs. pragmatism, the individual voice vs. social discipline. His story must be seen as personal testimony contributing to the ongoing debate among social democrats, syndicalists, libertarians, communists, pure and simple business unionists, conservative free-enterprisers and others, regarding individual needs, human liberation and the collective advancement of the common good in class society. His life story's embodiment of these broader themes will make this book of interest to Americanists in general as well as to those specially interested in the working class. Educators and the general public may similarly find it a valuable and nearly allegoric depiction of one man's journey through twentieth century working-class America. Perhaps Dennett's strongest message is the need for broad critical political education, democratic practices, ideological tolerance, and remembrance of long-range structural goals in the trade union and social reform movements.

Jeremy R. Egolf
Seattle, Washington
March, 1989

NOTES TO PREFACE

1. Despite the considerable research effort already expended, much still needs to be done on the history of workers in the 1930s and the CIO period. The principal overviews include Robert H. Zieger, "Toward the History of the CIO: A Bibliographical Report," *Labor History*, 26 (1985); Irving Bernstein, *The Lean Years: A History of the American Worker, 1920–1933* (Boston: Houghton Mifflin, 1960); idem, *The Turbulent Years: A History of the American Worker, 1933–41* (Boston: Houghton Mifflin, 1969); Art Preis, *Labor's Giant Step: Twenty Years of the CIO* (New York: Pathfinder Press, 1972); Walter Galenson, *The CIO Challenge to the AFL: A History of the American Labor Movement, 1935–1941* (Cambridge: Harvard University Press, 1960); Nelson Lichtenstein, *Labor's War at Home: The CIO in World War II* (New York: Cambridge University Press, 1982); Melvyn

Dubofsky and Warren Van Tyne, *John Lewis: A Biography* (New York: Quadrangle, 1978). See also the citations under note 4.

2. Wyndham Mortimer, *Organize! My Life as a Union Man* (Boston: Beacon Press, 1971); Nell Irvin Painter, *The Narrative of Hosea Hudson: His Life as a Negro Communist in the Deep South* (Cambridge: Harvard University Press, 1979); Al Richmond, *A Long View From the Left: Memoirs of an American Revolutionary* (Boston: Houghton Mifflin, 1972); Steve Nelson, James R. Barrett, and Rob Ruck, *Steve Nelson: American Radical* (Pittsburgh: University of Pittsburgh Press, 1981).

Other personal accounts of the Great Depression and CIO organizing efforts by sometime CP members include Harry Haywood, *Black Bolshevik: Autobiography of an Afro-American Communist* (Chicago: Liberator Press, 1978); George Charney, *A Long Journey* (Chicago: Quadrangle, 1968); Charles Denby, *Indignant Heart: A Black Worker's Journal* (Boston: South End, 1978); Len DeCaux, *Labor Radical: From the Wobblies to the CIO* (Boston: Beacon Press, 1972); and Junius Scales and Richard Nickson, *Cause at Heart* (Athens: University of Georgia Press, 1987).

Of course, not all early CIO leaders and activists who left their memoirs were Communists. Others who wrote their stories (generally from some form of social-democratic or liberal perspective) include Victor Reuther, *The Brothers Reuther and the Story of the UAW: A Memoir* (Boston: Houghton Mifflin, 1976); John Brophy, *A Miner's Life* (Madison: University of Wisconsin Press, 1961); David Dubinsky and A. H. Raskin, *David Dubinsky: A Life with Labor* (New York: Simon and Schuster, 1977); Frank Marquart, *An Auto Worker's Journal: The UAW from Crusade to One-Party Union* (University Park: Pennsylvania State University Press, 1975). See also Alice Lynd and Staughton Lynd, eds., *Rank and File: Personal Histories of Working-Class Organizers* (Boston: Beacon Press, 1973).

3. Jerry Lee Lembcke and William Tattam, *One Union in Wood: A Political History of the International Woodworkers of America* (New York: International, 1984); William E. Ames and Roger A. Simpson, *Unionism or Hearst: The Seattle Post-Intelligencer Strike of 1936* (Seattle: Pacific Northwest Labor History Association, 1978); Albert A. Acena, "The Washington Commonwealth Federation: Reform Politics and the Popular Front" (Ph.D. Dissertation, University of Washington, 1975). Robert G. Rodden, *The Fighting Machinists* (Washington: Kelly Press, n.d.) inadequately summarizes the 1940–1941 faction fight in IAM Lodge 751 (Boeing), which is also touched on by Mortimer, op cit. For a dated anti-communist account contem-

porary with the factional conflicts in the Woodworkers, see Vernon H. Jensen, *Lumber and Labor* (New York: Farrar and Rinehart, 1945).

See also Galenson, op cit., especially the chapters on lumber and brewery workers; Daniel Leab, *A Union of Individuals: The Formation of the American Newspaper Guild, 1933–1936* (New York: Columbia University, 1970); Charles P. Larrowe, "The Great Maritime Strike of '34," *Labor History*, 18 (1977), pp. 403–451, and (1971), pp. 3–37; Bruce Nelson, *Workers on the Waterfront* (Chicago: University of Illinois Press, 1988); idem, " 'Pentecost' on the Pacific: Maritime Workers and Working-Class Consciousness in the 1930s," in Maurice Zeitlin and Howard Kimeldorf, eds., *Political Power and Social Theory*, Vol. IV (Greenwich: JAI Press, 1984), pp. 141–182.

4. The more significant secondary literature on the Communist party generally and its relations with the CIO in particular from 1930 to 1960 includes: Irving Howe and Lewis A. Coser, *The Communist Party of the United States* (New York: Frederick A. Praeger, 1962); Harvey Klehr, *The Heyday of American Communism: The Depression Decade* (Stanford: Hoover Institute, 1984); Roger Keeran, *The Communist Party and the Auto Workers Unions* (Bloomington: University of Illinois Press, 1980); James Matles and James Higgins, *Them and Us: Struggles of a Rank-and-file Union* (Englewood Cliffs: Prentice Hall, 1974); Bert Cochran, *Labor and Communism* (Princeton: Princeton University Press, 1977); Maurice Isserman, *Which Side Were You On? The American Communist Party During World War II* (Middletown: Wesleyan University Press, 1982); Harvey A. Levenstein, *Communism, Anti-Communism, and the CIO* (Westport: Greenwood, 1981); Joseph Starobin, *American Communism in Crisis, 1943–1957* (Cambridge: Harvard University Press, 1972); David A. Shannon, *The Decline of American Communism* (New York: Harcourt, Brace, 1959); Zeitlin and Kimeldorf, op cit.

For a semi-official CP perspective, see William Z. Foster, *History of the Communist Party of the United States* (New York: Greenwood, 1968).

5. Mark Naison, *Communists in Harlem During the Depression* (Urbana: University of Illinois Press, 1983). Another useful local study of the Party is Paul Lyons, *Philadelphia's Communists, 1936–1956* (Philadelphia: Temple University Press, 1982); on the issue of decentralization in the CP, see especially Levenstein, op cit.

6. Because Lynn was for decades a hotbed for radical activity and stood at the leading edge of the industrial revolution, it has attracted an unusual amount of attention from historians of labor

and socialism. See Paul G. Faler, *Mechanics and Manufacturers in the Early Industrial Revolution: Lynn, Massachusetts, 1780–1860* (Albany: State University of New York Press, 1981); Alan Dawley, *Class and Community: The Industrial Revolution in Lynn* (Cambridge: Harvard University Press, 1976); John T. Cumbler, *Working-Class Community in Industrial America* (Urbana: University of Illinois Press, 1983). See also Ronald Schatz, *The Electrical Workers: A History of Labor at General Electric and Westinghouse, 1923–1960* (Urbana: University of Illinois Press, 1983); John H. M. Laslett, *Labor and the Left: A Study of Socialist and Radical Influences in the American Labor Movement, 1881–1924* (New York: Basic Books, 1970), ch. 3.; Henry F. Bedford, *Socialism and the Workers in Massachusetts, 1886–1912* (Amherst: University of Massachusetts Press, 1966), passim.

7. Several large Seattle AFL locals were left led during the late 1930s, including the University of Washington local of the American Federation of Teachers, Building Service Employees Union #6 (over 5000 members), and International Association of Machinists Lodges 79 (uptown shops) and 751 (the Boeing local). In its 1940–41 faction fight between the conservative international leadership and its local allies and a left-wing pro-United Auto Workers group (which included the Lodge's elected officers), Lodge 751 was reformed as District 751, currently the largest single body of workers represented by the IAM.

Dennett was not unique as an educated man in the leadership of the new CIO unions. For example, the Reuther brothers had several years of college and Donald Henderson, president of the Cannery Workers, was a former Columbia University economics professor. The five Washington State CIO Executive Board members suspended with Dennett in 1940 included two other college graduates: Bob Camozzi of the Newspaper Guild (University of Washington) and George Lane, the founding international secretary of the Alaska Fishermen's Union (Union Theological Seminary). Camozzi was a Party member but Lane was not. Dennett, Lane, and Camozzi comprised the WIUC Executive Board's Political Welfare Committee.

8. For the WCF, see Acena, op cit.; Acena's study is summarized in Klehr, op cit.

9. Lorin Lee Cary, "Institutionalized Conservatism in the Early C.I.O.: Adolph Germer, a Case Study," *Labor History* 13 (1972), pp. 475–504.

10. For the CP and blacks, see especially Naison, op cit., and Charles H. Martin, "The International Labor Defence and Black

America," in *Labor History* 25 (1985), pp. 165–194, and the references cited therein.

11. For the post-war changes in the Party, see for example, Starobin and Shannon, op cit. Party life in the period 1945–50 was characterized in part by intense, bitter and introverted internal fighting over the issues of "white chauvinism" and Earl Browder's 1944 dissolution of the CP. The anti-white-chauvinism campaign was very tangentially related to Dennett's problems with the Party; his expulsion was based principally on general disagreements regarding policy, organizational and personality matters.

12. We still need a full history of the Steelworkers union, but Peter Nyden, *Steelworkers Rank-and-File* (New York: Berkin and Govey, 1984), is informative regarding the repressive controls exercised by the steel hierarchy in the early '50s and sets the context for Dennett's experience. See also Paul F. Clark et al., eds., *Forging a Union of Steel* (Ithaca: Industrial and Labor Relations Press, 1987).

13. For the crushing of the left in the CIO and elsewhere during the 1948–55 period, see, for example, Robert Griffith and Athan Theoharis, eds., *The Specter: Original Essays on the Cold War and the Origin of McCarthyism* (1974); David Caute, *The Great Fear: The Anti-Communist Purge under Truman and Eisenhower* (New York: Simon and Schuster, 1978); Frank Emspak, "The Breakup of the CIO," pp. 101–140, in Zeitlin and Kimeldorf, op cit.

14. For example, Thomas Gobel, "Becoming American: Ethnic Workers and the Rise of the CIO," *Labor History* 29 (1988), pp. 199–224.

15. James Prickett, "New Perspectives on American Communism and the Labor Movement," in Zeitlin and Kimeldorf, op cit., pp. 3–36; James Weinstein, *Ambiguous Legacy: The left in American Politics* (New York: New Viewpoints, 1975).

16. Jeremy Egolf, "Popular Front Unionism in a Small Place: The Woodworkers of Pacific County, Washington, 1935–1941," (unpublished paper).

17. Nelson et al., op cit., and Scales and Nickson, op cit.

MY BACKGROUND

For a long time my friends have urged me to write about my experiences in the labor movement and my relations with the Communist Party, U.S.A. I am now free to report my exact experiences which contain information not widely known. I have kept many records that refresh and substantiate my numerous opinions and judgments, which probably vary at great length from the commonly accepted beliefs.

When I attempt to explain my joining the Communist Party, it seems to become unduly complicated because later developments clearly indicate belonging to the Party became a confusing exercise, with an end result of futility and betrayal. Even so, it was a unique experience that resulted in an inside understanding of why certain events happened the way they did. I think a review of the course I followed deserves to be made public so that others may benefit from my experience and better understand what happened and why.

I joined the Communist party in late 1931, and suffered through many stormy periods with a few breaks. I rejoiced in its successes, and was expelled in 1947 for many false reasons that will become self-explanatory as I recount the events that comprise my experience. There were times when it was almost impossible to remain a member and continue to fight for the causes to which I was dedicated. But I had a lifetime of roots which compelled me to search for and participate in the attempt to emancipate the working class from capitalist wage slavery.

I was literally born into the socialist movement. My father and my mother were enthusiastic followers of Eugene V. Debs. In the early 1900s Debs had the reputation for eloquently expressing the yearnings of the masses of working people to free themselves from exploitation as practiced under the capitalist system.

Shortly before I was born at Revere, Massachusetts, on April 26, 1908, my mother heard Debs orate about the political and economic condition of the working class and the ideas of socialism as a solution to the problems of capitalist exploitation that bore down so

1

hard on the poor. She was so impressed with what Debs advocated, she insisted on giving me the name of Eugene Victor in tribute to Debs. That great Socialist inspired many parents who named their children for him. But I think "greatness" has to be earned. It cannot be bequeathed.

I have always felt a close kinship with what Eugene Debs fought for, and have always felt humbled because I could never live up to his kind of greatness. As a child I had personal contact with Debs. In Old People's Hall in Boston around 1916, I was a scheduled elocution entertainer for the audience waiting to hear Debs. I recited poems of James Whitcomb Riley, such as "The Raggedy Man," because Riley and Debs were close personal friends. Debs shook my hand and hugged me as I came off the stage and he went on. His magnetism electrified the crowd. His presence made everyone rejoice to be alive. He transmitted new hope for a better future while condemning the present oppression of the workers.

I remember hearing the audience roar their approval when Debs condemned President Wilson for attempting to lead the United States into World War I. Debs called it an imperialist war for profits at the expense of the workers' lives. Wilson's 1916 election campaign claimed that, "He kept us out of war." Debs labeled that a lie and said Wilson was secretly planning to drag the United States into that war. History now knows that Debs was right. But the government prosecuted Debs for sedition and sent him to jail, an experience from which he never fully recovered.

"Sedition" was considered to be any opposition to the government's war effort. When the old socialist newspaper, the *Appeal to Reason*, reported in 1918 that Debs was locked up for sedition in Atlanta, I cried with a broken heart as a child because I personally knew that Debs was a kind and gentle man, and absolutely innocent of any crime.

My early years were lived in Lynn, Massachusetts, where I saw squalor and misery among honest, hard working people who lived, worked, and died without experiencing the real joys of living. I knew stories of child labor and abuse in the mills of nearby Lowell, Lawrence, and Haverill, Massachusetts. I remember the stench that came from the children who had been tending the filthy tanning pits where leather was made out of animal hides with urine, poisonous acid, and other chemicals which stunk on them all the time.

I had heard accounts of the military massacre of miners' families at Ludlow, Colorado, and tingled with resentment over those cruelties. I had heard about Eugene V. Debs being jailed for organizing railroad workers during the Pullman Palace Car Company strike in the previous century.

I had personally seen women shoe workers attacked by mounted police, resulting in injuries, bloodshed, and death. I remember my mother arming herself with two big hatpins with which to stab horses in the flanks to throw the mounted policemen to the ground. The women strikers would take a handful of cayenne pepper out of their handbags and throw it in the eyes of the downed policemen and jump on them with their "spike-heeled" shoes. Some policemen and women strikers were fatally injured in those encounters.

Every time I rode a streetcar to downtown Lynn I passed the glittering compound of the multimillionaire Lydia E. Pinkham family, who were ostentatiously displaying the class differences between them and the rest of us. We knew they made their wealth from selling patented medicine, Lydia E. Pinkham's famous tonic for women suffering general weakness and ill health. They had several houses for adults and several playhouses for children. All were kept in brilliant white paint and securely fenced off from the public with strong vertical iron bars and locked gates. We poor referred to this as their "jail," but truthfully we envied their luxury.

In school I was taught that education was the answer to all our problems. But later experience proved to me that there has to be more than knowledge involved in the emancipation of the working class. I learned from experience there are many obstacles in our way, such as lack of class-consciousness, inadequate understanding of the essence of authority, power, and privilege, all of which depend on who you are and what position you hold, and what you believe in.

My mother and father were both shoe factory workers. Their work made them sensitive to the suffering of the other wage earners on the job. The prevailing ruling capitalist class attitude in those days was to blame the workers themselves for being uneducated and poor. In an effort to overcome the indignity of being looked down on, many humble workers attempted to lift themselves up by their bootstraps by privately studying art, literature, drama, and music, in the hope of some day changing their mode of living with a more enriched culture. Many dreamed of ultimately going to California where its famous Hollywood glamorized life making everything appear delightful and pleasant. But few ever achieved that goal and had to endure the heartless contempt of the privileged classes throughout their lives.

My mother was born, lived, worked, and died in Lynn. She was the thirteenth child born to an Irish-Catholic family that suffered persecution by the American Patriotic Association (APA), whose aim was to discriminate against the Catholics and Irish immigrants. The APA desired to limit Irish men to unskilled labor, and women to scrubbing and cleaning. Her Catholic father was among those who were driven out of Belfast, Ireland, when the conquering Orangemen seized power there. Brought up in the Catholic church, my mother tried to follow the teachings of the then priests who preached hatred of all Jews and Protestants.

My mother had to go to work in a shoe factory, where she became an expert "back-stay stitcher" while in her early teens. The factory system destroyed her ability to remain totally loyal to her church because the male boss system established a permanent class hostility between the men bosses and the women workers. The Catholic Church's opposition to birth control made her life a constant turmoil because, after my birth, the doctor advised her to have no more children. In addition to that, one of her sisters had a coat-hanger abortion which, it seems, later induced a cancer that ultimately killed her. As a nine-year-old child, I watched her die in excruciating pain during her final two weeks.

Mother's entire life was a bitter experience because she had to endure more than her fair share of the unnecessary work. She often called my attention to the unfair burden she had to carry while working on the job and keeping house. She demanded that I learn how to take care of myself at an early age. She enthusiastically marched in the women's suffrage demonstrations, demanding the vote for women.

My father was born in New Brunswick, New Jersey, of a family whose ancestors immigrated to America about 1670. It was a proud family that traced its origins to William the Conqueror and included persons who participated in some of the Crusades. They had been affiliated with many different religious strains including Quakers, Church of England, Spiritualists, and mavericks not otherwise identifiable. My father took part in many different sports including wrestling, boxing, tobogganing, and swimming. I rarely saw my father in daylight when I was very young because he worked twelve hours a day as a foreman in the sole leather department of the A. G. Walton shoe factory in Chelsea, Massachusetts. He frequently walked the seventeen miles from our house to the factory. Somehow, he also made the time to distribute Socialist literature in various neighborhoods because he was an ardent follower of Debs.

My father's loyalty to the teachings of the Episcopal church against the "infallibility" of the Pope made it impossible for my parents to reach an amiable accommodation about much of anything religious. When the priests visited our home to urge my parents to send me to a Catholic school there was hostile warfare, even though some of the priests professed to believe in socialism.

My parents vainly sought some religion on which they could agree. They visited the services of practically every denomination and dragged me along. They finally found the mysteries of spiritualism to intrigue them, and accepted their church services as fulfilling their duty to worship God.

We witnessed seances, peculiar sounds, foglike images at distances that made it impossible to verify what was happening. But because I had been attending the Saturday nickelodean movies of the great Houdini performing his famous escape stunts, I thought Houdini's claim that he could duplicate any stunt the spiritualists performed and do it better to be more truthful than what the spiritualists offered.

Even though ideas about religion kept my parents hostile to each other, they did accept the teachings of the Socialist party as offered by Debs. Although Debs spoke militantly about emancipating the working class from capitalist exploitation, his presence and behavior portrayed the image of a cultured thinker devoted to his fellow beings. The Socialists' ideas built hopes for better things to come.

In my early years at school I was harassed by the teachers because my father was at times a challenging candidate to become a Socialist mayor of Lynn, Massachusetts. At one election he was considered to be so much of a threat that the Democrats and Republicans joined together on a "fusion" ticket to prevent his election over either of their possible single candidates. Sometimes when the whole class was sent to the gymnasium for exercise and recreation, I was pulled out of the line and sent back to my seat without explanation.

During the First World War, the Industrial Workers of the World organized the woolen mill workers in Lowell, Lawrence, and Haverill. Strikes stopped the production of blankets and coats for the military. The schools distributed a printed statement which declared, "I am a 100% American." We children were instructed to take that statement home and have our parents sign it. My father refused and told me to advise my teacher of this. For that, I was expelled from school. The truant officer visited my parents to try to get them to sign that statement. My father explained that he supported the organization of the woolen workers and steadfastly refused to bow to the wishes of the truant officer. I think it was about two weeks later that the school sent word to my parents to have me return to school. The teachers continued to show their hostility to me because of my father's refusal to buckle under to them.

Among the famous Socialists who were prominent in Lynn were Helen Keller and Charles Steinmetz. Because she had overcome her deafness and blindness, Helen Keller was held in great esteem. When she spoke in Lynn, it was a major event where she praised the ideas of socialism. General Electric's scientist Charles Steinmetz was famed because he successfully applied Nicolai Tesla's ideas about alternating current to practical electric motors. Steinmetz was also a member of the Socialist party in Lynn. He advised my father that the electric motor was the means by which socialism would be achieved because it would emancipate the worker from the drudgery of wage labor. It appears now that he was overly optimistic about that because, although some jobs are now physically easier, the main result has been enormous profits for capitalism.

To help overcome the monotony and drudgery that unfairly burdened her life, my mother pursued the study of operatic music with her beautiful and powerful contralto. She insisted that I obtain some cultural influences and required me to study elocution, music, and dance, which aided my later life by giving me greater assurance when making public appearances and speaking to large audiences.

My mother's efforts were thwarted when she was killed by an auto driven by a drunken soldier having his last fling before being sent overseas during the First World War. My mother died instantly on her thirtieth birthday, March 31, 1918. In her coat pocket was a new bag of marbles, a last gift to me. I was nine years old then. The soldier who killed my mother was on active duty; civil legal recourse was not open to us until after the war. A small cash settlement was eventually awarded for my care.

After my mother's death, my father suffered one adversity after another. First he fell ill in the flu epidemic of 1918. When he recovered from that, on his way to work early one morning he fell on an icy sidewalk and broke his leg. Shortly after he returned to work,

A. G. Walton, where he had worked for twenty-five years, gave him a pink slip in his pay envelope which stated that his services were no longer required. It was his forty-fifth birthday. There were no pensions for retired workers at that time. Then Congress extended the draft to include forty-five-year-olds.

Because my father was an active, dedicated Socialist who opposed World War I, he vowed that if drafted he would not fight in it to kill workers of another country in order to make profits for American business. But the war ended before he could be caught up in that situation. The manpower shortage caused by the draft opened up many jobs for my father, one of which was as a conductor on the Bay State Street Railway system. On that job, he soon developed blood poisoning from blisters on his feet. The doctors who treated him strongly urged him to get out of the city because it was so full of pollution and poison that he was in constant danger of infections that could cause loss of his legs or even prove fatal.

After the success of the Russian revolution, which aroused new hopes among the working class, Massachusetts' Socialists voted to support the left wing of the Party, which went on to form the Communist party. Although my father's sympathies were with the left wing, his health prevented him from actively supporting the new Party. And I must record that I had heard my father express some misgivings about what would happen to the new organization because the "old Socialists" were notorious for "talking every question to death" without performing the actions needed. In fact, my father was completely fed up with the "old Socialists" because of their endless talk without deeds.

Since he had grown up on various farms during his youth, my father longed to get back to the soil. So he wrote his father, who had settled at Crowley in Oregon's Willamette Valley about 1910. My grandfather Dennett encouraged us to come west and settle near him. We did move west just before the railroad strike of June, 1919. We lived with my grandfather for about a year. Moving west caused me to lose track of my mother's family, which I've never been able to pick up since.

We soon learned that my grandfather Dennett had suffered persecution because of his socialist beliefs. He was arrested in Portland, Oregon, for participating in the Socialist and Industrial Workers of the World (IWW) "Free-Speech" fight of 1912. Because of this, he was restricted to the borders of his farm by the sheriff of Polk County for the duration of World War I. A Secret Service agent named Hough kept track of him on his farm. My grandfather was something of an enterprising person who took advantage of every opportunity to make a commission by selling land near his farm. So he sold a small lot to Hough who built a small house on it and lived in it from time to time when he was checking on my grandfather.

My father finally invested all his savings, including the settlement from my mother's death (about $1600) in a nearby farm. My father tried to make a go of it by hiring out with a team of powerful Percheron horses to the contractors building the first paved highway nearby. But the mortgage on the farm cost more than he could earn outside, and the farm needed several years before the orchards we planted could produce income.

Dad managed to hang on to the farm until I finished high school and went on to the normal school at Monmouth, Oregon. But after I went away to teach in southern Oregon in the late 1920s, Dad was unable to keep up the payments on the mortgage, so it was foreclosed. Dad went into partnership with another farmer raising raspberries. He hung on that way for several years, but that farm also finally failed because of the economic scissors of high cost of producing and low receipts from production. Dad had to go on welfare until he died. My earnings never were enough to sustain my family needs and to help him. So we drifted apart during his later years when I became overwhelmed with problems I couldn't overcome.

During my high school years my father and I lived in some isolation and poverty that I was not very conscious about. A retired blacksmith neighbor who had been an active Socialist in a Newport News, Virginia, shipyard lived next to our farm. Almost every day that I went to school Bill Gath and his wife Annie would invite me in to have something to eat and to talk. During those talks he would make suggestions about books that I should read to enlarge my education. Among them were many pamphlets that had been published by the Socialist party in the early 1900s. Although I have forgotten the titles of most of them, one book sticks prominently in my memory. That was *Colonel Robert G. Ingersoll's 44 Lectures Complete*, which convinced me that religion did not offer a solution to our social problems. (I recently learned that other labor leaders were influenced by Ingersoll's writings as I was; among them was Wyndham Mortimer of the United Auto Workers.)

Those many readings convinced me that socialism had to be the next step in the upward march of civilization. The main question was, how? Our problem revolved around the class distinctions that existed in every neighborhood. Rich farmers and poor farmers lived side by side. Sharecroppers did most of the work. The rich farmers got most of the wealth—one-third of the crop for allowing the use of the land. Every year we saw farm auctions that wiped out some poor farmer family that had worked hard for a year trying to make a go of it, only to lose it all and fail in the end.

My path led away from the rural life because I could not see how I could earn a living at it. I had worked at all available jobs on the ranches around us. I worked on the then-giant 1000-acre Horst hop ranch "succoring runners" and training the good ones to go up the trellis set for them. I plowed with a three-horse team pulling a two-bottom plow for a neighbor who had to help me harness the horses because they were so big I couldn't throw the harness over the hame collar. I hired out at harvest time pitching hay and pitching bundles for a small threshing machine owned by a neighbor named Hamilton. I picked prunes and later became a dryerman. The pay averaged $1 a day, which left me in poverty all the time. From all those activities the best I could do was buy the rubber boots I needed to work on the farm, buy winter union suits, overalls, raincoat and mittens.

In all the farming communities, I observed the exploitation of children of the poor who tried to survive following the various harvest seasons for fruit, nuts, and vegetables. But no matter what they did they could not lift themselves out of poverty. The eastern factories and the western farms were equally cruel to the poor.

When I graduated in 1925 from high school in Rickreall, Oregon, the chairman of the school board, who was also a county official, strongly invited me to attend a Ku Klux Klan rally at the Dallas, Oregon, County Fair grounds. Out of curiosity I did go that event. I saw over 10,000 white robed and hooded Klan members burning a cross, waving the American flag, and pledging to keep Negroes and Bolsheviks out of Polk County.

That rally was an alarming shock to me. My father had told me how he, his brothers, and his father fought gun battles with the Klan in North Carolina in the 1890s. My grandfather was prospecting for gold claims for some northern company. The Klan attacked him because he was a northerner who would not join them in terrorizing Negroes. My father's family was eventually driven out of that area after several gun battles, during one of which the log cabin in which they lived was burned down.

My introduction to education at the Oregon Normal School caused me to broaden my intellectual pursuits. A favorite professor of mine was J. F. Santee, who stimulated a desire to get a good foundation in the principles of education by studying what the great philosophers taught. Santee's emphasis was on growth and development. Those concepts were very meaningful to me because they built on some of my high school readings, such as Jane Addam's *Hull House*, Victor Hugo's *Les Miserables*, Shakespeare's *Merchant of Venice* and Karl Marx's *Das Kapital*, which helped convince me that the problems of misery for the poor could only be corrected by changing capitalism to socialism.

The day the Italo-American anarchists Sacco and Vanzetti were executed, Professor Santee reviewed their case in our principles of education class. He pointed out the discrepancies in the court case and explained the cruelty and injustice being committed against anarchist immigrants. The whole class, including me, was in tears.

When teaching I tried to keep a social conscience in the forefront of my work, but found barriers against me and my way of thinking all over the teaching profession. I was shocked at the prejudice some of my teachers expressed against Negroes and Mexicans. One of the geography teachers made a remark to the effect that "the reason the people in Mexico were poor was because they were lazy." I protested vigorously that that was not the real reason; I knew many who worked in the seasonal harvests and the rate of pay was not enough to hold their families together. The teacher then added, "They even stop work entirely at noon to take a siesta," implying again they were lazy. I exploded at that remark, declaring that I had worked with them and knew they worked just as hard as any of the rest of us.

For my outburst I was ordered out of the class and almost expelled from school. I later had to apologize to the teacher and the class in order to return for the credits I needed to complete that degree requirement. The president of the Normal School, J. S. Landers, worked out that plan to restore peace. I always felt that it would have been more appropriate for the teacher to apologize to me and the class, but no such justice existed in 1927–1928.

Our family's broad intellectual interests pushed me to enter forensic competition in high school and later in normal school with considerable success. That public attention caused me to be elected student body president in both schools where I won student approval for opposing the arbitrary restraints on our social life as students. But I was always handicapped by poverty. I could not participate in those extra social activities that required any special expenditure.

When I later went on for a short time to the University of Oregon, I saw elite snobbishness in the fraternity and sorority groups. Their clannish behavior excluded those of us too poor to join them. There were a few students with some social conscience, but not enough to have any impact on the teaching profession.

During my first year of teaching, in 1928–29, the financial condition of the nation was undermined by the stock market crash. It was no surprise to the farmers (such as my father and grandfather), because they had been crushed ever since World War I by high costs of production and low market prices for their crops.

My low economic status, because of low salaries for teachers, blocked my efforts for higher education. I couldn't pay for the extras needed for more college education. I couldn't dress in the manner and live the comforts that prevailed among the "upper" class. My first marriage foundered on poverty and broke up in its second year.

My course recorded here, especially my life as an activist in the union and Communist movements, seems to me to be logical, normal, inevitable, and qualified by lifelong experienced class consciousness. I trust that recounting my experiences will help those who read it to understand my course, and to justify theirs.

ह&

THE TURNING POINT

ह&

By 1931 I had watched the economic system of the United States fall into chaos. Banks were discounting teachers' salary checks. Some school districts were beginning to reduce teachers' pay and fears were being expressed that bank failures were going to cause the whole economic system to collapse. President Hoover kept predicting that "prosperity is just around the corner." But stock brokers and bankers were reported to be committing suicide by the thousands as their "paper profits," stock and bank finances collapsed. Mortgages on farms were being foreclosed and breadlines in the cities held more people than the cities could take care of. I observed these developments with increasing apprehension that nothing but disaster lay ahead for the working people and my conviction grew every able bodied person should work to change a system that was failing.

My experience in teaching was not satisfactory to me. Nineteen twenty-eight to twenty-nine was spent in a one room elementary rural school south of Bandon, Oregon, where I worked with four, then six students. All I could do was see to it they each learned the basics in reading, writing, spelling, and arithmetic. We did make some progress in hygiene, and gained some appreciation of art and a desire to continue their learning. I urged the school board to consolidate the district with Bandon where the children could have better facilities than could be provided in that little one room school. I was offered a contract for the next year but gave up that idea in favor of the consolidation for the students. As a consequence I was too late in trying to obtain another teaching job for the next year, so was unemployed. I finally obtained a student loan from Ben Selling, a noted philanthropist in Portland. That allowed me to obtain a teaching contract for the next year; in the meantime, I attended the University of Oregon for the spring and summer quarters. I had to work on the side to make the small loan stretch for those two quarters. I waited tables in the dormitory and mowed grass for several sororities.

Late in 1931, while teaching elementary school near Portland, Oregon, I received a letter from my father, who was not a Communist party member at that time (although he did join much later), urging me to attend a conference in Portland to oppose the prosecution of some Communists under the Oregon Criminal Syndicalism statute. Our family had long opposed that law as being in violation of the U.S. Constitution because it made any efforts to organize workers or farmers into labor unions illegal. The cases then being prosecuted involved more than a dozen citizens and several aliens. Victims at the meeting were a Mr. Mitsif, a Mr. Popoff, and

Dirk de Jonge. The Immigration and Naturalization Service had begun proceedings against the aliens that, if carried out, would deport them to Bulgaria and Romania, where they faced immediate execution by right-wing dictatorships. So the defense of them was an actual matter of life or death.

I went to that conference, which was held under the auspices of the International Labor Defense, a Communist-led organization that defended the legal rights of workers. There I heard a lawyer by the name of Irwin Goodman declare his legal opinion that the Oregon Criminal Syndicalism law was unconstitutional, and he proposed to take his challenge all the way to the U.S. Supreme Court. He made a super-eloquent plea for audience support to carry the case all the way to win. And in 1937, the Supreme Court did agree with attorney Goodman's appeal, striking down the Oregon Criminal Syndicalism law as unconstitutional.

Mitsif, Popoff, and de Jonge spoke eloquently in their own behalf, contending that they were being prosecuted for their beliefs, but not for any illegal acts. A representative of the Communist party, Fred Walker, spoke spiritedly of the need for all believers in democracy to rally behind this legal case to insure that the principles of democracy be preserved.

It seemed to me that the least I could do was contribute small amounts of money and attend rallies for this cause which was obviously a just one. So I accepted invitations to attend many more meetings in Portland where I had the opportunity to talk with Communist leader Walker.

Because I was dissatisfied with the restricted life of a school teacher, I decided it was time for me to try to help change the evil oppressive system that blocked our growth and full development. I became convinced that the emancipation of the working class would not be accomplished through education alone, but rather that we would have to change the governmental power relationships. How to do that was very hazy and unclear, but the Communist party claimed to know how and cited their victory in Russia as living evidence proving their case. So I was persuaded to follow them. At that time I learned that their fundamental political program was the revolutionary overthrow of the capitalist system, replacing it with a socialist system which they claimed was succeeding in the Soviet Union.

When I decided to join the Communist party, U.S.A., in 1931 in Portland, Oregon, I was ordered to make up a Party name. I chose

Victor Haines. Victor is my middle name; Haines was an assumed middle name of my then-divorced wife. I soon found that it was not very simple or easy to join the Communist party at that time. It kept itself hidden from public access because of constant fear of illegal attacks and violence from a hostile public and public officials. The local Communist leaders at that time were very defensive and seldom available in public. They suspected every stranger of being a government agent out to spy on and betray them.

When I applied for membership I was told that the membership committee would have to investigate me. They questioned me at great length and challenged me as to why I was willing to take the risk of joining them when they were being prosecuted. I explained that my father had been a dedicated Socialist party member for many years; that I had studied Marx's *Das Kapital;* that when I was going to high school our family subscribed to many liberal and radical papers and magazines for years, including the *Daily Worker,* the *Butte Daily Bulletin,* the *Plentywood News,* the *Nation, The New Republic,* and *LaFollette's* magazine; and that all our sympathies belonged to the working class.

The membership committee suspected that because I was teaching school I had to be bourgeois. I had to inform them that school teachers were on the lowest rungs of the economic ladder, sometimes being paid less than day laborers. I advised them that I had carefully studied the six-volume Lenin library, that I rejoiced in the successes of the Russian Revolution and hoped we could bring about socialism in the United States of America because that logic meant turning our society from a dog-eat-dog conflict into a cooperative society, where people worked in harmony and helped each other instead of climbing over their corpses to get ahead.

Mitsif and Popoff, de Jonge's codefendants, were on the membership committee and they were extremely suspicious that new applicants were apt to be police spies attempting to infiltrate the Party to betray them. So they set up a special test for me. They ordered me to meet them on a dark night in a dark alley. At that time I was young, strong, and unafraid, so I met them as ordered. They walked me around several dark streets and alleys in silence for awhile. Then they warned me that the Party dealt severely with betrayers and spies. I sort of chuckled and laughed that one off. Then one of them put something to the back of my head and said, "In the Soviet Union they execute spies with a revolver to the back of the head." I asked him if he had a revolver. He answered, "no." I then told him he was playing a dangerous game with me and that I was through with it. They said they wanted to test my nerve, found me to be okay, and would recommend me for Party membership.

After the membership committee recommended accepting me, I was invited to Party meetings. I was shocked to learn the extreme cautions the Party followed to try to protect the place of meetings from becoming known to nonmembers. The first place to which I was invited required me to go to one address, where I was given a password which let me in at a different address. All this seemed unnecessary to me, but the leaders assured me they had to do it to safeguard the Party meetings from uninvited outsiders.

At that first meeting I learned that Fred Walker was the Section Organizer in charge of all Communist party activity in Oregon. He gave out assignments to many different members. I was ordered to attend a new members' class and a labor history class. These classes kept me quite busy outside of my teaching duties.

It soon became apparent that most of the other new members, who were mainly middle class liberal intellectuals, were learning asbtract ideas—book learning—in these classes, while I was finding confirmation and academic explanations of my own class experience. Before I realized what was happening I found myself teaching some of those classes. Then I was elected to attend a Communist party district meeting in Seattle. Fred Walker arranged everything, including a stop at a farm near Woodland, Washington, run by some Finns, to whom he was related by marriage, where we were treated to sauna baths and banquetlike meals both going to Seattle and returning to Portland.

I must confess that I listened carefully to everything that was discussed at that district meeting of the Communist party but did not begin to understand what was taking place. The impression I got was that all the good plans of the previous meeting were not carried out and everyone must do better in the next period. I heard words, such as: "opportunism," "sectarianism," "nihilism," "plenum," "co-opt," "factionalism," "chauvinism," "democratic centralism," "discipline," "dialectical materialism," and "agent *provocateur*" used in entirely different contexts than ever before. Organizational terms such as "unit organizer," "agitprop," "Control Commission," "Buro" were obscure, and the foreign-born people puzzled me because their logic seemed to be different from anything I had been taught in school. They explained that their discussions were polemical and dialectical, but that didn't explain it to me because I did not understand "polemical" or "dialectical." Those words were never used in normal school or when teaching.

It did seem to me that there were wide disagreements among the leaders who spoke and that those disagreements were not resolved in that meeting. Later I learned that my first impressions about those disagreements were accurate and that there were very real, severe conflicts among those leaders; some of this was what was later identified as factionalism—personal disagreements not based on principle.

The district organizer was Alex Noral, who had recently replaced Sidney Bloomfield whose health forced him to return to the East for medical treatment. Noral was looked up to in the beginning because he had just returned from the Soviet Union where he attended the Party's Lenin school in Moscow after the American Party's factional fight was settled by Stalin. The local Party people expected great leadership from someone who had the benefit of being educated in the Lenin school in Moscow. But Noral was sharply critical of almost everyone in the meeting and he demanded that they begin to act like Bolsheviks did in the Soviet Union. Most people present didn't understand what was meant by that demand. The organizational secretary, Ed Leavitt, who worked as a member of the Window Cleaners Union, spoke in a soft voice but made cutting remarks about some of the members' failures to carry out party assignments, and he disagreed with Noral on many points.

The chairman of the Control Commission, the disciplinary apparatus of the Party, was a Scotsman named John Laurie who worked as a boilermaker. His report announced punishment imposed on some members: some were reprimanded, some expelled, some given conditional membership providing they corrected their mistakes as directed by the Party officials and/or committees. That was all too strange for me to understand, mainly because I did not know anything about their so-called errors or violations of Party discipline, and it was in total conflict with what I had come to believe was our fair American system of justice, where the accused were considered innocent until proven guilty. Later I did become acquainted with many instances of unfair prosecution of labor activists in the American courts.

The financial secretary was a quite old man by the name of Jackson who complained that the district organizer was spending money the Party either did not have or could not afford. I did not understand then how they could do that, but later I learned that they borrowed money from sympathizers. The Party officials had no intention of paying it back, because they knew they would always be short of money in the future and there was no way they could repay it.

Walker went to great lengths to explain to me that the Party needed some new blood in the center of Seattle. He explained that Noral was demanding that he, Walker, become the district agitprop. Walker considered that to be an incorrect move because he had so many irons in the fire in Portland which he had to continue to attend to. He stressed that he just couldn't leave because there were not enough capable leaders in Portland to carry on all the campaigns he had started. Then Walker propositioned me to take the district agitprop job. I responded that I thought I really didn't know enough about that work to properly undertake its responsibilities, and besides I had plans to go on to college and get degrees in education and sociology. Walker scoffed at any future in education, stressing that it was much more important for me to work in the class struggle than in the classroom. He reminded me that my background belonged to the working class and that the Party needed me more than the children did. It was very clear that Walker had no intention of going back to Seattle to work with Noral.

A short time after we returned to Portland, Walker showed me a telegram from Noral ordering me to Seattle to become district agitprop. Walker advised me that that was a Party order and I had to obey or suffer disciplinary action. After thinking it over a couple of days I told Walker that I would give it a try after resigning my teaching job. I was so attached to the children I was teaching that I almost changed my mind as I was explaining to them that I was resigning from teaching to take on a much larger responsibility. About half the children broke down and cried, and so did I. But by then the "die was cast." I couldn't back out after making that commitment.

So in early February, 1932, I took my worldly belongings in two suitcases, the clothes on my back and one month's teacher's pay of $110 to Seattle and I reported to the Party office. Noral looked at me skeptically at first, then informed me that one of the women clothing workers had a room for me where I could stay for awhile and that I had to attend a District Buro meeting to be "co-opted" into membership in the Buro. The meeting occurred a day or two later and I was welcomed into the district leadership. I noticed that most of the Buro members spoke with accents indicating alien origins. I had no idea what I was supposed to do except that the Agitprop was responsible for educating new members, drawing up leaflets, making speeches when called upon and otherwise carrying out the Party line, which was published in the various official Party publications. I found it to be a full time job to read and try to understand those many publications.

I soon found out that in the ranks of about 250 Party members there were friendly, devoted, self-sacrificing people who gave everything they had for the cause, even to marching in protest parades where they knew in advance that they risked being beaten by hired goons or by the police, arrested and jailed. They gave their last dollar to support every Party campaign. They believed right and justice belonged on their side, protesting against imperialist war, supporting the shingle weavers' picket line, marching for unemployment insurance, saving the Scottsboro boys, organizing industrial red trade unions, and fervently defending the Soviet Union against threatened imperialist war.

ॐ

ORIENT TO HUNGER

ॐ

When I agreed to take on the job of District Agitprop Director I assumed that I would become a "professional revolutionary," which meant that I would be dedicated to Party work for the rest of my life. But I soon found out that I had no real idea of what that involved. I never had any financial income from the Party. At that time there was a common belief that living in a commune was ideal for a Communist. However, my experience was far less than satisfactory. I lived with a half dozen unemployed single men who depended on left-over food given to us at the wholesale distributors. We clothed ourselves with "cast-offs" whenever they could be found. None of the others understood why I would want a private corner where I could study, think, and work on plans for the Agit-prop Department. I was so busy with academic activities I could not do my share of scrounging for food and clothing. It became evident the others resented my lack of contributions for the group. There was no division of labor. They wanted each one to do everything in turn. I had to make other arrangements so I could study, concentrate, and plan. Group living interfered with my effort to do justice to my responsibilities. A private family finally took me in. That style of living proved to be best for me.

In 1932, something exciting was happening every day in Communist politics. National speakers were touring America on every imaginable issue, as well as on the national election campaign. At one time or other we met all the national leaders including Earl Browder, general secretary; William Z. Foster, chairman of the Trade Union Unity League; Herbert Benjamin, leader in Unemployed Councils; Jack Stachel, a labor leader; Elizabeth Gurley Flynn, an ex-IWW fiery organizer among textile workers; and Mother Bloor, famous for raising money for the Party by selling bonds payable after the revolution.

The local Party apparatus had to arrange the meeting place, get out the leaflets, borrow the money to rent the hall, meet the speaker, arrange for his/her accommodations, confer with him/her to satisfy the needs of that campaign, and learn all the latest instructions from the national office. Everyone had to show total deference to the touring speakers and try to obey their every command. The most important issue in every such affair was to raise enough money to cover the cost of putting on the meeting.

Strangely enough, one of the first political public meetings I was ordered to attend was significant but had nothing to do with the Communist party directly. The Puget Sound Savings and Loan Association had failed and closed its doors. A public meeting was advertised to do something about it. The Party district organizer, Alex Noral, had me attend to observe what went on and to let him know. He claimed to be part Indian and expected to inherit some money from the sale of some Indian land that he thought was controlled by that savings and loan association.

I saw a large group of people completely confused and without any ability to express their wishes or to obtain sufficient information to learn what to do. When the time came to convene the meeting, an elderly man dressed in expensive sports clothes walked up to the front of the room holding an elaborately decorated short swagger-stick, and tapped on the table for order. Someone near him nominated him to be chairman. Another nearby moved to close the nominations. The man at the table declared himself elected. Some people attempted to ask questions, but the chairman fended off every question by declaring that he was appointing a fact-finding committee to look into everything and report at a later time. I was never able to follow up on that development other than to notice that all reports in the papers pointed to a very dismal picture for the investors in that institution. My memory is that very much later the investors recovered about ten cents on the dollar deposited.

The most critical political issue in Seattle in 1932 was unemployment and acute hunger. The best information I could gather at the time was that the only people who were working and getting paid wages were city, county, state, and federal workers. And they were being pushed downward by successive wage cuts. The city of Seattle had three such cuts, each one about ten percent. The city and county workers were paid with warrants (essentially giving the workers IOUs) which the banks discounted by fifteen to twenty-five percent if cashed then and most people had to do so. One estimate at that time was that about 90,000 families were dependent on commissary food relief. That was probably close to half the population of Seattle.

The most prominent organization attempting to cope with the problem of unemployment and hunger was the Unemployed Citizens' League (UCL). It was organized in 1931 by Carl Branin, J. F. Cronin, and Hulet Wells of the Seattle Labor College (which had a Socialist party orientation and received the tolerant support of the Central Labor Council). By 1932, the UCL had enrolled more than 50,000 members organized around neighborhood commissaries that were somewhat self-administered as self-help, barter and relief agencies. The commissaries were supported by solicitations, and allotments financed by friendly businesses and sympathetic King County commissioners, especially Louis Nash, who was a closet Socialist. But as the city and county governments became impoverished and unable to furnish enough food and relief to the commissaries, the public authorities ordered arbitrary reductions in the allotments to families. This caused spontaneous violent protests from the people directly affected.

Nineteen thirty-two, being a big election year, saw every ambitious politician visit the local neighborhood Unemployed Citizens' League organizations. The leaders of the UCL sought the help of all the candidates to obtain more relief for their members. Many candidates made sympathetic promises. But the most controversial point was over permitting the Communist candidates to speak or to participate in the UCL activities. The Central Council of the UCL adopted a motion ordering all neighborhood locals to bar Communists from speaking at their meetings. But some Communists did break through that restriction because there was much dissension among the members over the failure of the leaders to block the relief cuts. I managed to speak to several neighborhood locals as an official representative of the Communist party. I was granted the floor by votes of the members at the meetings because many members wanted to know what the Communist program really was. Sometimes Marion Zioncheck, who was the UCL's attorney and a Democrat candidate for Congress, spoke, urging the local group to hear about the Communist ideas in the interest of democracy. I emphasized in my speeches that the Communist party advocated changing the economic and social system as the necessary ultimate solution, but while waiting for that it was necessary to resist evictions and utility shut-offs. These were the policies of the Communist Party's Unemployed Councils, which additionally advocated unemployment insurance and demanded union wages be paid for all work relief.

While in Seattle on a national tour, Herbert Benjamin, one of the national leaders of the Communist party and head of the Unemployed Councils, demanded that the local Communist party officials build the Unemployed Councils and vigorously oppose the Unemployed Citizens' League. He labeled them a "social fascist" organization intent on betraying the workers. This policy caused me severe problems later because it did not answer to the needs of the people in 1932.

PARTY POLICIES

The *Communist Manifesto,* written by Karl Marx and Friedrich Engels, starts out showing the conflict between the bourgeois class and the proletarian class by declaring, "The history of all hitherto existing society is the history of class struggles." Lenin expanded on Marx's writings showing all aspects of society to be various forms of class struggle. So this became the criterion from which the Party decided its policies. Failure to recognize the "class struggle" angle in every political situation opened the door to criticism. All of us tried to fulfill the obligation to give objective consideration to the class angle by using dialectical materialism. Disputes among us could arise over disagreement about the "facts" and also over the conclusions we made from the facts.

The Communist party prided itself on being able to reach the best conclusions about any political problems because it used dialectical materialism as its method of reasoning. The "materialist" part meant that the facts used in the reasoning process had to be real, not imaginary. The "dialectics" part was logical reasoning based on real facts. This formal method was glorified but seldom proven or demonstrated. When we could obtain the necessary facts as reality, the results, when estimating political situations, seemed to be correct. But most of the time we had to make decisions on the basis of limited information, so our decisions allowed faults to intrude more often than not. Too often we were ordered to carry out a policy or decision that had been made elsewhere or by some higher authority. The so-called "Party line", which precluded any possible changes, governed most of our activities. We were taught that our leaders were the wisest because they used the dialectical method of historical materialism. It was rare for the lowest structure of the Party to attempt to use this process, but it did come into play in the larger sections and districts. I did observe its successful use in the District Buro.

I soon learned that something identified as "democratic centralism" was the controlling principle of Party functioning. "Democratic" meant that everyone could take part in making the decision, and once it was made, any minority was obliged to abide by the majority. "Centralism" meant that all subordinate parts of the organization were required to obey the decisions of the higher bodies. This decision-making process occurred mainly regarding major policy questions. But when something important occurred everyone had to obey these principles. Failure to do so caused discipline to be imposed. Everything pointed to Lenin as the author of these rules which governed the Bolsheviks before they adopted the name Communist. As long as these principles were practiced as objective laws there seemed to be no fault, just ordinary logic. Justice and fairness depended on observing the material facts of truth and reality. But when applied capriciously it resulted in disaster to anyone who fell into disfavor (as I did later). Basically, the principle appeared to be majority rule, which seemed also to be espoused by American democratic ideals. Later I learned it followed the military conception of discipline, where the lower ranks were compelled to obey the higher ones.

When advocating a Party policy in competition with other political organizations, our tactic was to win the other rank and file members to our side by using critical attacks on the opposition leaders. This was known as the "United Front from Below." The Communist party was intent on securing its leadership over the working class by isolating the competition. Stalin openly advocated isolating those organizations whose policies were closest to the Communist party, because where the Party was in a "united front" with other groups, it was the aim of the Party to win control for itself. This attitude seemed to be well understood by the Socialist party because it almost always refused to cooperate with the Communist party in any joint effort. They maintained that no one should trust an agreement with the Communist party. Later, when the issue of opposing fascism became the most important question, the Socialist party shied away from any arrangement where the Communist party was involved. The Communist party took advantage of that situation to win the masses away from the Socialist party. The "United Front from Below" was paramount.

Party policies and decisions were always intended to be transmitted to the masses. That was done through the public channels open to us, such as daily newspapers and other publications, but we did not depend solely on those. We created what we identified as "our" mass organizations. They were public organizations, but they were mainly controlled by Party leaders as our "transmission" belts.

The most important was the Trade Union Unity League (TUUL). That was an effort led by William Z. Foster to exert influence among all labor unions by establishing red trade unions committed to the policy of "Defend the Soviet Union." Some of the greatest successes in red trade union organization occurred in the Northwest. A fisherman by the name of Emile Linden organized the Columbia River fisherman into a union which affiliated with the Red International of Labor Unions. Then he organized several groups of fishermen on Puget Sound. He died in an automobile accident before he could complete that work. His successors didn't have his perspectives and allowed those organizations to turn their backs on anything red. Their agreements were more in the nature of co-op plans, sharing the profits. The AFL opened its doors to workers in many different red unions in 1934 and 1935, which had the effect of checking the growth of the red unions. At that time, when there were indications the industrial union movement would begin, the TUUL ended its attempt at separate organization and dissolved.

Valiant efforts were made by Jim Murphy to organize lumber workers into red unions, and his propaganda and organizational efforts were a big influence on the later organization of the International Woodworkers of America. Murphy was politically destroyed by the Party for reasons not known to me. There were whispered claims that he was a drunkard and that he absconded with union money. That was the usual way in which the personal integrity of a prominent leader was undermined before he was expelled and politically destroyed.

The FSU ("Friends of the Soviet Union") was very successful in organizing groups to visit the Soviet Union. They came back with complimentary reports about the progress of socialism in the Soviet Union. I remember a Tacoma longshoreman by the name of Walter Larson who made glowing reports about the Soviet successes in production and the elimination of unemployment. But at the end he said he thought the Soviet men were lazy because the women were doing all the heavy work, including longshoring. The Party did not continue that tour.

A vitally important group was the ILD, International Labor Defense, whose main job was to organize the defense of workers and Communists arrested while participating in demonstrations on behalf of any group participating in the class struggle. There was a time when the American Civil Liberties Union could not be relied on to defend Communists afoul of the law. So the Party had to have its own instrument to protect its members. While the ILD did use lawyers, it put major emphasis on mobilizing masses of workers to militantly, physically demonstrate on behalf of those facing court problems. Many times they were successful. But too often they were not.

Locally we had recurring struggles to prevent the deportation of aliens who were members of the Party. The most frequently recurring case was that of Leon Glaser. He was a Russian Jew, prominent in the International Ladies' Garment Workers Union (ILGWU). Glaser was noted for being the most educated and articulate speaker in the Russian language around Seattle, and was an effective shop steward for the ILGWU. He also spoke English perfectly. He was frequently ordered deported, but the order could not be carried out because Russia would not accept him, and neither would any other country because he was a worker and a Communist party member. The Immigration and Naturalization Service always had to ultimately release him on technicalities dug up by the defense lawyers. Many protest meetings, where collections were taken to pay the expenses of his defense, were held in his behalf. The only legal case the government had against him was as a foreign-born member of the Communist party, not for any actions that could be classed as violations of law.

Lowell Wakefield, a Washington State native, was sent on a newspaper assignment to the South to investigate the arrests and convictions of a group of Negro youths who had been sentenced to death for alleged rape of white women in Scottsboro, Alabama. The facts Wakefield found completely contradicted the claims of the authorities, so it looked like another notorious southern lynching, only this time with the appearance of being legal. Wakefield's efforts on that case started a worldwide protest movement which ultimately saved the lives of all except one youth, who died in prison before the legal actions took effect. That campaign made the International Labor Defense and Wakefield famous. The Scottsboro campaign helped stir up vigorous opposition to the ruthless oppression suffered by black Americans throughout the South. Although major efforts were made to capitalize on the prestige that effort gave the Communist party, the black people hesitated to join the Communist party mainly because they did not trust the white Party leadership. Elevating blacks to top Party positions did not cure that problem.

The Party policy about the Negro question was very confusing. On the one hand, we argued for "self-determination" in the "Black Belt," but on the other hand, we could not outline any believable procedure by which to accomplish it. Many blacks made it known that they were more concerned with ending discrimination so they could live as equal human beings here and now.

The Party had close ties with many national language organizations. Among them were Finnish, Polish, Slav, Croation, and Jewish groups. They were mainly under the control of top Party leaders nationally. The strongest one was the Finnish Federation, but it suffered from an internal political struggle that ultimately reduced its influence. Some Jewish, Slavonian, and Croation groups maintained organizations for quite a long time and strongly influenced those immigrants to remain loyal to the Soviet Union. An insurance group, the International Worker's Order, serviced these language groups quite successfully for many years.

I gradually began to understand that I was not adequately informed about how Party policies were formulated or how to handle them. I was amazed at the amount of theoretical material available, in the form of outlines and study guides for classes, to teach Party policies to the members. They explicitly presented the teachings of Marx, Engels, Lenin, and Stalin and current issues. They dealt with strike strategy and tactics, and the use of the United Front from Below. I found them to be very informative and tried to persuade others in the district leadership that we ought to make full use of this material to raise the theoretical level of the entire membership, and to conduct public open forums where our leaders could make that information available to the general public. I ran into subtle opposition which was difficult to understand at first. Then I discovered that most of the active leaders were unfamiliar with the academic background of the Party theories and relied instead on current orders and directives from the top national leaders.

Being fresh from active teaching, I was intrigued with those study outlines and became totally impressed with the extensive effort the Party national headquarters had made to solve all the theoretical problems confronting us. As I studied the resources, they seemed to be logically sound. But when we tried to discuss our theories with non-Party people we ran into discouraging hostility. The Wobblies refused to accept any idea of political action to begin with, and insisted that only workers' control through industrial unionism would satisfy their abstract ideas of government. Our speakers continually competed with IWW leader "Big" Jim Thompson who frequently spoke on Skid Road on the corner of Washington and Occidental streets in Seattle—an area which has been redesigned by the city planners and has lost its identity with its past.

The Socialist party speakers condemned the Communist party for the cruelties committed in the Soviet Union under Stalin. We flatly denied that such cruelties were committed, because we didn't know any better at that time. So we counterattacked the Socialist party for failing to support the Soviet Union for establishing socialism in our time. Here again we accepted the claims of the top party leaders, little understanding the complexity of establishing a socialism that could be accepted as a real step toward our ideal of Marxian communism.

I visited the Socialist party open forum one night because the advertised speaker was Hulet Wells, an old line Socialist leader of the UCL. His subject was something about "what became of Marxism?" Wells made an entertaining speech expounding on Marx's genius in analyzing the capitalist system. But he ended with a declaration that it was a pity that no one had taken up the reins to continue to promote Marx's knowledge after Marx died. In the question period I asked him if he ever heard of Friedrich Engels. Wells said he did, but felt Engels really didn't do much for Marx's theories. Then I asked him if he ever heard of Lenin. Wells broke down and cried. Then he answered that he met Lenin when he visited Russia just after the revolution, and found him to be the greatest genius on earth. He admitted that Lenin did carry on Marx's work. My questions embarrassed Wells, and I was sorry to do that because I knew that he was one of the victims of the first World War. He served time in McNeil Penitentiary where he was tortured because he was convicted of sedition for opposing the United States' entrance into World War I.

Even though we were unable to convince everyone that the Soviet Union was truly on the path of socialism, our continued agitation and propaganda stating that the Soviet Union had abolished unemployment and was moving ahead, inspired the hope of the workers throughout the world. It had its effect, ultimately causing most of the active members to resign from the Socialist party and join the Communist party. We held forth a hope for a better world within our lifetimes, whereas the Socialist party leaders expended most of their effort criticizing and condemning the Communist party without providing any hope for political or economic improvement in the foreseeable future. We quoted Lenin, "Capitalism would not fall by itself, it had to be pushed over."

The Communist party contended that it was pursuing "scientific socialism" based on the principles of historical materialism as taught by Marx, in contrast to that brand of dreamers better known as "Utopian Socialists." The distinction we made was that the Communist party "made things happen" and intended to make the proletarian revolution happen—instead of waiting for it to happen, as the Socialist party advocated. The "old" Socialists argued that capitalism would automatically change to socialism by evolutionary processes, peacefully, claiming that was Marx's own theory. We replied that Lenin corrected that interpretation because capitalism had turned into imperialism, which would not willingly give up its power and privilege. Instead capitalism would make war to redivide the world markets at the expense of the workers.

Because I had read the foremost writings of Karl Marx, who argued that the working-class had the obligation to overthrow the capitalist system to save civilization for everyone (as stated in *The Communist Manifesto*) I searched in the Party literature for answers as to how that was to be accomplished. I found some hints that seemed logical, although most workers were not really convinced.

One such idea was that small strikes could be spread to become large strikes that would paralyze the capitalist system, leaving it no way out except to let the workers take over. Another part of that was that economic strikes could be turned into political strikes which would bring down the ruling class. Then there were suggestions that when the capitalists turn violent against the workers, the workers would fight back and unseat the capitalists. There is also the teaching that revolutionary trade unions could bring about the overthrow of capitalism with a "general strike." Those are all entertaining theories, but nothing in the United States to date has worked out as theorized.

In another vein, I found in some of Lenin's writings the idea that a revolutionary situation could develop in a capitalist nation when an economic crisis developed into a financial crisis, which in turn could become a political crisis where the existing ruling class became unable or unwilling to solve the crisis. Then if a disciplined political party with a revolutionary conscience existed, the system could be changed by a militant mass uprising. In a limited way that explained the situation that obtained in Russia when the Bolsheviks took power. Lenin also taught that support for socialist ideas among workers was not automatic, that the Party had to make a special effort to persuade the workers that socialism was the historical solution to the contradictions of the capitalist-imperialist system. This was what Lenin and his wife, Krupskaya, taught the masses through the old Russian Social-Democratic Labor Party for many years, and that was why the working class in Russia accepted Lenin's proposal to build socialism in Russia: they were prepared for it.

Later I noticed that Stalin expressed a different version of what took place in Russia than is projected in John Reed's *Ten Days that Shook the World*. While that is an exciting portrayal of what happened, it falls short of really explaining how the Bolsheviks took power. Stalin has reported that the Bolsheviks took power with well organized units of soldiers and sailors who felt betrayed by the czar's government, and again by Kerensky. And in recent years many leaders have admitted that the stability of their governments depends on their own internal military power. A famous quote from Mao states, "Power comes from the barrel of a gun." So anyone contemplating a seizure of power has to be able to overcome the military power of the existing ruling government.

It is a literary tragedy that so many writers refer to the Seattle Skid Road district as "Skid Row" because it completely distorts the meaning. The Seattle Skid Road was a place where logs were skidded down Yesler Hill to the waterfront where they were processed in a sawmill. It was the center of business activity in pioneer days. It was where the workers felt at home in their natural environment. It was where they elevated themselves. The conversion to Skid Row betrays a demeaning of the basic work that was done on the Yesler Hill skid road and in Henry Yesler's waterfront sawmill. The term loses any real meaning while forsaking its origin.

When I came to Seattle I was privileged to become a participant with the "Party institution" on the Skid Road better known as "Iron-Hat O'hanrahan." Iron-Hat became known that way because he always wore a black derby hat. He was crippled from polio and limped severely. He held forth at the corner of Washington and Occidental streets, where his brother had a cigar store. O'hanrahan kept a short stepladder and a soap box in his brother's store. He joined the Communist party after giving up on the Wobblies. So every Saturday evening when the crowds began to gather, Iron-Hat would get out the stepladder and soap box and offer the Communist literature for sale. Sometimes he would offer the whole batch for free distribution after his listeners' contributions were sufficient to pay for the bundle. Other times he would make a short speech baiting the Wobbly speaker Thompson. When the Salvation Army marched in to Skid Road, he would lead the crowd in singing some old Wobbly songs like "Solidarity," "The Cause of the Needy," "Hold the Fort," "The Red Flag," and "The International." Then he would bait any competition, especially Sister Doris and Sister Faye who played their mandolins and shook their hips while soliciting money for the religious missions they managed. Both were known in Alaska during the old gold rush aftermath. Sometimes an old sourdough would sidle up to one of them and ask, "Do you remember me, honey?" Faye and Doris kept on playing and singing, and shaking their hips.

I frequently had the Party assignment to speak on Skid Road because I belonged to the Skid Road unit of the Party. I usually enjoyed that challenge very much, although it sometimes caused me to lose my voice when the weather was bad or I attempted to speak too long or stayed too late answering questions from the audience. Frequently we had more than a thousand in that crowd, workers all.

The national leaders of the Communist party were demanding that we "Americanize" the Party because too many leaders showed their alien origin when they spoke to the public with a foreign accent. These leaders' immigrant backgrounds gave the impression that the Communist party was a foreign agency. That condition was inherited from the Party's early days when the main burden of the Party work was carried on by Socialist immigrants from all over Europe. In the early 1930s there weren't many native-born Americans leading the Party's local activities. Most of us had great difficulty trying to understand what the foreign-born with dialects were saying or meaning. And the political language of the Party made it very difficult to understand what was actually meant when spoken in a foreign accent. Many misunderstandings occurred because of the numerous language differences. Dialects and dialectics were logically confused.

A blood-curdling sight appeared in the Party office one day when Casey Boskaljon wearily walked into our presence. His clothes were torn in many places, his head had been shaved on top, a crooked swastika in red paint was on top of his head, his face was unshaven and he was a picture of total desperation. Slowly and hesitantly we were able to piece together what happened to him. He had been in the Yakima valley visiting various farmers, urging them to organize into the United Farmers League. Apparently he had begun to meet with some success because a group of anti-union leaders and city officials in Yakima decided to stop his activities. They captured him, shaved his head, roughed him up in the dirt, accused him of being a Communist agitator, and turned him loose down the road quite a way out of Yakima. He managed to hitchhike rides with several different autos, coming to Seattle over several days' time. We were not in a position to do much about what happened to Boskaljon. We did prepare accounts of this Nazi-like abuse of a farm organizer and released them to all the newspapers that would take them, but we could not provide enough explanation to attract much attention. Small notices did appear in the Communist party publications. Later I read in a Communist newspaper, the *New World*, that he became a working farmer in Eatonville, Washington.

My first political conflict within the Party arose when I attempted to correct the grammar in a draft anti-war leaflet that had been drawn up by the district organizer, Alex Noral. I thought it was unclear in meaning to an American public. Noral took violent exception to everything I said about the leaflet, and branded me a rotten intellectual, claiming that the workers would understand it without meddling from a school teacher. I lost that round but decided to put together a report on the work of the agitprop department since I had accepted the position of director. I read that report to a Buro meeting in the spring of 1932. The essence of that report was that the district organizer was in conflict with everyone and did not make an adequate effort to help the activists who tried to carry out the Party policies.

Noral responded to this report by adjourning the meeting and accusing me of being a factionalist, a Trotskyite, a rotten liberal, and probably a spy who sneaked into the Party to betray it. I was totally perplexed. Ed Leavitt, the organization secretary, came to my rescue by getting Noral to agree the next day to send me to Bellingham, where they had been begging for help. "To the sticks" was my discipline. Not knowing what else to do, I accepted that decision and went to Bellingham as soon as I could, still thinking of myself as a professional revolutionary.

To reorient myself I reread the *Communist Manifesto* and several books by Lenin and Stalin. These ideas stimulated me to a determination to do the best possible job for the Party in Bellingham. Stalin's *Foundations of Leninism* became my most studied guide.

ॐ

BELLINGHAM PARTY ORGANIZER

ॐ

I went to Bellingham, Washington, in the spring of 1932. There I found a very disciplined Communist party of seven members; an Unemployed Council of the same seven members; a Friends of the Soviet Union branch of the same seven members; and an International Labor Defense branch of the same seven members. They were certain that they were following the Party line in every particular, and complained that the masses were just too backward to act in their own behalf by joining our Party organizations. Our Communist party members faithfully carried out every Party campaign by peddling leaflets, pamphlets, and newspapers. But they had no public influence on anything. They were what I later learned to identify as a classic example of "sectarianism," with total loyalty to the working class and the ideals of the Communist party, but completely isolated from all other existing political activities.

I soon found out that in the city of Bellingham there were mass meetings of the general public with thousands of people gathering to hear discussions about socialism, unemployment, democracy, and many issues coming up in the 1932 elections. They were conducted by some active liberal people stimulated by an organization named the Equality Club, led by a Dr. Beebe. Beebe had sympathies with socialist ideas of Edward Bellamy's old "looking backward" variety. He was intellectually interested and active in current events.

Among the outstanding speakers invited to address these gatherings of between a thousand and two thousand people was George Vanderveer, a Seattle attorney respected for defending workers victimized for union activities. He was a strong drawing card to the public and he spoke from widespread experience and strong convictions with which he condemned the injustices of the capitalist economic system. Vanderveer had long ago established his fame by working with the Dunne brothers in Montana and by helping Clarence Darrow defend the IWW leaders who were prosecuted in such notorious cases as the Butte miners against the Anaconda Copper Mining Company. Vanderveer had led the 1917 defense of Big Bill Haywood and other IWW leaders prosecuted for sedition during World War I.

During the lecture, Vanderveer pointed out the cruelties of the capitalist court system which meted out injustice to the working class. He explained his activities in defending the labor victims. He condemned the economics of the capitalist system because they caused unnecessary hardships on many innocent people. His lecture stimulated widespread discussions among the public in Bellingham and the farmers in Whatcom County.

There was also a group of activists engaged in activities inspired by reports of how the Farm Holiday Association in the Midwest was resisting evictions and forced sales. In Bellingham, these activists worked together with the unemployed in an organization called the People's Councils, which was founded and organized by M. M. London after he found that the Unemployed Council, under the leadership and control of the Communist party, was not doing the job needed in Whatcom County.

I observed that London had gathered around him quite a few active workers who wanted to do something to defend the rights of the unemployed, even if it was not perfect. I found London's popularity was on a par with many civic leaders and he had strong roots among the masses. A few of our Party members in Bellingham had a lot of respect for London and his closest associates. One was an unemployed railroad worker, George Bradley. Others, Victor Bidwell and Einar Larson, were students at the Western Washington Normal School and provided essential technical help to make the organization function. Other unemployed workers providing a strong backbone to this organization were Dave Stauffer, Lester Nichols, Bill Cole, and women like Alice Hunt and Margaret Bergstrom, both of whom worked cleaning houses and scrubbing floors for others. These women contributed food and clothing to many workers who did the "Jimmy Higgins" work for the People's Councils. (Jimmy Higgins was a fictional grassroots activist of the early Socialist Party.)

By the time I arrived in Bellingham, the People's Councils had enrolled thousands of members paying minimum dues, meeting regularly, sponsoring mass meetings, actively resisting evictions, holding protest demonstrations against any cruelties they discovered and generally uplifting the morale of the general public. It seemed to me that the People's Councils were carrying on the most practical program that fit the situation. But I was under orders from Alex Noral and the national leader of the Unemployed Councils, Herbert Benjamin, to fight the People's Councils as being "social-fascist" betrayers of the people, and instead insist on building the Unemployed Councils to demand unemployment insurance and union wages for relief work.

Because there was such a wide discrepancy between what we were instructed to do and what was actually being done by other people, I felt that we were being left behind. So I wrote a detailed report in the form of a Party Section Resolution about that situation, and sent it to the national office of the Communist party with a request for advice as to what to do. They never answered me directly by letter, but the *Party Organizer* for Nov.-Dec. 1932 carried most of my section resolution, which I regarded as indicating agreement with our adopted policy of joining with the People's Councils in mass struggles. (See Appendix.) The *Party Organizer* titled my resolution, "In Struggle Workers Recognize Their Leaders." I always interpreted this as an endorsement of our policy from the National Office contradicting the policy of District Organizer Noral. By then I had urged our seven members to join the People's Councils and participate in all their activities and promote our Party line. At first our Party members were very reluctant and embarrassed to join the People's Councils for fear of being accused of violating Party discipline. But soon they found great satisfaction in being among the masses and agitating for our Party line. I also joined the People's Councils, made friends with the members and leaders, and took part in their neighborhood defensive activities against evictions and demanding relief help for the hungry people we found.

One activity I initiated for the People's Councils was to take an interest in the welfare of the Lummi Indians. I heard reports that they were suffering from lack of sufficient food and medicine. I took a committee from the People's Councils to the Lummi Reservation where we found sick people lying on bare dirt floors in their shacks, nearly starving from hunger, and very sick from lack of medical care. We gathered up a truckload of them and took them to the welfare office in Bellingham, demanding that these Indians be cared for. The welfare administrator called the police to try to intimidate us, but we sent runners out for reinforcements and hundreds of people came running to back us up, forcing the administrator to issue emergency orders for food and medicines for the Indians.

When we got back to the reservation, the Indians set up a committee of their own to work with the People's Councils. The welfare people resisted helping the Indians, claiming that it was the responsibility of the federal government. We assisted the Indians in directing their demands to the Bureau of Indian Affairs, who up to that time had avoided doing anything, but from then on found it necessary to provide food and medical care.

A short time later some of my friends in the People's Councils reported that they had been invited to a meeting of the KKK who planned to drive me out of town because of my relief activities. My friends later reported that they attended that meeting and were surprised that the leaders were unable to agree on any plan to act against me. My People's Councils friends joined the Communist party after that.

In Seattle the Unemployed Citizens' Leagues began to feel the pressure of the influence from the Communist party, which was publicly demanding that the state assume more responsibility for the care of the hungry and unemployed. The demand for a state hunger march became popular and spread throughout the state. In the People's Councils the idea developed that the Fourth of July was the appropriate date for the poor and unemployed to present their demands for relief to the state government in the capitol in Olympia. London promoted it.

When the People's Councils, through its affiliation with the statewide United Producers of Washington, decided to make that hunger march to Olympia, the Unemployed Citizens' Leagues throughout the state joined in that decision. (See Appendix.) The Communist party ordered its forces mobilized under the banner of the Unemployed Councils to join that march with instructions to promote the demands for unemployment insurance and work relief at union wages.

The Communist party district organizer, Alex Noral, was afraid that his new associates, who had recently come west from New York, were not seasoned enough to take over the leadership of that gathering when it got to Olympia. So he ordered Fred Walker, section organizer in Portland, Oregon, to come up to help because Walker had successfully led a recent hunger demonstration in Portland.

The three new district leaders of the Communist party—Lowell Wakefield, Alan Max, and Hutchin R. Hutchins—were fresh from the East and attempted to assume control and leadership of that demonstration which had gathered in Sylvester Park in downtown Olympia. But while they were attempting to assume control, M. M. London led the UCL, United Producers, and People's Councils members off toward the capitol.

When the Communist party leaders realized that a little more than half of the crowd had marched away, Fred Walker called on the rest of the crowd to march under the banner of the Unemployed Councils at a considerable distance behind the other group, so there was a distinct division in the ranks. Then when the Unemployed Councils group arrived at the capitol steps there was a lot of scuffling to control the top of the steps where the speakers could address the crowd.

Then the Communist party leaders, Wakefield, Max, and Hutchins, ordered me to get up on the top ledge to address the crowd and denounce M. M. London. They ordered me to label him and his associate leaders as social-fascist misleaders and betrayers of the workers. I was advised that I had to obey the orders of the Party district leaders who were there. They asserted that was democratic-centralism in practice, which was a fundamental principle of Party organization. Against my own judgment, I did as ordered. Of course, London and some of his followers heard my remarks, and made me pay for them when we got back to Bellingham.

London called a mass meeting where he reported what happened in Olympia, including my attack on him. The audience was with him and against me. Before the meeting I suspected that such an event could happen and decided that the only honorable thing I could do was to attend the meeting and face the criticism, which is what I did. But as the meeting progressed all the people sitting near me moved away several feet, leaving me completely exposed to their hostile stares. Nothing untoward happened in the meeting, but when I stepped outside to go home, I was surrounded by four People's Councils members who walked me down the street about a block before they started pounding and cursing me for what I had said about London in Olympia. Some of my friends called for help and several Party people rushed to my rescue after I had been knocked to the ground. I was skinned up a bit but not badly hurt. When I got up I told everyone there that I was ashamed of what I had done in Olympia (criticizing London), and that I was not able to avoid it then, although I would in the future—and I did.

I was able later to cement good relations with the leaders and members of the People's Councils by assisting them in every way. I had to draw the line at their request that I endorse the Democratic party. I steadfastly propagandized everywhere for the election of the Communist candidates and program, labelling the Democrats and Republicans as "Tweedle Dee and Tweedle Dum," an old Socialist party brand.

There was one incident at the close of activities in Olympia which almost erupted into a disaster after the main crowd left the capitol. A rumor circulated that the police were holding and beating a demonstrator in the Labor Temple. The crowd rushed to the Labor Temple to attempt to free whomever was being held. I was at the head of the crowd and reached the middle landing of the stairs in the Labor Temple when I heard pistols being cocked at the top of the stairs. I looked up and saw two policemen pointing their cocked revolvers straight at me. I felt imperiled and held up my hand to halt the crowd. I turned to ask the police to talk to us about the demonstrator they were holding and why they were holding him. The crowd did stop at my request and the police put away their pistols. I went up to talk to the police. Wakefield was yelling provocatively at them from the bottom of the stairs. When I got to the top, the police let the demonstrator go and he left the building through a back door. I reported that to the crowd below and everything calmed down. Later we learned that the demonstrator being held was actually informing to the police against our demonstration and identifying our leaders to them.

The Unemployed Citizens' Leagues, the United Producers, and People's Councils leaders failed to obtain a hearing with state officials on July 4th, 1932. Some of them came back on July 6th without their mass support and did meet with the governor, asking him to call a special session of the legislature. But he refused and all those efforts failed. So hunger and suffering continued through the following winter.

In 1932 the economic conditions in Bellingham and surrounding Whatcom County became so oppressive that masses of people were actively looking for broad political solutions to their general misery. All private industries were shut down and there was no indication when work would again be available there. The coal mine, the cement plant, the sawmills were all shut down, and there was no longshore work because there was no shipping.

The participation of the Communist party members in the mass activities caused many people to become receptive to the Party teachings that called for the replacement of capitalism with social-

ism, which we promoted by demanding immediate relief and ultimately revolution. It was very evident that all the working people
wanted jobs at better wages that would let them live decently. They
demanded the right to protest against injustices. They felt entitled
to a better future. We tried to respond to all the workers with appropriate communist literature.

The Communist party tried hard to plan effectively for the Hunger March of July 4, 1932. We knew we would face difficulties with
the UCL partisans because they advocated "self-help" as a solution
to poverty—something we militantly opposed. We thought our program was so superior to theirs that we would have a stronger appeal to all the demonstrators and we would win them to our side.
The Buro meeting where we planned that demonstration lasted over
thirty-six hours, because in those days, as long as anyone wanted to
say something about the subject on the table, we kept trying to analyze all the possibilities and dangers and to come up with answers
to solve every problem. Needless to say we misjudged the attitude
of the demonstrators and did not overcome the influence of the
UCL leaders and United Producers leaders, much to our embarrass-
ment.

After the march the District Buro met again and tried to analyze
what happened. We never did accept why the demonstrators did
not flock to our standard. Later I came to realize that parts of the
program of the Unemployed Council did not offer solutions to the
immediate needs of the unemployed. Our demand for unemployment insurance was remote and not responsive to the immediate
problems. The demand for union wages for work relief was closer,
but we did not adequately explain how it could be put into operation. We did not make a good enough case for the calling of a special session of the legislature. The other side focused on public
suffering as the need to call a special session of the legislature. The
failure to obtain satisfaction on that point was a hot political issue
that stirred up anger among all the people, which was reflected
later in the landslide vote for the Democratic party in opposition to
State Governor Hartley's and U.S. President Hoover's Republican
party policies. The Democratic party profited from that experience.
The Communist party did not.

We did resolve that a serious mistake was made when we allowed the demonstration to be split. We determined that we would
not allow such a mistake to happen again. We had a general con-
sensus that the march was a dramatic success as a mass mobiliza-

tion despite our failure to win the whole crowd, and that it was obviously necessary to organize another march which we would aim to lead and control. Next time we would focus more on supporting public welfare and food and medical relief, which were the issues uppermost in the minds of the unemployed.

During this period a large group of unemployed, hungry people led by Iver Moe in Anacortes, Washington, raided a grocery store and took the food they needed. Wakefield assumed leadership of the defense of those who were arrested because he was the head of the district International Labor Defense. Everyone acceded to his authority and his direction of the defense. Masses of workers from all around the area were assembled at the county courthouse in Mt. Vernon, in the belief that mass pressure would win the freedom of those who had been arrested. Some lawyers had urged that legal advice be used by the defense during the trial, as well as the mass pressure, but Wakefield contended the lawyers were not needed, and that the mass pressure tactic was the ILD policy. When Wakefield's policy did not win and Iver Moe was sentenced to prison, nearly everyone felt an error had been made; while in prison Moe turned against the Communist party for its failure due to admittedly incorrect policies. The Party itself severely criticized Wakefield and the policy he followed, branding it wrong to refuse appropriate legal defense when it was offered, as it was in this case. Another defense error was committed in the Frandsen eviction case at Seattle, where a policeman was injured. Some top Party leaders attempted privately to persuade the friendly prosecutor to "spring" the accused without sending them to trial. Those irregularities worked to the disadvantage of the victims. The Frandsen case was also lost in court and an accused was sent to jail for the assault on the policeman.

A second state hunger march was planned well (mainly by the Communist leaders in all the relief organizations), and carried out under the most adverse conditions possible on January 17, 1933. A State Hunger March Committee, with J. F. McNew as chairman, issued a leaflet distributed statewide that outlined a five-point program. This program demanded necessary cash relief and unemployment insurance; plans to stop evictions and discrimination against single workers, women and youth; and a proposal for a public works program. There was a bitter cold rain falling all the time we were on that march. The public authorities in Olympia adopted a hostile attitude toward the march and its leaders, and organized about 3000 veterans into a vigilante organization which blocked the entrance to Olympia and diverted us into Priest Point Park, just outside the city limits. After we were herded into the park the vigilantes posted a guard line to keep us confined in the park. To protect ourselves I organized our own guard line to match theirs. (See Appendix.)

I was left alone at the head of that picketline without advice or help from the other Party leaders. Later I learned they had been off to the capitol building where the legislature was in session. They were trying to get some response from the legislators to our five-point proposal, but they failed. Instead the legislature adopted the infamous MacDonald Bill, which cut relief. Those Party leaders were severely criticized by Alex Noral, because they left the mass of demonstrators without organized leadership, and they failed to correctly influence the legislature. While I was alone with the crowd in Priest Point Park, I had to rely mainly on my own thinking—which was that we came there to confer with the legislature—so I personally demanded that the vigilantes allow us to send a committee from the park to talk to the legislators (not knowing that our top Party leaders were already at the legislature, failing). At first the vigilantes flatly refused to allow anybody to leave the park. But as the first night of chilling cold rain fell on our exposed people, several became convulsive, dangerously ill and unconscious. We brought them to the lines facing the vigilantes and demanded that they take the sick people to a hospital. I told the vigilante guard captain that we held them responsible for the sick people. After the vigilantes took the first two groups, some newspapermen came up to our lines and asked if they could see what our conditions were like inside the park.

We were skeptical about allowing the newspapermen inside our lines, but I finally agreed and accompanied reporter Lester Hunt from the Seattle *Post-Intelligencer.* He came in with a photographer and flash cameras and got complete pictures of our conditions. I knew that was a risk, but I felt it was necessary to let the outside world know what our conditions actually were. I think later developments proved my point, because soon after Hunt left, the vigilantes told us that all women and children were to be evacuated because of the health hazards, such as no sanitation facilities, no protection against the terribly cold rain, and the hunger, exhaustion and evident sickness that existed. We were inclined to object to this proposal because it split our forces in half, but there was so much suffering among the people we had to accept that offer. I construed the vigilantes' order as them admitting their responsibility for our safety.

After the women and children and sick men were evacuated, some of the Party leaders came back from their unsuccessful trip to the capitol and became alarmed that some kind of violent attack was being planned against those of us left in the park. Then some Party leaders, led by Wakefield, rigged up a scheme to let the Party leaders escape from the park by means of boats in the bay at the park shoreline. When I heard about that plan, I told the vigilante captain opposite me on the picket line that they must evacuate all of us from the park before we died from exposure. He agreed with me, because he was also suffering from the exposure to that weather. We mutually set up a team to supervise everyone going back to their homes. That plan was carried out smoothly and agreeably even though there was great reluctance on our part to admit a second failure. See Appendix for supporting leaflets.

In February, 1933, I went to Seattle to attend a Communist party district committee meeting. While I was there, a demonstration at the County-City Building demanded our attention. So several of us joined the demonstration as soon as we could get excused from the district committee meeting, because it appeared to us that the leaders of the UCL had not mobilized organized support.

The leaders of the UCL had sent a small committee to the county commissioners' office to demand the restoration of some items recently cut. Most of the top leaders in the central UCL at that time were followers of the IWW policies that demanded direct physical action. They usually talked in favor of militant action, but seldom followed up on it. This time they did because the commissioners refused to meet with the protest committee. The IWW leaders sent out a call for more unemployed to join them in the County-City Building, to try to apply mass public pressure to meet the needs of the people. That call resulted in close to 3000 persons gathering throughout the building, which effectively blocked all business floors. Nothing could be done by any of the officials. (See Appendix.)

This went on for three days and two nights. Finally the health department declared the situation to be a menace to public health, and ordered the police to clear the building. The police took control of the elevators, came up behind us, and systematically took all of us squatters to the main entrances and turned us loose.

The crowd continued to demonstrate outside by circling the building for several hours. Shortly after midnight most of the crowd left feeling frustrated. I was in the building all the time, trying to coordinate the work of our Party leaders and their steering committee. I constantly urged various Party leaders to try to find the county officials, and to try to resolve this crisis of dwindling, necessary relief allowances. But all offices were locked up, leaving the mass of demonstrators out in the halls. And no one was able to get in touch with any of the officials at their home or the country club, or wherever they were hiding out.

As the crowd was being evicted, I spotted Alex Noral on the roof of a building across the street from the County-City Building. Because he was the leader of the Party, I rushed over to ask him if he had any suggestions for our Party fraction still in the building. (We referred to a group of Party members working in another organization as a "fraction.") But he never answered any question I asked. Instead, he told me it was a "glorious demonstration of the rising militancy of the working class and that's what a revolutionary uprising looks like."

I felt entirely differently about that experience. It seemed to me that the Party had failed to provide leadership. I felt perplexed because it seemed that there was nothing we could do. I saw it as an exercise in futility. The police moved that mass of about 3000 persons out of the building without much difficulty, although I did see one Wobbly leader carried away on a stretcher. I later learned his vertebra was broken by a police black-jack. Another Wobbly, Jack Boardway, told me that the injured one never did recover, and remained a paralyzed cripple for the rest of his life. That incident destroyed much of the IWW enthusiasm for militant leadership for that time, because they didn't have many leaders to spare as martyrs in a cause of whose usefulness or correctness they were uncertain.

Alex Noral sent stories to the Party national paper, *The Daily Worker*, glorifying the workers' militancy and prolonged occupation of the county-city building. He slanted the stories to claim it was a long step toward a workers' proletarian revolution. Public officials had locally branded that event as "anarchy" and warned the people not to allow a Communist revolution to take place. Most of the local newspapers condemned the unemployed for becoming so militant and paving the way for the Communists to take over.

Little did our critics know or understand that the Communist party did not cause that demonstration. Neither did we lead it. We did take part in it, to support it as it developed; we tried to sustain it. But it largely fell into the classification of a "spontaneous" demonstration. At no time did the demonstrators control or operate the building. We merely occupied it, and were thrown out when the authorities chose to do so without answering the hunger problem!

To me, the workers' militancy seemed to be without purposeful direction. I didn't think an honest claim to achieving anything could be made. There was instead a very negative result: none of the unemployed's needs were responded to, and we were forced to seek additional efforts to further organize the unemployed. We did that later.

In spite of two efforts which fell short of our objectives, we pushed forward with a third statewide march by getting motions and resolutions adopted in the neighborhood organizations. It was planned for March 1, 1933, and was successfully carried out while the legislature was in session. By this time, it was crystal clear to everyone, including leaders of every political persuasion, that something had to be done. The cities' and counties' finances were exhausted and and they were unable to meet any emergencies. (See Appendix.)

Because our local people in Olympia gave the city officials assurances in advance that our march would be for the benefit of the whole state and constituted no danger or harm to the city of Olympia, the city officials allowed the demonstration to take place in the old capitol building. We sent delegations to the legislature and invited legislators to visit our gathering. Some of them did, and they spoke pledging their support to us. The result of the march was an agreement between our committee, on which I served, and two of the most important leaders in the legislature to promote passage of a ten-million dollar bond issue to help the cities and counties over their crises. Representative Warren G. Magnuson, who later became a leading U.S. Senator, was chairman of the House Unemployment Committee, and Senator George Yantis was chairman of the Senate Ways and Means Committee. Both carried out their pledges to get the appropriation authorization adopted. Thus, we finally led a successful flight for a cause that was partly won, and yet we lost the leadership and credit to the Democratic party leaders. That was ironic because at that time the Communist party was very hostile to the Democratic party. The state did not sell the bonds immediately, but the authorization extended the financial credit, which afforded a minimum of relief. We did reap some gain by setting up a permanent state Committee of Action, dedicated to carrying on an active struggle at every relief station, to see that the hungry got cared for. The organization was unable to do as big a job as planned because it could not raise enough money. We did start a paper, the *Voice of Action*, which helped articulate the fight for more relief.

In the early years of Franklin D. Roosevelt's presidency, the Communist party was very critical of him. Then Soviet Foreign Minister Maxim Litvinov skillfully negotiated the United States' diplomatic recognition of the Soviet Union. From that time forward, the Communist party was less critical of President Roosevelt because the step of recognition was in accord with the defense of the Soviet Union, to which all Communists were dedicated. Litvinov was famous for promoting an international policy to "Quarantine the Aggressors."

At that time the American Communist party was affiliated with the Third International, better known as the Comintern. In the twenty-one conditions for affiliation was one that ordered each national section of the Party to submit to the authority of the ECCI (the Executive Committee of the Communist International). This committee, permanently located in Moscow and under the control of the Russian members, was led by Joseph Stalin. Everyone in authority in the American Communist party vigorously denied that that condition deprived the American Communist party of any of its autonomy, but the total history is replete with instances where the Russian Party did, in fact, dictate to the American Party on vital policy questions. These events caused several crises in the U.S. Party, during which some top American leaders either left voluntarily or were expelled.

It is very difficult to get the complete facts of such instances. I recall one furnished by Alex Noral. One time, when discussing the subject of discipline and what happened during the classic factional fight around 1930 between William Z. Foster, Jay Lovestone, Earl Browder, and several others, Noral recited his personal experience as one of the delegates to Moscow to settle that factional fight. The Lovestone theory of exceptionalism contended that the road to proletarian revolution in the United States would have to be different from the Cominterns' plans, which followed the pattern set by Russia. Lovestone's theory necessarily put the defense of the Soviet Union after the class-struggle situation in the United States, which was something the Comintern could not tolerate. Noral, who had been in the Foster majority faction, proudly declared that he was the first American delegate to stand before Stalin, and when Stalin asked if he unconditionally submitted to the authority of the ECCI, Noral proudly answered, "Yes." The American Communist party's majority faction agreed to stop the factional fighting and obey the directives of the ECCI, which rejected Lovestone's theory of "exceptionalism" for America, dissolved Foster's faction, condemned Trotsky's theory about permanent revolution, and accepted Stalin's theory of building "socialism in one country alone—Russia". Noral also told us that through the Comintern, the Soviet Communist party did subsidize much of the early financing of the American Communist party.

During the year that I was in Bellingham, the Party had grown from the seven original members to over 150 enthusiastic active members. The Bellingham new members were anxious to progress by study and activity, so I found a huge groundswell of support for a Marxist school.

I was swamped trying to teach new members' classes and promoting study of the Party's more extensive theories and practices. So I asked the district to help us with the school. In came Wakefield, Max, and Hutchins, who took over everything. I found myself out of step with all of them. In my effort to develop an understanding of Party policies, I had relied mainly on reading the current party periodicals—the *Party Organizer*, the *Daily Worker*, the *Communist*, the *Imprecor*—and Stalin's book, *Foundations of Leninism*. I later learned *Foundations of Leninism* was really Stalin's explanation of why and how he destroyed his opponents while he climbed to power after Lenin's death. His policy was to undermine those closest to him before they could attain enough influence to challenge him successfully. He systematically and consciously undermined them with detailed polemical (logical argumentation) analyses, which publicly destroyed their credibility as accepted leaders and turned his opponents against each other. The Moscow trials, which occurred in the mid- to late-1930s, carried out the execution of almost all of Stalin's adversaries who participated in the October 1917 revolution.

In the 1940's, Seattle attorney John Caughlan personally told me, when he returned from a trip to Russia, that he was convinced that those who had been executed were proven to have been guilty beyond any shadow of doubt. Soviet Premier Krushchev gave some explanation in 1956, but even he could not clear up all the politics involved, because he had himself actively aided Stalin's policies at various times when he was climbing the ladder to power. We learned that Stalin's prosecutions and executions were frame-ups and cruelties unprecedented in written history. But we Communists did not know or believe that in the 1930's, and the American Communist party never has contributed to a rational understanding of the terror that Stalin inflicted on the Soviet Communist party and others—probably because it could not be so explained.

By the summer of 1932, there was nationwide excitement over the demands of the WWI veterans in Portland, Oregon, who proposed the immediate payment of the bonus that Congress had promised at the close of the war. They organized the national Bonus Expeditionary Force and marched to Washington, D.C., to press their demands on Congress. President Hoover became infamous for ordering General Douglas MacArthur and Colonel Dwight D. Eisenhower to drive the veterans out of the nation's capitol by burning down their entire encampment at Anacostia flats.

A little later that year, the Unemployed Councils organized national hunger marches demanding unemployment insurance and jobs. When two of our younger Party members returned from one hunger march, they reported to me that they had talked to some of the national Party leaders about raising money for the Party. Somewhere they had picked up the idea that before the 1917 revolution Stalin had financed the Bolshevik by robbing banks, and they thought they could raise a lot of money smuggling sugar in and out of Canada. When our two delegates broached the subject to some of the national Party leaders on that hunger march, the answer they got was that "the Party would not refuse any money that was offered to them." I bristled with anxiety over this information, because it seemed to be fraught with danger of provocateurs, entrapment, and frame-ups against the Communist party. I feared they would talk about it to other people, so I ordered them not to.

When I reported this development to Morris Rapport, who had just come into the district in the spring of 1933 to replace Noral, on orders of the national office of the Party, Rapport immediately came to Bellingham. He "laid down the law" to those two members: under no circumstances were they to engage in any illegal activities, and they were not to discuss the idea with anyone else. I thought Rapport's discussion with those two members backed me up solidly, and thereby expressed endorsement of my work. But to my surprise, a short time later, and without explanation, he ordered me to return to Seattle—I assumed to resume district agitprop work. I thought I was doing a good job in Bellingham, and had visions of doing even better because we had just completed a Party school with the help of Wakefield, Max, and Hutchins. But I found myself at odds with some of the teachings of that threesome. Wakefield was too provocative, and advocated more demonstrative mass activities with militant force on picket lines that would intimidate our opponents. Max seemed intellectually detached, because he concentrated on promoting the FSU. He tried to be persuasive through logic and reports that the Soviet Union was measuring up to our ideals by promoting culture and satisfying the cultural needs of the people. He played "Frenesee" on the piano whenever one was available. Hutchins insisted that every Party member had to accept without question everything he claimed Marx advocated or wrote.

Some of the members complained to me that Hutchins couldn't explain or justify some of Marx's economics. We understood that he had spent over two years in the Lenin School in Moscow, and should be able to explain rationally Marx's ideas about economics. I had always assumed that any of Marx's doctrines or teachings could be logically reasoned out and explained. But Hutchins presented us with the idea that there are many parts of Marx's teachings that could not be so rationalized, and that we were obliged to accept those teachings without question. When I sounded out Hutchins about that idea, he warned me that Party discipline could be imposed on me if I did not accept what he taught. Having specialized in teaching, I knew he was logically dead wrong. Later I learned that Rapport considered Hutchins to be incorrect on almost everything about the Party line.

Reluctantly, I obeyed Rapport's order to return to Seattle. I later found out there was considerable criticism of everything about my work. Rapport had picked this up by nosing around skillfully, and he decided that it was time for me to leave there. He also found some good, new, young leaders among the Brockway family to take over the responsibilities of developing the Bellingham section of the Party.

When I returned to Seattle, it turned out that I was not really wanted in the district office as the agitprop. I was ignored, pushed aside, given no assignments, and left to exist as best I could in the Skid Road branch of the Party, where I did do a lot of agitprop work. But all attention was on unemployment. I sensed there must be something else I should do. I degenerated politically and drifted into the infamous Seattle soup line, where I lived with others on two inadequate meals a day.

During this time I found out that Noral had written a Party policy resolution in September of 1932 that condemned my work in Bellingham as violating Party policy by "actual collaboration from the top . . ." with the "fakers" (People's Councils). So the ground was completely cut from under me politically, with no chance for me to correct it. Noral made it appear that I had deliberately violated Party policy; he never acknowledged that the *Party Organizer* published an account that specifically endorsed the policies I pursued in Bellingham.

Without any specific assignments, I was at a loss for direction. I was under the impression that I was in the Party as a professional revolutionary but I found myself being left out of the revolution. I did find useful activity helping Iron-Hat O'hanrahan on Skid Road. And I spent a lot of time helping the Marine Workers Industrial Union (MWIU), under the leadership of Jimmy Archer, Ernie Fox, Walter Stack, Blackie Cannelonga, and others, distribute leaflets up and down the waterfront—which helped lay the foundation for the later organization of all the marine unions. We thoroughly penetrated all the ships and docks in Seattle, demanding industrial union organizations, rotary hiring, equalization of earnings, and affiliation with the Red International of Labor Unions. Also I helped Bill Dobbins, president of the Central UCL, by doing quite a lot of secretarial work for him.

A few months of that frustrating Skid Road existence in a sort of nether-nether land caused me to look for some way to break out. The work I was doing was very useful and kept me quite busy, but it did not have a long-range perspective, and it was not what I thought I had bargained for when I agreed to come to Seattle the first time to become the district agitprop. My reading of party literature convinced me that I should be doing better work, and more of it. Rapport was demanding that the Party get off Skid Road and root itself in the neighborhoods and factories according to the latest national party directives. Unemployed and subsisting on the soup line's two inadequate meals a day, I couldn't do that. So, when I saw a notice on the bulletin board at the soup line asking for interviews with persons who had any kind of skill or work experience, I signed up. It was the CCC.

૨**

THE CCC

૨**

I was sworn into the Civilian Conservation Corps in Seattle, April 17, 1934, along with about a hundred others. Within a few days we were sent to Lester, Washington, which was about sixty railroad-miles east of Seattle in the Snoqualmie National Forest. The first work I was assigned to was building access roads through the Snoqualmie National Forest and down the Green River Gorge. That work was under the direction of the Forest Service. My foreman was a Mr. Vose, who taught us how to pace ourselves when climbing mountain trails. My first work was as a "powder-monkey," setting dynamite charges with caps and fuses to break up the hard rock on the edge of the Green River Gorge. The 1745th Company also built camps at Speelyi Creek, Yale, Washington, near what used to be a classic Mt. St. Helens, and on Lake Sullivan near Metaline Falls and the Pend Oreille River, in the northeast corner of the state of Washington.

A short time later, while the camp was being constructed close to the community of Lester, I was transferred to the camp administrative staff as assistant educational adviser. The camp commander, First Lieutenant Otto A. Huefner, was under army orders to fill out his complement of staff according to *Table of Organization* regulations. I had the best qualifications for the educational work, so I was upgraded. I worked hard and long conducting classes, publishing a camp mimeographed paper, *The 1745th Post,* and counseling members about advancing their educations. The main work of our company was to build camps, fire breaks and access roads, and to fight fires. We were a "lead" company because we were all "LEM's"—Local Experienced Men. That company had skilled men qualified to efficiently do almost any kind of heavy construction work, anywhere.

The national headquarters of the CCC sent lots of material to the camp urging the members to upgrade their education and schooling. We did not have much success along that line, but through the camp paper we were able to keep morale quite high. The most troublesome educational problem was that most of the older men had difficulty with reading and spelling. When I urged them to use the dictionary, they complained that they couldn't find the words because they couldn't spell them. I had to work with individuals personally to help them use the dictionary until they could find the words they wanted.

During one of the first roll calls, I inadvertently almost betrayed myself by answering to my Party name, Haines, which was called for another person who also answered. Company Commander Huefner repeated the name, and I kept quiet. The incident passed without further notice, except that a couple of the members remembered me "soap-boxing" on Skid Road for the Communist party under the name of Haines. They assured me that they would keep mum about it, and I think they did. I never made that mistake a second time, and I never found out whether it was remembered by the company commander. I did learn later that a Seattle policeman visited the camp at Lester. He came to warn the commander that there must be some Communists in the company, because we all came from Skid Road, where the radicals congregated. I later thought that policeman fingered me, although nothing was ever said to me directly.

One sunny Sunday afternoon, I walked a short distance from camp and came upon a cluster of trees still standing straight and turning to stone. There was a spring nearby that was supplying dissolved silica, which was being drawn up in the tree sap and converting live trees into what appeared to be a standing petrified forest. It seemed paradoxical that some trees were alive on one side and turned to stone on the other side, and standing among others that had already collapsed and fallen.

A short distance further on that path I came upon a pile of small bones that I identified as the remains of a baby deer. As I walked on, I suddenly came within ten feet of a bright yellow cougar, sound asleep. My footsteps awakened the cat, who slowly arose, stretched, and looked at me. He turned away, walked ahead of me, and turned off the path. The forest service leaders had advised us that those cats had the trick of circling to come up behind their prey or human enemy. So I turned around to go back to the camp. But near camp I encountered that same cat again. When he saw me, he turned off the trail again and disappeared. I had no camera to record the incident and no weapon for protection, so I was nervous until I was safely back in camp.

When I took my first furlough, the 1934 waterfront strike was on. There was considerable support for the strike among our CCC company, because most of the men had been waterfront workers themselves at some time. When it became known that I was going to Seattle, quite a few of our members offered me a few dollars to take to the strike headquarters. It totaled $38, which I delivered to Jimmy Archer of the MWIU.

Several of the strike committee leaders there asked me if there had been any effort to recruit strikebreakers in our camp. I had to report that there had not been any overt attempt that I knew about, and expressed a belief that it would not happen with our members. I reported that many of them had natural sympathy with the strike because they were mainly waterfront and lumber workers, out of jobs.

Later there was a problem that arose when the union carpenters in Metaline Falls, Washington, inquired about who was building the CCC camp on Lake Sullivan. When they asked me one time when I was in Metaline Falls, I replied that so far as I knew it was the CCC members doing all the construction. They told me that was a violation of the agreement the government had about any and all construction, namely that any job of that kind had to be done with union carpenters. Later Commander Huefner accused me of stirring up that trouble with the carpenters, and held it as one of the reasons he had to get rid of me.

As assistant educational advisor I conducted classes in reading, writing and some arithmetic. Later I added social science and "Contemporary Social Movements"—a term coined by Jerome Davis, which I borrowed from my college studies. This class got me into lots of trouble with the camp commander. The class was attended by most of the members because they were older men who had met so much adversity, they were thinking about what ought to be done to overcome the unfair economic conditions. The camp commander also attended the first few sessions, where I introduced the subjects discussed in Jerome Davis' book, including fascism, socialism, communism, and capitalism. After the third session, Lt. Huefner called me to his office to tell me that I should not teach that class. I argued that it was a class I took at the University of Oregon and that I got credit for it in my sociology major, and that there was such an interest in the subject I felt obligated to continue the class. I tried to present the ideal that everyone should be informed about the different systems of government so they could make informed judgments about current political issues. Huefner vigorously disagreed, contending that even discussing the subjects was undermining the morale of the members in the camp, and might lead to some of them accepting or approving theories other than capitalism. After a deadlock in our thinking was reached, Commander Huefner advised me to get on a truck and leave camp. I declined to leave that way because it would go down in the record as AWOL, "absent without leave"—a black mark on my record.

The company I was in was just beginning to be converted from a LEM unit to a regular unit of young men recruited from the depressed areas of the East. This is probably a major reason why Camp Commander Huefner was determined to get rid of me, because I would not fit in with the new organization being planned.

Shortly after that session with Huefner, he conducted another "hearing," accusing me of many different offenses, all of which I charged were false and groundless. When I told him all of his charges were false, he retorted that it didn't make any difference, because they looked good in the record. He had another member of the company, George Leighton, take a stenographic record, which he said he would submit to the higher authorities to justify his next step—a direct order for me to leave camp immediately with an administrative discharge. So on July 12, 1935, I returned to Seattle hoping to find some way to lift the stigma of the administrative discharge. I never did succeed, although I tried. On July 21, 1935, I mailed my appeal to the Ninth Corps Area. The answer, dated August 29, 1935, was a total rejection of my appeal with advice that there was no further recourse for me. That experience with the army in the CCC taught me the military style and methods, which were invaluable later, when I was drafted and did army administration clerical work in World War II. I already knew how to make army payrolls, do correspondence, and keep service records.

When I got back to Seattle, I gave a great deal of thought to what I considered to be the problems with the CCC and the Communist party policy about it. I had heard that in some places the Young Communist League had led violent demonstrations against the army administration and there was a lot of confusion about what the Party policy should be with regard to the CCC.

From the beginning, the army's general attitude toward the CCC was that they really constituted a "reserve" army that needed to be trained so it could fill in the ranks of the regular army in case of war. Elementary squad drill was widely advocated, and actually practiced in some companies. Where that happened there was usually some resistance from the enrollees. In some camps the military drilling was welcomed. Much depended on the preparations.

The Party's general attitude, as expressed through its Young Communist League, was hostility and opposition to the military training often proposed as a program for the CCC. The Party clung to a belief that the CCC must maintain a civilian orientation to avoid American preparation for imperialist war against the Soviet Union. The CCC was a part of the unemployment relief plans of that period; it could have been a major step toward total militarization had there not been such overwhelming public opposition to it.

When I arrived back in Seattle the Party ignored me, so we never exchanged ideas of what ought to be the Party policy toward the CCC. From my experience, I considered it to be a magnificent opportunity to pick up the general as well as political education of the "dropouts" of that period—if the army administration could be persuaded to not smother it in military formations and squad drilling. The work program under the Forest Service was enormous and gratifyingly successful. The roads and mountain trails constructed were many years ahead of the Forest Service schedule, and the forest fires put out provided vast protection to America.

ટ**ᴫ**

A WATERFRONT WORKER

ટ**ᴫ**

The discharge from the CCC left me with only a few dollars cash in my pocket. That condition led me to head for Skid Road, where I felt certain to find some of my old friends and probably some from the CCC. I succeeded in finding a cheap "flop" in a Skid Road hotel, and got food in the bargain-priced "short-order" eating places there. Soon I found one that hired me to wash dishes and scrub floors. After a few weeks, the woman who owned the place became dissatisfied with my work, and gave me an excellent recommendation as she fired me.

I wandered around Skid Road a few days before I met up with several of my former CCC buddies who socialized by drinking beer together while making the rounds. Late one night, when we got hungry, somebody suggested that we go somewhere to eat. James Cleaver, a former member of our CCC company, insisted that it would be his party. Cleaver said he knew where we could all eat and it wouldn't cost us a cent. He took us to the waterfront. We followed him to the galley of a Puget Sound Freight Lines boat that was working cargo at a dock. Cleaver asked the cook to feed us. The cook did. He gave us a first class meal of juicy steaks with all the trimmings. Before I could finish eating, I felt the boat begin to move. I was startled by that feeling, and rushed out on deck where I saw my friend Cleaver on the dock smiling and waving to me and shouting that I was taking his place to work on the boat. He said that was the only way he could get relief from the job, and that he had been working for over a month and had to have a rest. While I was trying to think what I could do next, someone in the pilot house shouted, "Cast off the breast line." One of the other deck hands pointed to a line sinking in the water a short distance from the dock, and told me that was the breast line. It was my job to haul it in and coil it up at the cavil so it could be used when the boat tied up at the next dock.

I caught on to the duties quickly because the other crew members willingly told me what to do and when to do it. They coached me to become a deck hand, seaman, traveling cargo-handler/trucker, and longshoreman. I have always referred to that experience as having been "shanghaied." At that time, and every time I think about it, it seems incredible that it could happen to me in 1935, but it did. It embarked me on an extensive practical experience in trade union work.

The first time we returned to Seattle I was sent to the Coast Guard office to get ordinary seaman's papers to qualify me to remain on the job. The papers were issued immediately without any difficulty, and I still have papers issued in May, 1937, and August, 1938.

My work on the freight boats made me think of my earlier experiences in 1932 and part of 1934 distributing leaflets and talking with seamen and longshoremen, and urging them to join the Marine Workers Industrial Union and affiliate with the Red International of Labor Unions. I wondered what would happen if I advocated that line to the crew I was working with now. It was a challenge to try to apply my theoretical knowledge to the actual job with real workers. I soon found out that those abstract ideas didn't register with those workers. I had to find out just what was on their minds.

The first problem I encountered was that the workers, while sympathetic to the idea of the organization of a union, had practically no confidence that the Ferryboatmen's Union they belonged to was actually going to do anything to improve their conditions. The union's leaders seemed to be so remote from the workers that there was a great deal of skepticism about them. Captain John M. Fox was the main official; Ralph Goldsmith was the job dispatcher; and Max Wedekind was the patrolman, organizer, and dues collector. I later learned that Fox had borrowed money from his own personal life insurance to sustain his efforts to organize the tug boats, freight boats, barges, and ferry boats on Puget Sound. I also learned that C. W. Deal, coast president of the union, and executive board member of the International Seamen's Union, had served on the federal government's National Recovery Administration (NRA) committee that had set the code standards with the big shipowners. These standards covered the operation of the entire marine industry regarding minimum wages, maximum hours, and other working conditions, including sanitation.

The Black Ball System had the big ferries on the Bremerton Navy Yard run. The Kitsap Navigation Company had the smaller ferries, better known as the "Mosquito Fleet," which serviced the islands and small ports throughout Puget Sound. Ed Lovejoy had most of the Puget Sound Freight Boats. Fred Marvin had a couple of freight boats. All of them were operating under certification by the Coast Guard.

Marvin often obtained his crews from the federal penitentiary on McNeil Island. Those workers did not have civil rights. They inherited a condition that compared with slave labor because they could not go ashore; they could only return to the penitentiary.

Captain Fox had a deep-sea master mariner's license, and had previously skippered deep-sea oil tankers. He got interested in or-

ganizing the union on Puget Sound after a short experience on the
ferries in San Francisco. He tried to prepare the Puget Sound shipowners to accept the total organization of the crews working on the
inland waters; he promised that he would help them in many different ways, such as by compliance with the provisions of Section
7-A of the NRA, which established the legal rights of workers to
organize and bargain collectively.

But he found that none of the shipowners were willing to sign a
labor contract that would establish equitable wages and conditions.
He conferred with the labor leaders in the Seattle Central Labor
Council, who advised him to go for arbitration, and they recommended a Judge Gaines to be the arbitrator. Fox accepted that advice and persuaded the companies to go along with that choice.

When I went to work on the Seatac for the Puget Sound Freight
Lines about September 1st, 1935, everybody was anxiously waiting
for the arbitrator to hand down his decision. It was long overdue.
We were working for $49 and a few cents a month, with no limita-
tion on hours and no facilities to maintain decent cleanliness—no
showers, and nothing but a bucket to wash clothes in and to hold
water for bathing. There was one very attractive condition: the food
was excellent, plentiful, and couldn't be complained about. But the
other conditions forced frequent turnover in crews, accompanied by
continuous grumbling and excessive drinking when ashore to relieve the monotony, misery, and bare existence. I had experienced
better working conditions before, and told the men I was working
with that it was unfair and unnecessary for anybody to be treated
the way we were. They took a liking to what I said and elected me
to go ashore to hear the results of the arbitration when it was to be
reported. Rumors had reached us that we had been betrayed by the
arbitrator, and the workers told me to go ashore and do something
about it.

It so happened that before going ashore that time we had been
handling sack lime and sack cement, which made us very dirty. We
felt miserable. But I didn't have time to go anywhere ashore to clean
up because the meeting was being held in the Labor Temple in Seattle right away. Fox was greatly distressed by what he saw when he
looked at me and some of the others who came with me. Also
present was C. W. Deal, the coast president of the union. Both
talked to me about why I came that way and what else we had to
complain about. I told them briefly before I spoke to the meeting. In
the meeting I called attention to the filthy condition we were in,

and reported that the crews on the freight boats wanted bathing facilities, clean linen and blankets for the bunks, and the regulation of work hours so we could live like human beings. The people at the meeting roared approval of what I said.

When Captain Fox reported the decisions of the arbitrator, he expressed his judgment that Judge Gaines had given everything to the companies and nothing to the union. In the face of that report and my complaints, both Fox and Deal declared their belief that no one could accept the arbitration award. That surprised most people, because the previous general assumption was that you had to accept the decision of an arbitration. But here we were with an arbitration award that we could not accept, and the leaders of the union agreed with us.

Several members present, including myself, suggested that the best thing we could do was to strike against the arbitrator's decision. When the strike motion was made, it carried unanimously. Both Deal and Fox endorsed the strike and asked what we wanted to do about it. I proposed that we elect a strike committee and notify the companies that we rejected the arbitration decision and were ready to negotiate a better agreement. I was elected chairman of the strike committee and negotiating committee.

The next day we organized picket lines and notified the companies that the strike was on. Fox quickly made arrangements for distress relief. Deal communicated with the companies that it was a legal strike, and that he sanctioned it in his position as a member of the executive board of the International Seamen's Union to which we were affiliated. I led our publicity committee to the newsroom of the Seattle *Post-Intelligencer*, and gave a verbal account to the reporters—who did such a good job that we got headlines for several days.

Soon after the strike got under way and my name as chairman of the committee became known, some of my old Communist party friends made a point to find me, even though I had been out of contact with the Party during my hitch in the CCC. They warned me that Deal and Fox were enemies of the workers because they had refused to support the general strike in San Francisco in 1934. They had become known as "Dirty Deal" and "Finky Fox," and my friends said that my first job was to get rid of them. That information bothered me quite a bit because it seemed to put a stumbling block in the strike path, and I had no direct personal information that would justify such a course.

After thinking over the "sting" the Communist party people injected into the situation, I sounded out the workers' feelings about Deal and Fox. I found the workers wanted to trust them. So I advised my Communist party friends that Deal and Fox supported the strike and the workers trusted them, and anything that would undermine them at this time would sabotage the strike and the demands of the workers. The Party leaders in the Trade Union Commission, led by a person known to me as Harry Jackson, disagreed with my position. They tried to get some other Party members in the union to harass Deal and Fox with motions demanding that the officers report what they were doing in secret meetings with the employers. These Party members tried to create suspicion that I was joining Deal and Fox in selling out the workers behind their backs. I believed there was no truth in those accusations against Deal and Fox, so I demanded that the Party members either support the strike or get out of the way so the workers could win something. Under that pressure, the Party did support the strike and stopped attacking us. Then the Party members signed me up in the Communist party again because they wanted some leverage on that strike. I signed up because I wanted to be in a position to deal directly with them as the occasion required.

I had to take everything that was told to me with a grain of salt, because my last association with the Party had been rather tenuous and there had been some vilification secretly carried on against me. I knew firsthand how disagreements could become obstacles to any progress. So I reserved judgment as to the integrity of Deal and Fox. They soon learned that I had prior membership in the Communist party and was currently associating freely with known Communists on the waterfront. So Deal and Fox confronted me with an accusation that I was working for the Communist party, not the union.

I believe it was their intention to try to force me to step out of the leadership of that strike situation. I had a very frank talk with them and admitted I had been a member of the Communist party. I fully understood how the Party operated, and I felt I had enough experience with them to know how to conduct myself in whatever situation we found ourselves. I reminded Deal and Fox that the members were solidly supporting me as well as them, and that I thought our best strategy would be to pull together and follow democratic policies throughout the strike. By that I meant that all of us would be free and open with the membership on all questions we had to decide, and that we would submit all major policy questions to the members and abide by their decisions. I frankly advised them there were Communists in positions of power in the Maritime Federation who we might need as we progressed, and that any redbaiting would disrupt getting any help from the other unions. Nearly every marine union had Communists who exerted a strong influence on the policies those unions pursued.

I advised Deal and Fox that I had been appraised of the Party's criticism of their activities in San Francisco during the general strike. I considered the purpose of those tales to be to prejudice our judgment against each other. For that reason I felt we were on equal terms. And if we were half as smart as I thought we were, we would not allow extraneous events to influence our judgment about each other. I promised them that I was dedicated, and always had been, to the democratic process, and that meant judgments of people's worth and effort had to be based on specific things they did, not on unverified rumors. I proposed that we would make our decisions on the basis of the best information known to us at a given time. Each situation or problem should be submitted to the strike committee and/or membership before we attempted to make a commitment. I declared myself committed to that policy, and suggested that if they would do the same, we would work things out. While we might disagree, we were all under obligation to abide by the wishes of the membership.

Deal and Fox said that my suggestions were the most unusual they had ever heard from a Communist, that they had never run into any Communist who talked that way before. They expressed doubt that I could fulfill this kind of commitment because they thought the Party would always interfere. I assured them I was perfectly free and was an independent enough person that I could be true to my word. They declared themselves to be willing to give our relationship an honest try. We did function that way throughout the strike. We did not always agree with each other, but we were always open with the membership, making complete reports on all developments and negotiating sessions.

Because of my open admission that I had Communist party experience and knew something about the Marxist teachings on capitalism, socialism, and revolution, as well as trade union strategy, during the strike I was frequently asked how the Communists expected to bring about a revolution in the United States. I patiently explained that hardly anybody could claim to know all the answers to that question, but generally we anticipated that the ruling class would initiate violence against the workers whenever the workers made demands for improvements in wages and conditions of work. At that time the workers would have to decide whether they would defend themselves or surrender. I pointed out it was characteristic of all labor disputes that at some time the government intervened, and usually on the side of the employers, so we had a responsibility to prepare to ward off such intervention and to protect our members from betrayal.

During the first few days, the union picket line showed unanimous strength. Some of the shipowners tried to get the workers to stop the picketing. One even showed a pistol he carried to try to intimidate our members, but they told him to stay away, and he did. There were no negotiations during the first couple of weeks because the shipowners would not even agree to meet our negotiating committee. Finally, Captain John Fox got the two largest owners, Alex Peabody and Ed Lovejoy, to agree to meet with us in a room in the Baroness residential hotel in Seattle. The shipowners got to the meeting place first. As I entered with the negotiating committee, Alex Peabody declared in a loud voice, "Damn you, Dennett, I know you are a Communist, but I am a capitalist and will fight you to the last drop of my blood. I admit the Communists' theories sound great and they will probably prevail some day, but I will keep them back as long as possible." Then I said, "Okay, captain, now let's negotiate." He answered, "Never," and the meeting broke up, hopelessly deadlocked.

The strike had reached a crisis point when Governor Clarence D. Martin of Washington State intervened by ordering the strike leaders to his Olympia office to try to find some way of ending the strike. After telling us a few ribald stories that were somewhat entertaining, he announced that he was prepared to set up an impartial tribunal to hear our complaints and render a decision. Governor Martin appointed a Commission of Review and Arbitration composed of Timothy A. Paul, a superior court judge from Walla Walla, Washington, chairman; Mrs. Pearl A. Wanamaker, a state representative from Coupeville, Washington; and Dr. Sherman L. Devine, a Presbyterian minister in Seattle, Washington.

My Communist party friends had previously advised me that the governor would probably try to push us back into arbitration, where we could expect to be betrayed again. So I told the governor that the decision made by that arbitration tribunal would have to be fair and equitable or the workers would strike against it again. The governor assured us it was his intention that the arbitration tribunal would render a fair and impartial decision that we could live with, and he would back it up.

Deal and Fox were anxious to end the strike as soon as possible, because there was beginning to be too much public pressure against us for the inconvenience it was causing commuters. Also, I realized that the workers were very poor financially. The union was very new, with little reserve resources and no allies. I agreed with the others on the strike committee to gamble on a new arbitration, provided the union was willing to put on the strongest possible case. Deal and Fox assured me they had hired the services of the best organization that existed to help unions present their cases to arbitration. It was the Pacific Coast Labor Bureau, headed by Henry Melnikow. Melnikow had presented the case that resulted in the decasualization of the Longshoremen on the Pacific Coast and settled the 1934 strike. That impressed me as the best possible arrangement we could make, because the Pacific Coast Labor Bureau had already established its integrity in its dealings with the maritime unions. They had a staff of experts that my radical friends could not challenge.

I was certain I could compile evidence about our working conditions on the freight boats convincing enough to compel the arbitrators to rule that those conditions had to be corrected. I went back to work on the boat and kept a log of everything we did at work. When the company learned that I was keeping a log they brought in their ship's log, thinking it would contradict me. Instead it confirmed what I contended, particularly the point about working unlimited hours, and it contained an admission that there were no bathing or other sanitary facilities available on board ship.

The Pacific Coast Labor Bureau was able to make good use of the information I gathered. It was vital to winning big improvements on the freight boats. But the freight boat evidence did not apply to the ferry boats, and the case presented for them was not very persuasive. They did not gain as much as they felt they were entitled to.

When the new award was announced, I had to declare, "the terms for the freight boats were a good step forward, but the lack of progress on the ferries made the settlement go down sour and painfully for me." But I felt that we had to accept it for now, and try for improvements in the next negotiations—which was what we did.

The members voted almost unanimously to accept the award, and the next year's negotiations brought some improvements for the ferry boat workers.

One immediate change that occurred following the strike of the Ferryboatmen's Union was the "death" of the Mosquito Fleet, the Kitsap Navigation Company. The strike was blamed for that, but the truth was the Kitsap Navigation Company had been losing money for a long time before the strike, due to the fierce competition from the big ferries of the Black Ball System. The improved working conditions imposed by the arbitration did increase the costs to the company to a breaking point, and the company had no hope of becoming profitable in the future. At the same time, bridges were being planned that would permit the consolidation of traffic lanes by the larger vessels of the Black Ball lines, which improved the service and squeezed out the smaller vessels. Service between Seattle and the Bremerton Navy Yard was greatly improved.

During the strike and arbitration, the owners of the Kitsap Navigation Company, led by Phillip McBride, pleaded that they could not endure any increased costs. That point caused the union much concern, because any loss of jobs would hurt the union. On the other hand, the union could not in good conscience yield to the demands of the company because that would legitimize substandard wages for the workers. Even with the award the wages were too low in our judgment. The regulation of working hours increased the costs and caused the Kitsap Navigation Company to give up.

Immediately after voting to accept the decisions of the Governor's Commission of Review and Arbitration, both parties discovered that the commission left it up to the parties to work out the details on how to comply with the decisions. It took several weeks for the union to obtain the information from each vessel that was necessary to settle the rules that would apply to each problem. The arbitration decision was based on the NRA Code, which had been established May 23, 1934. I stayed with that problem of interpreting and applying the decision's rules to each boat until everything was agreed to and written up as the "Report of the Committee of Nine." I was chairman of that committee.

When the union hired the Pacific Coast Labor Bureau to prepare its case for presentation to the arbitrators, all of us actively gathering evidence engaged in lengthy discussions about the economic and legal issues with the specialists: Henry Melnikow, James Landye, and David Selvin. Frequently those philosophical and political discussions roamed far and wide in pursuit of answers to the many problems arising in the union movement. There was a massive upsurge in union organization all over the nation, and many people, including the workers themselves, were concerned about what the unions would do ultimately and where they were going.

Henry Melnikow, president of the Pacific Coast Labor Bureau, stimulated our discussions at every opportunity. He revealed that he got his start working as a counter-espionage agent for the United States Army in Paris during World War I. At the close of the war, he became associated with a reputed "liberal," Stuart Chase, who tried to resolve some of the labor-management problems in a democratic way with the government. He supported what became known as the "Plumb Plan," which provided for government ownership of the railroads, union representation in the administration, and use of arbitration to solve deadlocks. The plan was endorsed by the railroad unions and the American Federation of Labor, but was rejected by Congress and the employers. In that effort, Melnikow learned something about matching cost of living with wages as a means of settling labor disputes. The more we discussed and explored these ideas, the more intriguing it became.

Melnikow had several "aces up his sleeve." One of the young lawyers he hired was a fellow by the name of James Landye. Landye came out of the University of Oregon law school, where he had studied under Dean Wayne Morse, who was widely acclaimed for his knowledge and teaching of the law. Landye got Morse and the employers on the Columbia River to arbitrate a labor dispute in which the employers thought they had successfully argued that they could not afford to increase wages as the union proposed, and would have to go out of business if the union won its claim. Melnikow presented evidence proving that the existing wages did not meet the cost of living for the workers, and Wayne Morse, the arbitrator, handed down a precedent-setting decision to the effect that wages were a first charge upon any industry and had to meet the cost of living as a minimum. The employers didn't like it, but they complied with the decision and did stay in business.

Later, Wayne Morse clearly established rules defining how arbitration in labor cases should be conducted to comply with legal responsibilities. The rules he established for arbitrations have been highly successful in settling the disputes that have arisen between

the longshoremen and the waterfront employers on the Pacific
Coast for over fifty years. The main principle Morse established was
that any question submitted to arbitration must have its limits
clearly defined, so the arbitrator will have to render the decision
within the provisions of the labor contract, and cannot wander away
from the subject of the dispute.

Melnikow and his staff of specialists were very successful in
processing disputes in arbitration before Morse within the limits of
the labor contract—and especially in defining the jurisdiction of the
longshoremen according to the cargo "point of rest." That meant
that the work of moving cargo from the dock to the ship and from
the ship to the dock was the jurisdiction of the longshoremen. Sam
Kagel became an outstanding arbitrator, using Morse's rules for the
longshoremen and the waterfront employers on the Pacific Coast.

While the establishment of fair arbitration was very reassuring,
I became concerned about the political isolation of the then-named
Ferryboatmen's Union from the other maritime unions because of
the hostility hanging over from the 1934 general strike in San Francisco. Deal and Fox were condemned then, and there was some lin-
gering Communist party hostility often expressed that the other
unions, such as the Longshoremen, Seamen, and Marine Engineers, should take over the Ferryboatmen to get rid of Deal and
Fox. I argued in the Party against that idea, saying it was contrary
to the Party policy of supporting industrial unionism as opposed to
craft unionism. My point was strong and won support among the
Party district leaders. The Party trade union advisers constantly
warned me that Deal and Fox were unreliable, and that they would
cut my throat unless I cut theirs first. At the same time, the employers kept pressuring Deal and Fox to get rid of me as a dangerous radical. It was inevitable that something would happen, and
it did.

About a month after the strike was settled, I was working on
the Belana, of Puget Sound Freight Lines. The captain, Lewis, told
me as we got to port in Seattle one day, that he had to let me go
because the company didn't want me around anymore. When I
asked him if he had found some fault with my work, he said, "No."
Then I told him that was discrimination because of my union activity and I would have to fight it. I took the problem up with Fox
right away, insisting that he process a grievance on my behalf. He
showed signs of wanting to avoid processing a grievance for me,
but I insisted it had to be done to protect all the others who were

active in the strike. Fox dragged his feet in taking the matter up with the company, and the company took an inordinate length of time to reply to my complaint. During that long interval I was ashore, busy almost every minute, meeting with committees in the Maritime Federation, which was anticipating a major conflict with the waterfront employers. I was also elected a delegate to the Seattle Central Labor Council, which met every Wednesday night. Such constant activity gave me invaluable experience in working with the officers and leaders in all the maritime unions and the Central Labor Council. I was able to help many of the union leaders draft and distribute leaflets and issue news releases about numerous union developments taking place.

After too long a delay, Fox did obtain a settlement from the Puget Sound Freight Lines which allowed me to return to work, but on a different boat, the Seatac, on which I had previously worked. Fox and I had many conversations about the different aspects of the problems associated with the organization of the Ferryboatmen, especially how he expected to survive when the other marine unions were making hints that they ought to take over the jurisdiction of the Ferryboatmen's Union.

At the same time I was also taking part in frequent meetings of the Washington Commonwealth Federation (the WCF) because in 1936 the Communist party was very actively working to affect the fall elections. There I obtained valuable information about, and became oriented to, the political situation.

The WCF had been founded during the summer of 1935 by commonwealth builders, technocrats, labor activists, liberal democrats, and others on a platform of "production for use," old age pensions, public power, unemployment relief, and support for collective bargaining and the rights of strikers. At that time the state AFL convention in Port Angeles endorsed the WCF. That move encouraged many local unions to affiliate with the WCF, and to participate in wide-ranging political activity within the Democratic party. That endorsement was obtained by the determined efforts of the Communist party fraction in that AFL convention. We recognized the WCF as a form of popular front organization capable of carrying out the anti-fascist policies we considered to be our major political responsibility at that time.

I was an Inlandboatmen's Union delegate to the WCF's April, 1936, convention, and there I was elected chairman of the Resolutions Committee. The Communist party and other like-minded people had enough votes in the committee to secure endorsement of a resolution supporting the candidacy of Governor Benson of Minnesota for president of the United States. But in the middle of the convention we learned that Benson was dying of cancer, and that the Communist party nationally was going to run its own candidates who would encourage support for the reelection of President Roosevelt. We immediately changed our presidential candidacy resolution to reflect this, which caused some confusion among the non-Communists.

Throughout the convention, Morris Rapport, the Northwest district organizer of the Communist party, was in the antechamber of the meeting hall, coordinating the activities of Communist party members who attended the convention as union or unemployed delegates. He used runners to relay information about the proceedings and to issue policy directives. Howard Costigan, executive secretary of the WCF, was speaking the literal truth when he later stated that, at this convention, "I first saw the Communist line going one way and then I saw it go the other way and I wanted to know what was going on." So he asked for membership in the Party. We also succeeded at this convention in having the constitutional ban on participation by Communists lifted. Until it was dissolved in 1944, the WCF had a very influential role as the left wing of the Democratic party in Washington State. Through it, the Communists were able to exert influence on the course of Democratic party politics. From 1938 through 1940, I functioned as one of the WCF's vice presidents. During this time I was invited to Communist Party Buro meetings, and later was elected to membership.

During 1935, 1936, and 1937, Earl Browder vigorously led the American Communist party on a course he identified as "Twentieth Century Americanism." He directed us to integrate our political activity with local progressive political activists. He insisted that Party work be more open and democratic. He abandoned all reference to promoting revolution as a means to overthrow capitalism. These directives strengthened and reinforced our activities in the Washington Commonwealth Federation and Democratic party. Rapport reported to us that he had satisfactory meetings with Democratic Party National Committeemen and women, and with several state and county public officials, where they exchanged pledges to help each other in the anti-fascist campaigns. The Central Committee of the Party, in charting our political direction, approved local control for us in the Northwest. The issue constantly before us was if or when the WCF would break from the Democratic party and go "independent," like the American Labor Party did in New York. We never reached the breaking point, and we stayed within the Democratic party.

IBU JOINS MARITIME FEDERATION

Because of what happened between Deal and Fox with the other maritime unions during the 1934 general strike in San Francisco, the other unions maintained a reserved hostility toward Deal and Fox which was stimulated by the Party. I advised Fox that I considered this latent hostility to be a major threat to his efforts to organize the unorganized marine workers on Puget Sound. He agreed, but saw no clear way to overcome it. I promised to do my best to help, and eventually was quite successful in protecting the members of the Ferryboatmen's Union (which soon after changed its name to Inlandboatmen's Union).

I found an opening to work on when I learned there was a very sharp policy split between Harry Lundeberg of the Sailors' Union, who was also president of the Maritime Federation, and Harry Bridges of the Longshoremen's union. The basic split was over adhering to a contract that contained terms and conditions that were adverse to a union. Lundeberg had begun advocating "Job Action" to break those adverse conditions. Bridges insisted on living up to the contract until the next negotiations, at which time all the unions could work together to make the desired changes. It was a desperate conflict that threatened the life of the Maritime Federation, because it was divisive if one union acted alone.

The Communist party leaders sided with Bridges' position and were firmly against Lundeberg's position as anarchistic. Also, the Party had soured in its trust of Lundeberg. During the formation of the Maritime Federation in 1935, the Party had often invited Lundeberg to participate in the Party's maritime top fraction (a caucus of Communists who had achieved high positions in the marine unions) where strategy and policies were worked out. But when Lundeberg committed himself to the job action tactic, which would place all the other unions in jeopardy, the Party withdrew its support of him.

When I suggested that the affiliation of the Inlandboatmen's Union to the Maritime Federation could help stabilize the strength on the side of the Longshoremen, the Party fully agreed. I pointed out that the Inlandboatmen tugboats serviced all marine traffic up and down the coast, and were vitally needed in any long-range plans. But the Party leaders were stubborn in their hostility toward Deal and Fox. Because of this personal antagonism, the Party didn't want to even raise any question with Bridges about affiliation of the Inlandboatmen to the Federation, despite the strategic merits of the proposal.

So I thought I'd try Lundeberg first. I approached him through an appointment made by Ernie Fox, a Communist party member I knew who was working as a Sailors' Union port patrolman and acting secretary to Lundeberg. As soon as Lundeberg understood what I wanted to talk about—the Inlandboatmen joining the Federation— he referred to us as "tule-sailors" from the "mud-flats" and demanded that we get rid of those two "phoneys," Deal and Fox, before the Federation could consider admitting the Inlandboatmen.

After that rebuff, I asked Party members I knew to help me approach Harry Bridges. But they were against my approaching Bridges, indicating their belief that Bridges would have to be just as against Deal and Fox as was Lundeberg. It seemed to me that the Party position was all wrong to allow consideration of individual personalities to interfere with strengthening the position of the rank and file workers such as myself in those respective unions. So I went to the hotel where Bridges was staying, hoping to run into him, and I actually did "bump into him" on purpose. I identified myself as having recently come off a successful strike of the Inlandboatmen and asked if he would let me discuss our affiliation problem with him. He answered, "Sure, but let me get a few minutes rest before you come up to my room," and he gave me his room number.

I immediately phoned Deal, told him I had an appointment with Bridges, and asked him if he was willing for me to propose a meeting between them to work out a plan to affiliate. Deal expressed surprise that I had that appointment, and expressed further doubt that Bridges would agree to any meeting between them or affiliation of the Inlandboatmen to the Maritime Federation, but he did give me an okay to try.

Bridges was resting on his bed in the hotel room when I knocked a little later. When he said, "Come in," I did, and I immediately told him I thought it was necessary to consolidate the local waterfront workers with the Maritime Federation but had been turned down by Lundeberg. Bridges expressed a belief that we couldn't trust Deal or Fox because they did not support the general strike in San Francisco in 1934. I answered that I had talked to Deal about that, and Deal's version was that Bridges had cut his own throat in San Francisco by approaching Deal and Fox antagonistically, without anything having been done by the old Ferryboatmen's Union. Bridges chuckled and said, "Well, maybe we did." I found him to be flexible, and willing to plan for the future and let bygones be bygones. I pointed out that the Inlandboatmen's Union was an industrial union, combining navigation, deck, and engine departments into one union; that it had the tugboats organized; and that it was an essential element in the movement of all vessels coming or going in Puget Sound and all ports up and down the coast. Bridges agreed to the logic of the situation right away, and agreed to meet Deal to try to work out something.

I then phoned Deal again, asking him to come to the hotel where Bridges was staying. I told him that I would meet him at the entrance and the two of us would go up to Bridges' room together. Bridges was still alone when I knocked again, and he invited us in. I opened the conversation by saying I had heard each of them express doubts about the other being willing to heal the breach between them, but I thought both of them were big enough to do it for the sake of the members of both unions. Each grinned and glanced skeptically at the other and then at me. I kept going, to press the points that the tugboatmen were an essential link in the marine industry, were organized in the Inlandboatmen's Union, and wanted to affiliate with the rest of the marine unions in the Maritime Federation where they belonged. That would be a positive step forward, which would close the gap that existed.

Bridges said he agreed with my reasoning on that issue, but would like to know how we felt about the policy of job action that Lundeberg was advocating to change an existing contract. Both Deal and I expressed opposition to that idea, explaining that we thought it would create chaos in the industry. Bridges then expressed his willingness to have the Longshoremen support our application for affiliation to the Maritime Federation, if that was what we really wanted. Deal readily agreed that he wanted to heal the breach, and told Bridges that he would be glad to work to consolidate the Inlandboatmen's Union with the Maritime Federation. I told both of them that I had a very unsatisfactory conference with Lundeberg, and for that reason I believed we would have to work very carefully to avoid letting Lundeberg block our affiliation plans. Each of us carried out our promises to the other. The Inlandboatmen's Union became affiliated to the Maritime Federation of the Pacific and to each of the district councils, and it actively participated in Federation affairs. I was elected one of the Inlandboatmen's Union delegates to the Maritime Federation's Puget Sound District Council and to the third convention (1937), and became an active member of the publicity committee.

In the summer of 1936, everything indicated that the waterfront employers were going to try to break up the Maritime Federation unions. Everyone was very concerned about what Harry Lundeberg would do during this crisis, because he had become so hostile to the Longshoremen and Harry Bridges. He appeared to be willing to sacrifice the Maritime Federation unions to get what he wanted for the Sailors' Union alone.

All these maneuvers and struggles to iron out a consistent policy forced me to rethink what I had been advocating from Communist party policy and red trade union tactics. We had been taught that our policy should be to develop a revolutionary trade union consciousness. But I found that the workers wanted our unions to serve them. So we advocated the organization of industrial unions, which brought all the workers of a plant or industry together to pool their strength, in contrast to the many divisions created by the craft union form of organization. I learned that the craft unions resisted being combined in industrial unions because they contended they would lose the right to bargain for benefits due them because of their special skills and needs. Besides, they did not trust the unskilled workers, and exhibited a certain amount of the contempt and low esteem society generally exhibited for the "lowly" unskilled worker.

I remembered the various reports on the significance of the general strike in San Francisco in 1934. Some news reports construed it as a preliminary step toward a worker's revolution. There were reports that some Communist leaders in San Francisco were quoted in Communist party papers in the Soviet Union as having led the workers close to adopting revolutionary tactics and policies. Later, when I had an opportunity to talk with some of those who led that general strike, I came to the conclusion that it was no more a step in the direction of revolution than was the 1933 unemployed workers' three-day occupation of the Seattle County-City Building. Neither had any element of "governing" nor any lasting influence on government. The general strike was an important event in the life of the unions that illustrated they could work together for self-defense, but their goals and purposes were very limited, and most leaders disavowed any ambition to take over the government.

Events since that time seem to me to clearly indicate that some Communist party leaders greatly overestimated the meaning of many events when the workers fought hard in defense of their unions. It is obvious by now that most of the developments in union organization in the United States in the 1930s, 1940s and later lacked any political direction toward a socialist revolution. I think that reveals that there is something way out of line in the teachings about, and results expected of, trade union organization by the Communist party. Actually, the main thrust of the union efforts in the early 1930s was a determination: to obtain the legal rights to organize and bargain with employers; to stop the employers' wage-cutting policies of that time; to turn the members' economic position around; and to raise their standard of living for the benefit of their families, especially their children, by using Section 7-A of the NRA—which later was incorporated into the National Labor Relations Act.

ða

1936 SEATTLE LABOR DAY PARADE

ða

Between 1935 and 1936, labor unrest and political dissension nation-wide sifted into the lowest ranks of organized and unorganized labor. Communist party influence was widespread, because we were the most active of any political group promising a way out of the economic crisis. Our many activists kept agitating for industrial unionism and trade union democracy. We promoted our primary responsibility to oppose imperialist war. It was part of the effort to instill in the ranks of the working people a determination to defend the Soviet Union from all imperialist attacks, because the Soviet Union was the first socialist nation dedicated to emancipating the working class. We Party people had been thoroughly indoctrinated with the idea that sooner or later the capitalist nations would launch a military attack on the Soviet Union to destroy it because it was a socialist example. That agitation had considerable influence among the maritime workers because they could directly observe increasing military preparations among most of the big maritime nations—the U.S., Great Britain, Germany, and Japan. Military maneuvers by Hitler's Germany and Mussolini's fascist Italy were crushing a socialist republic in Spain and Hitler was making noises about expanding for *lebensraum*. *Mein Kampf* had been published, outlining Hitler's ambition to crush the Bolsheviks and the Jews, and to let the German Aryan race rule the world for a "thousand years." Many thinking people, including workers, became vitally concerned that Hitler meant to crush his opposition as he had written in *Mein Kampf* ("My Battle"). That meant trouble for everyone else throughout the world.

At the same time big businessmen in the United States had turned against President Roosevelt, even though his emergency policies had saved their businesses in 1933. But the so-called "Liberty League" wanted to halt the increasing influence of organized labor and to obtain greater profits for itself. The Liberty League considered President Roosevelt to stand in its way because he supported

Section 7-A of the National Industrial Recovery Act. Section 7-A promised that workers would have the legal right to organize and bargain collectively. There were too many instances where the official corporate employer attitude was still that labor unions were illegal. (Section 7-A was later expanded as the National Labor Relations Act (passed in 1935), which was guided through Congress by Senator Robert Wagner of New York under enormous pressure from his constituents. The Communist party exerted constant pressure on Wagner by mobilizing many unions there to express the workers' needs.)

The CIO was being launched. There were beginnings of mass upheavals in all the mass-production industries, including auto, rubber, glass, steel, mining and others, and dire predictions were constantly being made by the press and public officials that the nation was on the verge of total destruction because of the growth of organized labor and the New Deal.

It was clearly evident to all who would pay attention that private industry was demanding that the government help it beat back the workers in the rising unions. The organization of the Pacific Coast Maritime Federation was relatively new. It indicated a new conscious solidarity of the workers. It was a positive indication that the workers were on the move. The employers became alarmed when they saw this strength of the workers. Even so, many of us were inexperienced and made many mistakes when it came to dealing face to face with the big employers, and more so when dealing with powerful government agencies that combined their "carrot" proposals with a "big stick" threat that, if we didn't accept their proposals, all "hell would descend upon us." The most notorious leader in the government attempting those tactics was General Hugh Johnson, who was promoting the Blue Eagle (symbol of the National Recovery Administration) and demanding that the unions submit to his dictation. He and the employers were shocked into hysteria in 1934 and 1936, when the maritime unions refused to be intimidated by his threats and went out on strike to defend their rights. The workers in the new unions wanted to support President Roosevelt in opposition to the employers' big business hostility—no matter how much they threatened us.

Because I was a delegate to the Central Labor Council, as well as to the Puget Sound District Council of the Maritime Federation, I carried policy questions back and forth between these councils to the delegates in each, and learned to coordinate the activities of the

marine unions with those in the Central Labor Council. Soon I became chairman of the marine caucus in the Central Labor Council,
and established working relations with the officers of the Central
Labor Council, as well as with the Maritime Federation. When we
had a problem, motion or request to present to either council, I followed the practice of discussing the idea with the chairman before-
hand so we could have an understanding of how and when the
motion would be considered. I usually submitted motions or requests in accordance with an agreement with the chairman. That
procedure allowed us to proceed without misunderstanding. At
first many of the motions I presented were voted down by the conservative majority in the Central Labor Council. But as the summer
of 1936 wore on and our problems became more mutual and inter-
locking, my motions, backed by the large marine caucus, were favorably, although sometimes reluctantly, received. Most of my
motions and proposals had a direct bearing on trade union problems, although I made many efforts to inject political issues, such as
condemnation of Hitler or Mussolini and support for the Spanish
Republic, into the proceedings. I was constantly stimulated by discussions and political policy decisions made in the Party Buro meetings. The Party district organizer, Rapport, taught us to confirm
dialectical (logical) conclusions by testing with material facts.

Most of the opposition to my efforts came from the half dozen
leaders left over from the old Seattle general strike of 1919. Some of
them still held "old socialist" beliefs that were hostile to anything
communist. Included among them were Bert Swain of the Operating Engineers, Dave Levine of the Jewelry Workers, Jimmy Duncan
of the Auto Mechanics, Sam DeMoss and Claude O'Reilly of the
Teamsters and the council secretary, Charles Doyle from the Paint-
ers. They had lived through that famous period in 1919, and they
had a real fear that events of the 1936 era were pushing us into another big confrontation with the employers, which would lead to
another general strike. They were against it because their experience in 1919 scared them—they didn't know what to do with a general strike or how another like it could be controlled or contained.
They were afraid of a socialist revolution. Each of them openly discussed their fears with me many times, claiming that the workers
did not gain anything from the general strike. I came to understand
their fears that such a strike could get out of hand. But I pressed
forward anyway, in the conviction that the unions had to fight on
behalf of their members.

As my efforts expanded in the councils, I got the feeling that the members were anxious to see us take some action that would indicate our class solidarity, and our strength and determination to resist the attempts of the employers and the anti-labor government agencies to take away our recent gains—especially the provisions of the National Labor Relations Act. I was meeting regularly with the top leaders of the Communist party, as well as with almost all the top union leaders, and I sensed a feeling of anxiety and apprehension everywhere as I searched for answers and to do something useful and worthwhile. I began to feel that the whole labor movement was anxious to influence the entire community to respect us and our rights. I felt pressure to try to get the whole labor movement to demonstrate its strength, to protect itself from the expected employer attacks.

As Labor Day was approaching, I asked various officials what they planned to do that day. Nearly all of them said they were going to have a picnic just like they usually did. I began to ask various leaders if they ever considered marching in a Labor Day Parade. Some of them answered that they used to do that many years ago, but they found it easier to just have a picnic. I began to suggest that maybe it was time to break out of the old shell and show their strength by having a big parade for all the unions. We'd let the employers and the government know that we were strong and were able to use our strength to defend ourselves. Local union officials began to express interest and some enthusiasm for the idea. Some suggested that we could hold the parade in the morning and still have a picnic in the afternoon. We reached a point where I sensed that there was almost unanimous acceptance of the necessity of holding a Labor Day parade.

Without forcing a commitment or motion, I reported to the marine caucus that I had found widespread support for having a Labor Day parade. The marine caucus in the Central Labor Council immediately endorsed the idea, and authorized me to present the idea to the Central Labor Council. Much to everyone's surprise, almost every delegate in the Central Labor Council voted for the parade. Because there was no opposition, I pushed forward to ask the chairman to appoint me to head the committee to organize the parade, and to give me credentials to solicit support from the various locals.

Chairman Claude O'Reilly granted my request and Secretary Charles Doyle issued the official credentials immediately. There were a few expressions of doubt that the parade could be put together in the little time we had left, but I assured the council that the maritime workers were solidly supporting the idea, and that we would have a parade to be proud of. I carefully approached the large Teamster organization to join the maritime workers to insure a creditable performance. There was considerable uncertainty as to what the Teamsters would do, because they suspended holding meetings during the summer. But several of the local officers, including Claude O'Reilly of the big Teamster Local #174, pledged to mobilize their members for the parade, and they did.

The parade committee authorized three ideas as appropriate themes for the parade: 1) "Free Tom Mooney"; 2) "Point out William Randolph Hearst as 'Public Enemy Number One' "; and 3) "A funeral for the Washington Industrial Council" (who were the employers, not the later CIO Industrial Union Council).

After I obtained the endorsement of practically every local union in the city, I drew up charts and plans for assembling the parade and the marching route. Then I went to Mayor Dore to apply for a parade permit, and asked if the city would let us have the police drill team to lead the parade. Dore was surprised that we asked him to deal directly with us, but he cooperated fully. He made a few phone calls and got the parade permit issued right away. Dore asked me to let his army officer assistant organize the parade. I showed my plans to the army officer who was there, and after looking them over, he endorsed them, saying there was nothing more needed.

The parade came off as planned. One estimate was that about 25,000 marched. All the units were assembled on various streets that converged on Second Avenue from Skid Road. They marched up Second Avenue to Bell Town, at the north end of downtown Seattle, where they were demobilized and dispersed in an orderly manner.

A fellow by the name of Victor Hicks, from the Teacher's Union, gave yeoman assistance in assembling the units and seeing to it that no errors crept in. Hicks saw to it that we had a reviewing stand on a flat-bed truck between Pike and Pine streets. The organized women's auxiliaries saw to it that we had a parade queen, as beautiful as every other queen.

I never got to watch the parade as the workers marched because I was busy seeing to it that all units were in their assigned positions. Many years later I did see motion pictures that had been made by regular news services, and they were inspiring.

 え♦

THE P-I STRIKE

え♦

During the summer of 1936, some of the employees of Seattle's Hearst newspaper, the *Post-Intelligencer* (the P-I), began organizing the Newspaper Guild with the help of David Selvin. I had become acquainted with Selvin during the 1935 ferry boat strike, when he was a research specialist on the Pacific Coast Labor Bureau. Hearst responded by discharging two very well liked and courageous workers: Everhardt Armstrong, drama critic and writer, for alleged insubordination, and "Slim" Lynch, photographer and sports writer, for alleged inefficiency. Firing these two aroused the anger of the entire labor movement, and was interpreted by those of us in positions of leadership as a first attack signal on the rest of the workers in Seattle. Our Labor Day Parade preparations gave us the opportunity and vehicle to publicize the guild's cause to the entire labor movement and to win the support of the general public. By August 12, 1936, the Seattle Newspaper Guild members found themselves committed to strike, because the guild had asked the Central Labor Council to put the *Post-Intelligencer* on the unions' unfair list, which it did Wednesday night, August 12, 1936. Hearst, instead of negotiating a settlement with the guild, was actively organizing the employees in the editorial section of the P-I into an anti-union group, with the help of top business reporter-writer Fred Niendorf.

The inescapable outcome of these events was strike action and a move to mobilize the widest possible support for the guild. Although I was not a guild member nor a newspaperman, I had furnished reporters with vital up-to-the-minute news about activities on the waterfront, thereby becoming personally known and trusted. As an influential delegate spokesman for the marine section in the Central Labor Council, a member of the publicity committee of the Maritime Federation's Northwest District Council, and a bona fide waterfront worker with publicized experience in recent successful strikes of the Ferryboatmen, I was the only outsider invited to the meeting where the guild had to make the decision of whether to go on strike. It did on August 13, 1936.

After a very long discussion which reached an impasse, the guild members seemed to be unable to make a clear-cut decision. At that point, they invited me to speak to help them think out the situation. I told them that whenever we had to make that decision, we had to realize that there were no guarantees about the outcome except those that we made by rallying our friends to help us and mustering our courage to do what had to be done. I informed them that in the maritime industry we were facing a similar conflict with the Waterfront Employers Association, and we knew that we would have to fight back. I pledged to the guild that I would do everything in my power to get all the maritime unions and the Central Labor Council to help the guild win its strike. I pledged to see to it that there would be enough waterfront workers on the picket line the next morning to make a powerful show of strength, to prevent scabs from attempting to publish the P-I. I also advised them I would help mobilize the Washington Commonwealth Federation (of which I was a well known active member), which reached far and wide in the community. I would find ways to get support from the Democratic party public officials and members, and try to get the whole city against Hearst. I emphasized that the guild members should lead all activities, and let us know where they wanted support. That meant that the guild would have to control the picket line and organize its publicity in its own way. I suggested that relief procedures should be started immediately, so the members would be properly provided for from the very beginning. At the end of my talk, the guild voted to strike immediately.

I took advantage of the guild strike to enliven the morale and interest of every union in the city in building up the Labor Day Parade. It was natural that "Down with Hearst" became the principal theme of the Labor Day Parade. I spoke encouragingly about the progress of our plans at each meeting of the Central Labor Council. I reported regularly to the Maritime Federation District Council. I spoke at every neighborhood meeting of the Washington Commonwealth Federation that I could attend. I was invited to Communist party District Buro meetings, where my progress reports were analyzed and where I received advice and counsel from other, more experienced, leaders, especially from Party District Organizer Morris Rapport and Trade Union Secretary Harry Jackson. Each place where the guild strike was discussed, I emphasized the importance of everyone participating in the Labor Day Parade in order to make it a success. As enthusiasm for the success of the Labor Day Parade kept building, more and more leaders and members in the ranks began to become enthusiastic about the possibility of winning the strike against Hearst.

The first day of the guild strike against the *Post-Intelligencer*, I visited the picket line fairly early in the morning to make sure that promises made the night before were fulfilled by large numbers of longshoremen and other waterfront workers being present. I spoke to several of them, warning that we wanted masses present all the time to insure that no violence was committed against the Newspaper Guild members, because they were our fellow workers and not used to the rough and tumble tactics which could be expected from Hearst's hired gunmen. The longshoremen's union sent several work gangs, whose presence boosted the morale of the guild members. Then a sizeable group of Teamsters joined the picket line, mixing with the Longshoremen fraternally. Soon the Teamsters spotted an armed strikebreaker guard who had previously killed one of their pickets during a brewery strike in Tacoma. Needless to say, the Teamsters saw to it that the armed strikebreaker did not carry out his intention to intimidate the guildsmen. It was reported that the Teamsters defense squad gave that armed strikebreaker a severe physical lesson. That strikebreaker had to be withdrawn from that assignment by the Hearst management, to protect him from the wrath of the Teamsters who kept up a constant vigil, watching for any other hired gunmen. The Longshoremen, Teamsters, Washington Commonwealth Federation, Democratic party, and several church organizations led by Reverend Fred Shorter of the Church of the People, all backed the guild strikers. With Mayor Dore officially and publicly supporting the guild, the city of Seattle was overwhelmingly against Hearst.

During my checkup that first morning to make sure our marine workers were there in substantial numbers, a slender fellow stepped up to me and asked if I knew what was going on. He looked like a stranger, somewhat out of place, so I answered skeptically that I thought I knew, and asked why he wanted to know. He quickly said that he was from out of town and had some responsibility in the Newspaper Guild national office, and that he couldn't seem to find anyone who could fill him in on what was actually going on. I immediately sensed that he could be a Communist party member in the national guild office, so I told him I could furnish some information, but that I had no authority and was working solely as a supporter in the strike. Then I suggested that this was a serious political situation that deserved the attention of experts. He said that was what he wanted. I construed that to mean that he wanted to contact the Seattle leader of the Communist party, so I took a chance and led him to the Communist party office where he met Morris Rapport, the district organizer. They talked over the situation for a long time.

This inquiring person turned out to be Jonathan Eddy, the national secretary of the Newspaper Guild and a Communist party leader in it. Eddy thanked me for putting him in touch with the highest authority of the Communist party in the Northwest. In the discussion that started between Eddy and Rapport, I quickly learned that the national leaders of the guild were opposed to a local strike against Hearst. They had a different plan, which would be to coordinate a national strike against Hearst. They felt this local strike was doomed to failure, because they would be fighting without the pressure planned in a national strike. Eddy expressed a belief this local strike would delay their effort to organize against Hearst nationally. At this point, I excused myself from that meeting because I had promised the guild that I would help keep the picket line going. Later I asked Rapport if his meeting with Eddy caused any change in our local plans. He told me we had to keep going on the course already started. Rapport told me that he assured Eddy that the local Communist party was strong, that the labor movement was strong, and that the political situation was in favor of the guild. Later I learned that Rapport considered the strike to be a blessing in the political arena, because it stopped the circulation of the Hearst anti-Roosevelt propaganda in the P-I. As the strike progressed and pressure kept building up to end the strike, the major objective of the Communist party was to keep the strike going until after the fall election, which was the best help we could give Roosevelt.

Eddy was confronted with some organizational disputes among the other high guild officials regarding the local guild strike. Eddy and Morgan Hull, a guild organizer who came in after Selvin left, disagreed on strategy, and those differences were never resolved. The local guild members matured rapidly under the constant pressure on them. Richard Sellers became an outstanding organizer with the help of Forrest Williams, Art French, Cliff Erickson, Raymond Holmes, Slim Lynch and others.

As the strike dragged on week after week, there was much fear that the guild members would be starved out. Contributions for their support never were enough to provide for their needs. The local unions were willing, but few had very much spare money in their treasuries. Strong appeals had to be made to community organizations, including churches and neighborhood political groups. Howard Costigan, executive secretary of the Washington Commonwealth Federation, used his radio news program to advise the entire community of the guild's plight, struggling without adequate financial resources. Such news reports helped solicit needed funds. Being a radio newsman, Costigan was a member of the guild and could speak with creditable knowledge about the situation.

The only weakening in the ranks of labor occurred when the increasingly powerful Seattle Teamster leader, Dave Beck, advised Mayor Dore that he wanted the strike settled soon, even if the guild did not gain anything from Hearst. He said the business people were suffering since they could not get their advertising contracts published in the P-I. That made Mayor Dore nervous, and caused him to send word to the local guild leaders that he was going to have to send the police to end the picket line very soon. I was in the committee that responded to the mayor's threat. We diplomatically pointed out that the entire labor movement and the whole city were supporting the guild, and it would be an act of folly to break up such a strong political combination. We pointed out to him that it was politically wise to keep the P-I closed until after the election. Reluctantly he agreed with us, and he delayed any more pressure against the strike until after the election. By that time, Hearst changed his strategy from fighting us to attempting to find a way to get along with us.

When Roosevelt won that election, Hearst sent word that he was ready to settle. The guild was not actually ready, but hurriedly arranged to reach an agreement on most local issues. Hearst was unwilling to settle the cases of Armstrong and Lynch, claiming that he could not act regarding them before the National Labor Relations Board reached a decision on those two men's "unfair labor practice" cases. He was still unwilling to admit that he had committed unfair labor practices.

Then Hearst made a very skillful political move by replacing the old local management with John Boettiger and his wife Anna (the daughter of President Roosevelt) to manage and edit the *Post-Intelligencer*. That move enabled Hearst to reestablish good relations with the community. The Boettigers exercised skill at establishing open relations with practically every political element in the community which had supported the strike. Their efforts were successful to a very large degree in reestablishing a working relationship all around.

When the guild had to resolve its issues to negotiate an agreement with the Boettigers, the officers felt the need for outside help. They asked me to sit in with them, and the Boettigers agreed to it. This was probably because I had been so influential in the Central Labor Council, I had had a prominent hand in the Labor Day Parade (which had lambasted Hearst very hard), and I had participated in local politics through the Washington Commonwealth Federation.

I actively participated in the negotiations, exerting most of my efforts on getting the salary scale raised from the then too common wage of under $20 a week. The first raises seemed quite large proportionately, because the base pay was as low as $5 a week for copy boys.

After the negotiations were completed, the Boettigers established a regular practice of having Howard Costigan (executive secretary of the Washington Commonwealth Federation), Hugh DeLacy (president of the WCF) and me (a vice president of the WCF) to their home for dinner and an evening of discussion. We reviewed any and almost all political matters of mutual interest, which mostly involved goings on in the Democratic party and the doings of Democrat office holders. All of us understood that it was to our mutual benefit to reach common understandings about political positions, and to preserve our mutual interests in promoting what the Communists called a "democratic front against fascism." Anna communicated that information to her father, President Roosevelt, through her mother, Eleanor. Sometimes we also received advice or information that helped guide our decisions and avoid conflicts with President Roosevelt.

One sticky political issue that caused all of us dining at the Boettigers great concern centered on the American League Against War and Fascism. DeLacy, Costigan and I pressed the argument that America's foreign policy, which had allowed Hitler to build a huge war machine and use it to help crush the Spanish Republic, was a policy that would come back to haunt the United States. Those discussions led us to an agreement in 1938 to have Anna speak to a league mass meeting, in Eagles Auditorium at Seventh &

Union in Seattle. Her pitch was that she knew that her father was doing his best to safeguard America from war, and that everyone must have faith in him. We were disappointed that she avoided mentioning the need to lift the embargo against Spain. Our later Communist party analysis was, in effect, that her speech contained nothing that we could rely on. It did help the American League Against War and Fascism, led by state Senator N. P. Atkinson, to win a wider range of public respectability, but the increasing isolation of the Communist party and its allies at the onset of World War II negated most of that public relations effect.

At the time, both sides profited much from the exchanges at the Boettigers' home because it permitted us to understand each other better and to make allowances for our differences without crossing into open conflict. But inevitably we revealed our membership in the Communist party because the policies we advocated were consistently supportive of the published Communist Party policies. John Boettiger knowingly pointed that out to us.

The dinner invitations to us stopped after John Boettiger accurately accused us of being Communists.

ટ૱

FOLLOWING THE 1936 ELECTION

ટ૱

The lines of class conflict in the Northwest and on the Pacific Coast sharpened following President Roosevelt's successful 1936 reelection campaign.

Early in November, 1936, violent attacks were made on striking members of the Lumber and Sawmill Workers Union at McCleary,

Washington, a little company town in Grays Harbor County on the road from Olympia to Aberdeen. The McCleary Lumber Company had refused to deal with the lumber union since the 1935 general strike of timber workers. One hundred fifty-two union men were locked out of the McCleary mill in an effort to destroy the union. The company recruited scabs, mostly from the drought-stricken midwest.

In September, 1936, the union repeatedly contacted the company to negotiate recognition, but were rebuffed. The union workers then reestablished a picket line. The mill owner, Henry McCleary, openly pledged to use force to drive every union man out of town. It was reported that many non-union employees were given arms. Non-union employees made several attacks on pickets, inflicting injuries. When reports of violence against union members became known, timber workers from other communities came to McCleary and took positions on the picket line to give courage to non-union workers who might want to support the union.

According to newspaper reports in my files, peaceful pickets were brutally clubbed and tear gassed on November 4 by Washington State Patrol officers; the attack came at 8:45 p.m., just 24 hours after the end of the national election. The attack was signalled by Chief Cole, the head of the State Patrol. The first to be gassed were a group of twelve women, one of whom had her leg cut by flying gravel. As the pickets retreated, police fired a tear gas gun directly into the face of a pregnant woman who was unable to move as quickly as they demanded. She was clubbed down. Her husband, coming to get her, was beaten in the doorway of their home. A Mrs. Geer received a shoulder injury and Homer Evans sustained a severe concussion. Other injured persons included Paul Hasbrook, Paul Carr, and Mrs. Goodpastor. All those injured were union men or their wives and all were residents of McCleary, not reinforcements from other towns.

After the picket line was smashed, non-union workers were transported in State vehicles through what had been the picket line. There were rumors that the non-union workers were actually professional strikebreaking strong-arm thugs recruited from Seattle. The violence continued through the next day.

The attack by the State Patrol came as a complete surprise. No strikebreakers were attempting to pass through the picket line before the attack. The only previous violence in the strike had occurred two days earlier when a picket was stabbed seven times in the back by a scab. Judge Wright of Montesano issued an injunction against picketing at McCleary's mill in nearby Shelton and a temporary restraining order on picketing in McCleary and proceeded to hold a hearing on an anti-picketing injunction for the town of McCleary.

McCleary came under defacto martial law. State Patrolmen continued to be stationed there for several weeks. Local businessmen complained that their activities were interfered with by the State Patrol. Although the town was on the main highway from Olympia to Aberdeen, all strangers passing through were stopped by the police, photographed and told to leave town. According to a newspaper report, a party of men who stopped before a beer parlor for a drink were told, "Get out of town and stay out. We're taking your license number and if you light in town again we're going to run you in. Now I'm going to give you until I count to five. If you're not gone we'll give you the works right now."

In response to the vicious State Police attack, the leaders of the Grays Harbor timber unions and of the Maritime Federation arranged a mass meeting at Aberdeen. Howard Costigan met with several of the injured and pledged that the Washington Commonwealth Federation would launch a campaign to get rid of the state patrol as a strike-breaking agency. The state Department of Labor and Industries investigated the incident, with no result.

J. S. Hofman, Hugh DeLacy, and I were at that time the Political Welfare Committee of the Seattle Central Labor Council. We conducted our own investigation of the McCleary affair, confirming all the facts stated above. Along with several leaders of the southwest Washington labor movement, including William Brackinreed (president of the Grays Harbor Central Labor Council), John Davis (Secretary of the Grays Harbor Sub-District Council of the Maritime Federation), and William Plested (President of the Lumber and Sawmill Workers' Grays-Willapa Harbor District Council), we conferred with Governor Martin on November 17.

Before the election, Martin had promised me and the other members of the Seattle Central Labor Council Political Welfare Committee that when state authorities were sent into any troubled area they would have orders to protect the lives of all workers equally, as much as the property of the owners. Now, we told Governor Martin that we wanted an immediate public investigation to be followed with appropriate action. The governor stated that the affair caused him more trouble than any other single act for many months and complained vigorously that he wanted not to spend any more time on it. Governor Martin's position was essentially, "This regrettable incident will be repeated if any town is invaded by a mob." Plested intimated that a statewide timber strike to aid the McCleary workers might occur if the governor failed to take action. The governor would not commit himself to anything, but merely hinted that something might be done in the future.

When we reported back to the Seattle Central Labor Council, the Council agreed that the State Patrol was not tending to its normal highway safety duties but was usurping the duties of small town peace officers without cause. The Council directed us to organize statewide labor protests against the Governor's actions. We urged Martin to immediately suspend Chief Cole and all officers on duty at McCleary during the picket line incidents, to publicize the results of the Department of Labor and Industries investigation, and to enact laws that would provide criminal penalties in the instance of any further breaches of peace by officers of the law.

All our protests were to no avail at that time. However, there were later repercussions for Martin, who, although he was a Democrat, we had come to regard as being pro-business rather than an enthusiastic pro-labor New Dealer. During the 1940 election campaign, Governor Martin invited me to his office in Olympia to make promises to me in my capacity as secretary of the state CIO Council. (At this time, I was also vice-president of the WCF and one of the three members of the state CIO Political Welfare Committee.) The meeting was arranged by Joe Ruddy, who operated a marine fumigating business in Seattle.

Governor Martin told us that the polls indicated he would be defeated in the coming election unless he made up to organized labor. He realized our controversy over the McCleary conflict had not been satisfactorily resolved, and promised that, if elected, he would see to it that it did not happen again. I had to advise the governor that his mistake about McCleary was a bitter pill that labor could not swallow; it still stuck in our "craw." At the time of this meeting with Martin, most of the McCleary workers belonged to the International Woodworkers of America and, still unsuccessful in gaining bargaining recognition from McCleary, were in the process of taking their case all the way to the NLRB. Martin expressed profuse regret over the whole McCleary affair, and admitted it was probably to late to try to convince organized labor that he had a change of heart. I thanked him for his promises and advised that there was nothing that I could or would do to help his election, because it was too late. That fall, he was defeated by the Republican, Arthur Langlie. Martin had dug his own grave.

During the winter following the McCleary strike, the Waterfront Employers Association hardened its determination to weaken the maritime unions. They refused to negotiate settlements with the maritime workers over disputes that had been accumulating since 1934. So the Maritime Federation of the Pacific felt forced to strike, to defend its right to organize and bargain collectively. As a delegate to the Northwest district council, I participated in the work of the publicity committee, keeping the members informed of every development as we learned about it. I also took my turn on the picket lines.

From the beginning, the Maritime Federation was threatened with division within the ranks over nearly every policy issue. Lundeberg of the Sailors' Union of the Pacific continuously expressed hostility to anything proposed by Harry Bridges or the other unions. Lundeberg branded nearly all proposals as too political. That allowed the U.S. government representative, Hugh Johnson, to promote a wedge. He condemned the marine unions for refusal to accept government intervention; he claimed the strike would undermine President Roosevelt's economic recovery program. That claim did not intimidate the marine unions. It was clear to us that General Johnson was trying to use government pressure to impose the will of the employers against the workers, in conflict with the provisions of the National Labor Relations Act.

Our argument in answer to Lundeberg was that we had to mobilize our political strength to counter the dirty politics of the employers, who were in collusion with the government. Harry Bridges stated the idea that our economic strength on the picket line was the best political argument we had. Our rank and file members agreed with Bridges.

General Johnson failed to break the strike. He and his supporters tried every trick in the book to get the unions to open the picket lines to let "emergency" supplies through to some claimed disaster area. Alaska and Hawaii were frequently cited as in dire need. With considerable skill, the marine unions responded to each emergency demand, and allowed necessary food and essential supplies to be shipped to the out-ports as mutually agreed upon.

That strike lasted through the worst of the winter, when the Employers Association finally realized they could not break the solidarity of the maritime workers even though Lundeberg was breaking away, and a new issue—the CIO's industrial unionism versus the AFL's craft unionism—was looming large. The CIO threat was the threat of larger and more extensive organization of workers everywhere. My participation in the strike and, at this time, in the debate on the CIO was minimal, because I was pushed into the Seattle city elections of February, 1937.

During the P-I strike many new labor leaders emerged. They showed great ability to activate their own groups and enlisted other groups to support them. Those in the Newspaper Guild who have been previously recognized included Dick Sellers, Cliff Erickson, Art French, Ray Holmes, and many others.

Victor Hicks from one of the teachers' unions showed versatility in reaching the other teachers' unions and groups of government workers, and showing the proper way to aid the P-I strikers. Hicks was young and enthusiastic about our political efforts, and suggested that we ought to promote a ticket of a teacher and a strong labor leader for election to the Seattle City Council. Hicks already had a name to suggest: Hugh DeLacy, a prominent member of the University of Washington American Federation of Teachers local union (which he had helped to organize two years before). DeLacy also had working-class experience from working as a marine fireman on deep-sea vessels, and as a laborer in the building trades.

Hicks also called attention to Earl Gunther, vice president of the Central Labor Council and a delegate from the stagehands' union, because he had exerted a strong influence on the other "old-time" leaders during the P-I strike. The names of DeLacy and Gunther for the city council caught the favor of those who had been activists throughout the P-I strike. Then Hicks went so far as to push me as manager of the political campaign, because I had an established contact in every union from the Labor Day Parade, as well as in the Democratic party through my activities in the Washington Commonwealth Federation.

I reluctantly accepted the task of managing the DeLacy-Gunther campaign because my personal situation was impoverished. But John M. Fox, head of the Ferryboatmen's Union, offered to furnish a campaign office and to help me with my personal financial situation enough so I could get by. DeLacy found a secretary by the name of Betty Forrest from among the university professor's wives. She worked as a volunteer throughout the campaign.

When we made the public announcement that DeLacy and Gunther were running as a team for the city council, the Central Labor Council leaders warned me that no "double" team had ever won an election, and they wouldn't support this one either. In fact, they refused to support Gunther singly, even though he was vice president of the Central Labor Council. Some of the council old-timers told me that it looked like an effort to get some "reds" on the city council. Some of them knew that Gunther had worked with William Z. Foster during the steel strike of 1919. They professed to know nothing about DeLacy, the University of Washington teaching assistant, but scoffed at the idea that a Phi Beta Kappa teacher would be any good on the city council. It seemed to me that it was necessary to again approach the local unions for endorsements without having a collision with the old-timers in the Central Labor Council, although I kept up a dialogue with them about our progress all during the campaign.

To get things started, I drew up a short list of ideas, collected from the neighborhood political organizations and some of the local unions, for a political platform. They were:

1. Restore the wages of city workers that had been cut during the early days of the Depression.

2. Rejuvenate the old, worn-out streetcar system with a newly developed vehicle known as the "President's Conference Car," which could operate almost noiselessly and smoothly.

3. Build a viaduct across the railroad tracks on Spokane Street (twelve pairs). The West Seattle Democratic Club, led by Mrs. Margaret Haglund (wife of the well known restaurant operator, Ivar), had advised me that their most urgent problem was overcoming the hazards of crossing those sets of tracks from West Seattle to downtown. DeLacy later found out that the terms of the city franchise with the railroads required that when a time came that a viaduct was required for public safety, the railroads were legally obligated to pay the costs. Ultimately, the city council compromised on that issue and helped the railroads pay for the Spokane Street Viaduct, which was built much later.

DeLacy and Gunther approved these proposals and developed several others which we put together in a mimeographed letter announcing the opening of the DeLacy-Gunther campaign. The letter was then sent to all the local unions and to the social and fraternal organizations. The following three points were added to the above by DeLacy and Gunther:

1. For efficient municipal service.
   a. Lower telephone rates.
   b. Modernize the streetcar system to give safe, efficient, low-cost service with adequate protection to the men who work in industry.
   c. Apply modern engineering to insure traffic safety.
2. Economic relief. Provide aid to the unemployed.
   a. Free streetcar service to all certified for public assistance.
   b. Initiate a building program with federal aid.
3. Apply organized labor standards.
   a. Full support to the progressive program of President Franklin D. Roosevelt and Mayor John F. Dore.
   b. Sponsor community forums on controversial public questions.

Favorable responses came from almost all the local organizations, together with enthusiastic endorsement of candidates DeLacy and Gunther and their program. We followed that up with solicitation for funds, and most of the organizations made small contributions, which enabled us to buy radio time and place ads in nearly all the local neighborhood newspapers very early in the campaign. It became very evident that there was a strong ground swell for new, clean political leaders the public could trust. We pushed the idea of having new, incorruptible, educated people in city politics, instead of the old deceitful corrupted servants of the "invisible" government. In the beginning of the campaign the usual avenues of publicity ignored us. We couldn't get DeLacy's and Gunther's names mentioned in the daily newspapers nor on the radio. But when it became evident to everyone that DeLacy and Gunther were picking up a lot of support from the "man in the street," we caught the first hints of a coming interference from the University of Washington administration.

The discussions we had in the Communist Party District Buro led us to anticipate that the university would be manipulated by the conservative element in the city to do something to interfere with DeLacy's campaign. We correctly estimated that they would try to force him to either drop out of the council race or resign his teaching position. So we advised DeLacy to be ready for that move by having an application for a leave of absence, for the period of the election campaign, ready when it became necessary to fight back.

Events worked out as we anticipated, and DeLacy was ready for them. We had arranged for DeLacy to have his letter cross in the mail with the university letter. When the university's "suspicious" letter came, we had DeLacy send off his request for a leave of absence without opening the letter from the university.

The letters did cross in the mail on a Wednesday night, the night the Central Labor Council regularly met. I got in touch with the city editor of the *Seattle Star*, Charles Daggett, and offered him a scoop on the firing by the university and DeLacy's request for a leave of absence if he would cooperate with us. We publicly emphasized the point that an educational institute was attempting to illegally deny a teacher's civil right to run for public office. Daggett agreed, on condition that I keep the news from the rival morning papers until he could publish it in his afternoon paper. I agreed, and that meant not letting news of the letters get out on the floor of the Central Labor Council that night. But I received an order from the Party trade union secretary, Harry Jackson, to break the news to the Central Labor Council that night, and to fight for a motion to condemn the University of Washington. When I tried to persuade him it would be better not to do that, without revealing the deal I had with Daggett and the *Seattle Star*, he gave me a direct Party order that I must do as he directed or be disciplined by the Party. In spite of his threat, I kept my silence in the Central Labor Council that night and saw to it that no one else breathed a word about the letters crossing in the mail. I privately asked Chairman O'Reilly not to recognize any motions about DeLacy that night. He was very cooperative and did not allow anyone to mention DeLacy.

The next day, the *Seattle Star* carried top headlines about the university firing DeLacy, thereby interfering with his political right to seek public office. The other newspapers came to us to get the story, and to look at the letters and publish their contents. My decision to violate a Party order from Jackson was vindicated by our newspaper campaign successes, so no Party discipline was inflicted on me. Spokesmen for the university tried to cover up their dirty hands in this attempt to remove DeLacy from the race, but they failed, mainly because we kept up a running crusade for clean politics. The resulting picture to the public was the university using crooked politics to obstruct the efforts of a clean, incorruptible young professor to run for public office.

The League of Women Voters and other groups sent questionnaires asking for our candidates' stand on many issues. The candidates answered in detail, apparently to the satisfaction of the inquirers. The issues were about amortization of city bonds, proposed purchase of the private power company Puget Sound Power and Light, tax equalization, etc.

Once, during the latter half of the campaign, an unidentified group invited DeLacy to an unexplained conference. DeLacy asked me to go with him because he had some misgivings about it. It turned out to be in a dark room in a remote area, where half a dozen men proposed to finance the whole of DeLacy's campaign if he would promise to help promote legislation favorable to the slot machine industry. DeLacy turned to me for the answer. I told them that we were sound financially and did not need any other help. That effort to corrupt DeLacy failed. No other efforts were made.

Although Gunther's name was carried with DeLacy's throughout the primary campaign, we were unable to stir up as much attention for Gunther. The result was that DeLacy was comfortably nominated and went on to win in the general election, but Gunther lost out. Our success with DeLacy inspired the local unions and fraternal groups to carry the campaign all the way. Our campaign was successfully carried on by promoting a progressive united slate of Scavotto, Norton, and Delacy.

DeLacy established an honorable record that won praises from all the city workers and all the unions that had contracts with the city. Despite DeLacy's publicly reputed Communist connections, the teamsters' unions under Frank Brewster and Dave Beck became his staunch supporters because he carried out his campaign promises—which resulted in restoring much of the wages lost in the Depression cuts.

ॐ

THE CIO MOVEMENT

ॐ

My experience in the CIO began in the Inlandboatmen's Union on June 12, 1936, when we received a letter with a resolution from the United Mine Workers of America, District 10, signed by Sam Nichols, president; Richard Francis, secretary-treasurer; and William Dalrymple, international representative. The letter requested endorsement of the CIO, and asked our support for an endorsement at the state Federation of Labor convention July 13, 1936.

Because I had long been an advocate of industrial union organization from the Communist party perspective, I took the lead in my union, urging support for the Mine Workers' resolution. My motion carried unanimously. It was logical that our union would support this resolution because we were already an industrial union. All unlicensed personnel on the vessels working on Puget Sound were in one union and worked together successfully.

At the state AFL convention, all our efforts were thwarted by the entrenched craft unions and the ruling of the previous AFL national convention that the subject was not one for State Federations or City Central bodies; the decision could be made only by International organizations.

One of the convincing points made by the craft union leaders during the discussions was that the skilled workers would lose some of their bargaining rights. John F. Dore, then mayor of Seattle, injected his political judgment on this subject in the convention by say ing, the "Industrial Union was an organization opposed to unionism." I recall he went on to say that he owed Dave Beck a debt for support in his election and, "I am going to pay it back in the next two years." (He did that, by having the police siding with the AFL against the CIO on picket lines in the city.) By the close of that convention, there were ominous indications that the splits in the labor movement were going to interfere with the unions' organizing the unorganized.

Because the AFL had failed to organize the unorganized workers by 1935, masses of workers were spontaneously joining together
and petitioning the AFL to establish them in unions. But the AFL
was not responding fast enough to satisfy the needs of the workers.
Idle factories were reopening and the masses of unskilled workers
were getting back on the payroll, anxiously looking forward to
progress. These masses were the formerly unemployed, who had
conducted hunger marches under the leadership of the Communists
in the Unemployed Councils and other organizations, and who had
learned to demonstrate militantly for their needs. One of those
needs was that Congress enact legislation providing a legal basis for
workers to have the right to organize and bargain collectively. That
became the famous Section 7–A of the NIRA, and went on to ultimately become the National Labor Relations Act. The Communists
had taught the unemployed the tactics of mass, collective activity,
and had urged them to press for their legal rights to organize and
bargain collectively. The WPA (Works Progress Administration)
unions were organized by the Communists out of the Unemployed
Councils.

Many people may not be aware of it, and others would probably
like to bury this information, but before the United States Communist party adopted the policy of building the "democratic front
against fascism" in 1935, the Communist's openly declared aim was
to overthrow capitalism, although we didn't know exactly how to do
it. There were many different partial answers; one that stood out
was about the Unemployed Councils. I personally heard Herbert
Benjamin, who was a publicly known Communist, the national
leader of the Unemployed Councils, and a leader in the national
hunger marches, advise local leaders in Seattle that the Unemployed Councils in old Russia were the basis of the 1905 rebellion,
which was a dress rehearsal for the successful revolution of 1917. He
claimed that the workers, soldiers, and sailors organized the Soviets—the Russian word for Revolutionary Councils—from the Unemployed Councils of that time. So the main purpose in organizing
the Unemployed Councils in the USA was to build a revolutionary
base, from which could be launched a Soviet type revolution in
America, using those workers.

I think it must be beyond doubt or question that these facts
were collected by the various intelligence gathering agencies in the
army, navy, Coast Guard, immigration service and FBI, all of whom
watched the Communist party, and who had their agents inside

also. They relayed that information through channels to President Roosevelt. These facts regarding the Unemployed Councils personally known to me, convince me that "the die was cast" for the CIO before it was born. It is my carefully considered judgment that President Roosevelt was fully aware of the need to mobilize the working people to be against the fascists, and that he was equally concerned to see to it that the working people broke away from the Communist influence. The January, 1987, issue of the *American Atheist* has a report on page 38 that, "According to Hoover's [the FBI 'J. Edgar'] notes from a meeting on August 24, 1936, Roosevelt desired to control the activities of subversives in the U.S. particularly fascists and communists. On September 6, 1936, the FBI was placed in charge of policing subversives."

From my later experience with John L. Lewis and the CIO, I am convinced that President Roosevelt asked the labor leaders, Green, and then Lewis, to get control of all the workers in order to keep the workers' loyalty to the capitalist system, and at no time did either Roosevelt or Lewis propose to emancipate the workers. They devoted their best efforts to tying the loyalty of the workers to the capitalist system through the industrial unions.

I think John L. Lewis and his closest associates practiced deceit on the workers in the CIO from the very beginning. The radicals, especially the Communists, misled themselves and their allies by representing the CIO as a step toward socialism and the emancipation of the working class.

There are many indications that Roosevelt and Lewis had a "gentlemen's" agreement in 1936, that in return for Lewis supporting Roosevelt's reelection, Roosevelt would see to it that the government would not hamper or interfere in Lewis' efforts to organize the CIO. In fact, there was a general feeling among the unorganized workers that President Roosevelt would help them get organized. Some CIO organizers gave that impression.

Enormous successes occurred during the CIO's first couple of years—1935 and 1936. During that time, the auto workers in Michigan militantly surged ahead with organizing and demanding recognition. Wyndham Mortimer spearheaded that drive, which led to a direct confrontation when the public demanded the workers' picket lines be crushed by National Guard or federal troops. Governor Murphy was already on a hot spot when John L. Lewis came to Michigan at the request of Mortimer and took his stand with the auto-worker pickets. Lewis was willing to actually place his life in danger at that point. But his courage won the day for the auto workers. Mortimer told me that that act by Lewis saved the organization of the auto workers, because Governor Murphy advised everyone that it would be folly to have soldiers shoot Lewis because such an act would spread fire among the workers nationwide. Knowledge of that attitude also restrained President Roosevelt from intervening with United States troops.

But when the violence of the "Little Steel Strike" occurred in South Chicago on Memorial Day, 1937, the publicity of that event (the killing of several pickets by police) shocked the entire nation, especially the workers. The employers damned Roosevelt for letting that violence happen. Lewis expected Roosevelt to support labor's side, but Roosevelt responded to that crisis by saying, "A plague o' both your houses," to which Lewis countered, "Which house— Hearst or Dupont?" Neither expression did justice to the situation, and each changed direction from then on. Lewis felt especially betrayed because he had contributed $500,000 to Roosevelt's election in 1936, and felt that he deserved better consideration from Roosevelt because of that.

Up to that time, many of us in the CIO had been advised by "insiders" that Lewis was in line for greater political influence in the Roosevelt administration; it was possible he would become secretary of labor. Some with a prejudice against women were hoping to get Frances Perkins out that way. But the course of events pushed Lewis and Roosevelt further and further apart, to the disadvantage of the working people.

From advocating militant revolutionary tactics to adopting united front agreements with every group willing to fight the rise of fascism was a long step that the Communist party took in 1935. The rise of Hitler to power in Germany in 1933 precipitated a reign of terror against Communists, Jews, Catholics, Protestants, and every group which resisted his policies. The entire world underwent a major political upheaval. News reporters like William L. Shirer were reporting that the Nazis were imposing a bloody reign of terror, using naked violence to impose their will on all others. Those who resisted the Nazis were imposed on in every way possible. At least six million German people, as well as six million Jews, lost their freedom and ultimately their lives in that savage Nazi seizure of power, which was the opening chapter of World War II.

In an attempt to consolidate their power, the Nazis concocted a transparent fraud and blamed the Communists for the Reichstag fire. That scheme backfired in 1935 when Communist leader Georgi Dimitroff won an acquittal in the Nazi court itself by proving that it was the Nazis under General Goering who planned the fire, using a mentally deficient Dutch worker by the name of Van der Lubbe to commit the bungling deed.

For that success, Dimitroff was promoted to top leadership in the Communist International. There he outlined a new united front policy for all Communist parties throughout the world. The new policy focused activity toward the defeat of the existing fascist governments and aimed to prevent the rise of any more. Previously, the Communist party official policy prohibited all its sections and members from working with any rival organizations, such as the Socialist and the Social Democratic parties. Stalin, who controlled the political policies of the International at that time, had stubbornly refused to permit the German Communist party leaders to make any deals with the leaders of the German Social Democratic party. Many now believe that had the Communist party and the Social Democratic party in Germany worked together at that time, they could have prevented Hitler's rise to power and all the subsequent events of World War II.

The foremost achievements of this change of policy were the building of the "Front Populaire" in France and the advocacy of Democratic Front policies that changed the public behavior of Communist leaders and parties throughout the world. In America, it converted the old pro-revolutionary policies into more social-democratic ones, permitting and directing Communist leaders to enter into limited agreements with leaders of the Democratic party and any other organizations, particularly labor and fraternal groups, solely on the basis of their commitment to oppose fascism.

The inner functioning of the Communist party became consciously pro-democratic. It did away with many of the Party activities that could be considered "secret" and "conspiratorial." Communist district and national leaders met openly with Democratic party national committeemen and women to discuss policies that would win the masses over against the fascists and cause United States government officials to promise publicly to follow an anti-fascist policy. Most political leaders recognized that the attitude of the working people was the most critical element in deciding which way the United States would behave toward fascism. But at that time, the masses of workers in the United States were mainly uninformed, unorganized, anti-political and unable to determine their own destiny. It was all too painfully evident that the organization of the workers in the United States was the most urgent issue before us.

Conscious of the menacing political events caused by the rise of Hitler and fascism, we Communists took the lead in using every opportunity to promote a united anti-fascist policy among all workers, whether they were organized in unions, fraternal groups, or political organizations. At first the Socialist party leaders withheld their support, because they believed the Communist party would betray them. But when the CIO was launched by John L. Lewis, the Communist leadership ignored nearly all resistance—inside or outside the CP—to working with non-communists. There were a few difficult legacies from the Communist party past which had to be overcome. President Roosevelt played a big part in removing obstacles to anti-fascist unity. He recognized the necessity of uniting the nation and did unify it (with a few exceptions, such as the World War II concentration camps for American-born Japanese).

President Roosevelt and Congress felt the mass pressure of the workers, and reluctantly accepted the principle that workers should have the legal right to organize and bargain collectively. So we got the National Labor Relations Act, which established our legal rights. But the passage of the law did not automatically result in union organization. In fact, most unions had to sustain their claim to the right with militant picket lines because the employers opposed recognizing the unions as long as they could.

During June, 1937, the third convention of the Maritime Federation occurred in Portland, Oregon. The CIO called nationally for the marine unions to leave the AFL and join the CIO. So the most urgent issue before the federation was which way it would go. The Communist party organized a large "fraction" (a caucus of Communists and our close allies) to meet the night before the convention opened. The purpose of the meeting was to consolidate our strength, so we could put over an endorsement of the CIO. Harry Bridges and several non-Party delegates came to that meeting to lay before us the conditions for affiliation to the CIO that John L. Lewis set forth. Bridges had just been designated by Lewis as the CIO director for the Pacific Coast. We understood that Lewis selected Bridges instead of Harry Lundeberg in the belief that Bridges was the stronger leader. We also understood that Lundeberg became determined to prevent an endorsement of the CIO because he had been passed over by John L. Lewis.

The Party was glad Bridges won the appointment because the Party strength in the Longshoremen's Union gave us an advantage in trying to persuade the other unions to go along. But Bridges was the target of some of the dirtiest tactics the government ever engaged in.

I was present in Harry Bridges' hotel room in Portland, Oregon, for a conference on strategy in the third convention of the Maritime Federation when the "bugs" were discovered. Henry Schmidt, a longshoremen's delegate, got an inspiration to have some fun with whoever was listening by carrying on an imaginary conversation with Joseph Stalin. He thanked Joe for the gold shipment and promised to make good use of the money. At the end of this conversation someone made a loud noise over the bug hoping to blast the ear drums on the other end. Then we all had a good laugh about the absurd situation.

When news of the bugs in Bridges' hotel room became public, every group that sympathized with labor roundly condemned the Immigration and Naturalization Service for violating Bridges' civil rights to privacy in his residence. The convention later took similar action and called upon Secretary of Labor Frances Perkins to have the government put a stop to such antics. That event, by reducing the moral prestige of the government, weakened the effort to deport Bridges as an undesirable alien.

I served as secretary of the resolutions committee throughout that convention, and still have my penciled notes showing that the convention was almost evenly divided over whether to join the CIO. Lundeberg and his able assistant, Bob Dombroff from Seattle, hammered hard against committing the maritime workers to a course of direct political action involvement, which they claimed would result from joining the CIO. Despite the division among the convention delegates, it was a widely known fact that every organization that had polled its membership found the overwhelming majority favored withdrawal from the AFL and immediate affiliation with the CIO.

The most disappointing result of the convention was the failure to promote greater unity between the East Coast and West Coast unions. The positive stand taken by practically every delegate provided a powerful stimulus to repeated and continued efforts on the part of the East Coast and West Coast delegations to get together and iron out existing differences. We reached a memorandum of understanding among those representatives, in which each agreed that they would cease the publication of any (more) statements in the union press that would reflect negatively on the other organization. We also agreed that mutual interplacement of men on intercoastal vessels would be practiced, instead of attempting to settle these questions by either claiming jurisdiction when the other already had the crew aboard. But all the plans for a national federation failed when the principal leaders on the East and West coasts were unable to reach the necessary agreements. We could not reconcile the differences in structure. The National Maritime Union (NMU) combined deck, engine, and stewards sections. On the West Coast, each section was a separate union unwilling to amalgamate with others.

John Brophy, the CIO representative present, let it be known that the CIO was opposed to the organization of a National Maritime Federation. He proposed an alternative in the form of a marine section within the CIO that would serve as an umbrella for all the marine unions. That was the ultimate decision, which went into effect much later.

The menace of fascism was strongly understood by marine workers because they could see it was destroying the Spanish republic, and there were many seafaring workers fighting in Spain on the side of the republic. That's why the convention voted for a coast-wide demonstration on August 2, 1937, to support the Republic. Several fraternal delegates from all over the world, some in disguise, spoke urging the demonstration. Their protest was against the Neutrality Act of the United States, which denied aid to democratic nations. The Fascists had no restraints and were destroying Spain. That demonstration was successfully carried out on the West Coast.

The question probably debated most thoroughly on the floor was whether or not to endorse Labor's Non-Partisan League (LNPL), and similar local political organizations, like the WCF in Washington and the OCF in Oregon. The debate centered around the question of whether or not labor unions should take direct political action. This question was decided in the negative, despite the fact that the overwhelming majority of delegates favored making the endorsement. But the distribution of voting power was weighted in favor of the smaller organizations. So when a delegate in a smaller organization, who held the balance of power, was called out of the convention hall by a telephone call at the time the roll-call vote was taken, we lost the vote to endorse political action with Labor's Non-Partisan League. Later in the convention proceedings action was taken to establish congressional lobbies in Washington, D.C., indicating that in practice the maritime unions were quite aware of the importance of safeguarding labor's political rights as a complement to safeguarding labor's economic rights. Various measures to impose greater restrictions on all maritime workers such as the "Fink book," a continuous registration of discharge from a job, were being promoted in Congress at that time.

During the general push for CIO organization, the Maritime Federation District Council #1 in Seattle caused the organization of the Alaska Cannery Workers in 1936–37. The several Fishermen's unions that delivered fish to the Alaska canneries observed that Filipino, Japanese and native Alaskan cannery workers were being exploited by gamblers and labor contractors. To overcome that condition, the fishermen proposed that the Maritime Federation sponsor and supervise the dispatch of cannery workers to Alaska. Conrad Espe, a fisherman, was elected to organize the cannery workers and to bring some order out of the chaos that had prevailed in the past.

Espe found quite a few agricultural workers, who normally migrated each year from California to Seattle, to work in the Alaska canneries. They formed a stable committee and obtained a union charter for the Cannery Workers and Farm Laborers Union Local No. 7, affiliated with the United Cannery, Agricultural, Packing, and Allied Workers of America (UCAPAWA), led by Donald Henderson in the CIO.

The gamblers and labor contractors did everything they could to destroy that union. Virgil Duyungan, the local union president, was attacked and killed by gunmen in a restaurant in Seattle's Chinatown. He had expected to be attacked, so he had armed himself with a pistol to fight back, and in that exchange he managed to kill his assailant, a labor contractor. The local union secretary, Aurelio Simon, was also killed in that exchange. When I heard the news on the radio, I went to the morgue to verify that those were the bodies of the men I knew. It proved to be true. Their bodies were riddled with bullet holes.

As executive secretary of the Seattle Industrial Labor Union Council, I organized a huge funeral procession. It was supported by all the unions in the Maritime Federation, and they marched on every street in the Seattle Chinatown area. We marched with lively bands and large banners to show our solidarity with the Cannery Workers in their fight against the racketeers. The union spirit of that group of workers was revived and has carried on ever since.

Duyungan's successors had to fight hard for several years before they eliminated that clique of underworld characters. The Second World War interrupted the organization of Japanese cannery workers because the United States government imprisoned them in detention camps. After the war that union was again plagued by criminals and redbaiters. Since then the union has had to obtain protective affiliation with the International Longshoremen's and Warehousemen's Union.

After the third maritime convention, reports from Spain indicated that the Loyalists were suffering heavy losses, while defending themselves from Franco's onslaught. Franco was getting unlimited support from German Nazis and Italian Fascists. I gave serious thought to joining the Abraham Lincoln Brigade of pro-Loyalist American volunteers to Spain, because I felt that was more important than the CIO. I submitted an application to Morris Rapport, the Communist party district organizer, who had control over recruiting for the Spanish war. He stopped my application, and told me that the Party considered that the Spanish republic was lost, mainly because the syndicalists, anarchists and Trotskyists in Barcelona and Asturia refused to unite and support the Socialists and Communists fighting to defend Madrid. Because of that split, which was causing the Loyalists to be losing the battle against Franco, the Soviet Union was withdrawing from the fight and the Abraham Lincoln Brigade was being sent back home to America late in 1938. At that time Rapport was notified that his son was killed while fighting for the republic before the decision was made to withdraw. Spain was another case where a progressive cause was lost because diverging allies refused to work together.

To me, everything happening in that period, 1936–1939, points out that allies must work together or suffer failure. The Socialists and anarchists in Spain both lost, separately. In Germany, the Communists and Social Democrats both lost, separately. In the United States, the AFL and the CIO both lost in the larger arena of establishing a progressive future. In each case there were logical reasons for not uniting, but in each case both groups lost because of their refusal to unite against their common enemy. I'm certain that Roosevelt and Lewis had some kind of agreement, but it too was broken, and the workers' immediate interests suffered because of that rift.

Some employer leaders became hysterically alarmed that the workers would go beyond union organization and attempt to carry out some of the Communist ideas of "workers' control" on the job that had been planted among them when they were unemployed and engaging in militant hunger marches. There were reports that some European unions were demanding and getting seats on the boards of directors running some big industries. That scared most American capitalists and politicians, who demanded that the government prevent that. They considered it a step in the direction of socialism. In the Seattle area, the Industrial Council, an arm of the chamber of commerce, circulated hysterical warnings against allowing organized labor to obtain any power for its workers or, especially, its leaders. Warnings were also made earlier against the effects of NRA industry code agreements which were made under government supervision.

In the Northwest, Dave Beck's teamster organization took an active part in the organization of the many different NRA industry code agreements. In that way, many light industries became tied to function by agreement with the Teamsters. Some chamber of commerce leaders became alarmed over this, and expressed fears that business was going to lose control of their industries. But when the CIO came into the picture, the chamber of commerce made its peace with Beck and the teamster organization rather than accept the CIO, which was alleged to be Communist controlled.

The AFL pursued obstructionist tactics in September, 1937, by ordering all Central Labor Councils to expel the unions that supported the CIO. My union was among those that were so separated from the main body of organized labor because the Inlandboatmen voted CIO. For a brief time we bridged the gap of our separation by holding regular Wednesday noon luncheons, open to progressives in the AFL, where we discussed current events, sometimes with special programs by out of town visitors. The unions affiliated with the Maritime Federation of the Pacific continued to function in a limited way, but we found it difficult to deal with the local city and county governments. So we organized a Seattle Unity Council, which had the support of a few AFL unions for a short time. However, soon the national AFL ordered those local AFL unions to leave the Unity Council. Then we had to reorganize into a strictly CIO city labor council. That later led us to organize the state CIO Council, because we also had to engage in political activities with the state legislature.

Because I was prominent in all these efforts, I was elected the full time first secretary of the state CIO Council. At that time we thought it politically wise to humor John L. Lewis' regional director, Richard Francis, by electing him president, but he did not lend any support to the state council. Instead he most often identified himself as the direct representative of John L. Lewis, using his title of CIO regional director, instead of president of the CIO Council.

The Washington State Industrial Union Council (CIO) was always too weak financially to make any public impression; we actually had too few members from which to draw per capita tax. My salary was $25 a week and my stenographer's was $20, and I constantly fell behind in my personal finances because our income did not support us.

We did not have the number of members needed to obtain full leadership in organized labor. Our political influence went beyond our organizational strength, however, because of our successes in the Washington Commonwealth Federation and the failures of the AFL, whose political ties were mostly with old line Republicans. We had to fight for our lives on the picket lines because Dave Beck's teamster "goons" constantly challenged us. The police, under Mayor Dore's promise to help Beck, always helped the teamsters, thus leaving our ordinary workers at the mercy of Beck's "goon-squad" of strong-arm gangs. Bridges had publicly indicated it was the intention of the International Longshoremen's and Warehousemen's Union (ILWU) to organize warehouses anywhere off the waterfront, to "march inland." Beck vowed to keep the Longshoremen's Union from moving inland, and indicated that he intended to move in on the waterfront to take the warehousemen away from the ILWU and Bridges. In spite of all efforts, neither side could carry out its intentions. The CIO lumber workers had a harder time of it, because the teamsters succeeded in stealing the jurisdiction of the log haulers in several places where we could not put up enough defense. We didn't have the truck drivers.

I tried to counter-fight the AFL and teamsters' jurisdictional raiding tactics by going before every business, social, fraternal, and political organization in Seattle, advocating public support for democratic trade unionism. That did help limit and decrease the violence the AFL was committing against the CIO.

My experience in the CIO was exciting from beginning to end because my practice had to test long-held theories that did not work out. As an active Communist, for years I had spent much effort agitating and propagandizing in favor of industrial unionism, without really comprehending the many different facets involved. The basic principle of the Trade Union Unity League, led by Communist leader William Z. Foster, was mobilizing the masses of workers to defend the Soviet Union. The formation of the Maritime Federation of the Pacific was supported in the beginning by Foster because it looked like it was a move toward revolutionary industrial unionism. It later turned out not to be because the separate unions functioned as a federation instead of as a single unit. Then when the CIO came along, we had to swing our support there because it held forth a greater promise for united strength. The Maritime Federation did demonstrate that united, the marine unions were able to make more progress than they had ever made individually. The successful strikes in 1934 and 1936 convincingly demonstrated that together the unions could defend themselves from concerted employer attacks.

When the CIO was beginning, widespread labor upheavals inspired industrial organization. All of the workers in a plant or factory would join together and demonstrate seemingly unlimited strength to win recognition and obtain collective bargaining. Most of those contracts in the beginning did not satisfy the needs of the workers because the pay scales were too low. Employer recognition of the union was the first consideration of the CIO leadership; wages and working conditions were secondary. Later strikes and negotiations made some improvements, but rarely what the workers expected and demanded.

The craft unions in the AFL already had higher wage scales than the CIO could obtain in their first negotiations. The AFL took greater advantage of the National Labor Relations Act in the belief that those legislated benefits really belonged to the skilled craft union workers more than to the unskilled, mass-production workers.

The CIO found that it had to back up NLRB cases with militant picket lines. Unfair labor practice cases were always fought hard to the bitter end. The Communists had laid the foundation for militant activity when we were advocating the building of red trade unions, because our main objective was to defend the Soviet Union. We fully believed that the capitalist nations would ultimately try to destroy the Soviet Union by a military attack, at which time we trusted that the workers in America would rise up and oppose such an imperialist war.

In the state of Washington, we built the CIO in spite of overwhelming odds against us. The Communist party had exerted its total effort to the building of industrial unions in the past, and when the CIO came along, it continued that course with much success. The CIO supporters were very often thwarted by the legal and political struggle the AFL waged against us. They brought in many special organizers, and Dave Beck extended his jurisdiction of the Teamsters' charter to include everything on wheels and a lot more. We referred to his charter as "made of rubber" because he stretched it to cover anything he wanted to control.

When local unions in the AFL tried to switch to the CIO, the AFL lawyers were frequently able to obtain court orders that stripped the locals of all their money resources, returning it to the AFL. Beck directed his whole organization, which was quite large, to convincing employers with unorganized workers, such as downtown department store managers, to fear the CIO as a gang of reds about to start a revolution. Beck moved in on the retail clerks and signed contracts with the employers guaranteeing continued service by the Teamsters. When an employer was reluctant to sign up with the Teamsters, there was a suggestion that the Teamsters would not give delivery service if the business went CIO. The CIO was in no position to compete with the Teamsters in the state of Washington, even though there were a few independent truckers who tried. We couldn't give them the support they needed to survive.

ò⬠

MORE CIO AND WCF

ò⬠

I was a delegate from the state CIO Council and the Inlandboatmen's Union to the first four CIO national conventions, and I was very favorably impressed with the grandeur and potential of a progressive program as presented skillfully by the various leaders. There were promises of great ideas and programs for the future. I signed the original charter, which founded the CIO, at the first convention, in Pittsburgh in 1938.

Each convention was conducted like a political convention of Democrats or Republicans. Demonstrations were always timed to give the longest to Lewis. Much of the hoopla was from hired demonstrators trying to whip up enthusiasm; it was so transparently artificial it had very little effect on the delegates.

John L. Lewis always made very inspiring speeches to each session of the convention, which did stir most of the delegates with a belief that the CIO was going to create a new and better order of life for the working class. However, many of the United Mine Workers delegates personally told me that they were skeptical of Lewis' promises. They had gone through bitter struggles against him in the past in Kentucky, Illinois and Pennsylvania, and they had doubts that Lewis would perform as progressively as he spoke. From the very beginning, I was made aware of the fragile relationship between the Communist progressive activists and the conservative organizers who controlled the administrative machinery of the CIO. Convention entertainers from the social-democratically oriented New York area unions often expressed ridicule, criticism, and contempt of the Communists.

At the first convention I met Roy Hudson, whom I knew from his visits to the Northwest as the Party labor adviser. I found him at the CIO convention directing Communist members on what to do and whom to see. The usual answers he gave me about my problems were to the effect that I should work through Lee Pressman, the CIO attorney who had the best access to Lewis. Hudson told me that Pressman was one of "our," meaning the Communist party, people. But when I discussed my political problems of division between LNPL and the WCF with Pressman, he turned my questions aside, saying that nothing could be done to budge Lewis.

Locally, I got an advantage for the CIO over the AFL because the AFL nationally and locally opposed the enactment of Social Security and unemployment insurance laws at that time. The AFL alleged that those proposals came from the Communists. But the CIO nationally announced its support for those programs despite the alleged Communist origin. As secretary of the state CIO Council, I gave the labor endorsement testimony to the state legislature, which secured the passage of the acts that allowed those laws to take effect. The state AFL refused to testify for those laws in the Washington State Legislature, and remained aloof from all those legislative efforts. Later, however, when that legislation became effective, the AFL sought and obtained many key administrative positions actually controlling the use of those laws. The CIO did not have qualified candidates with inside political influence to seek those positions.

My direct experience with Lewis was in 1938, 1939, 1940 and part of 1941. As a delegate to the first four national conventions of the CIO, I became acquainted with most of the national CIO leaders, especially Lewis, through conferences over various parts of the CIO program as it applied in the Northwest. Those meetings forewarned me that the organizational foundation of the CIO under Lewis had no intention of, or planning for, carrying out locally the progressive promises proclaimed in the speeches to the convention.

At one point, one of the Party leaders asked me to talk to Walter Reuther to suggest that it would be a good political move for him to introduce the resolution supporting China and opposing the shipment of scrap iron to Japan. Reuther readily agreed, and did it. During my discussion with him at that time, he questioned me at great length about the situation for organization in the Seattle Boeing aircraft plant. I had to advise him to stay out of it because the machinists union had it under control. They had originally been asked by the Maritime Federation to do that job and they were doing it. The Seattle "left" in the CIO was on good terms locally with the AFL Machinists, so we felt it was unwise to interject contention from a far-away source, such as the UAW. Reuther was disappointed with my report, but he accepted it as realistic and asked me to keep the UAW informed of developments there. I did so through Wyndham Mortimer, the left-wing UAW representative assigned to organizing west coast aircraft plants.

There were a few jurisdictional disputes between the Sailors' Union of the Pacific (SUP) and NMU on the West Coast, but most of them were resolved by the workers themselves. I became involved in one case where the SUP kidnapped an NMU crew and hid it in the Arlington Hotel in Seattle, intending to force the ship's captain to accept a West Coast crew in order to sail from here. But I obtained authority from the national office of the NMU to attempt to recover the NMU crew and to escort them to the ship, which had moved to Tacoma. I had two independent CIO truck drivers go with me to the Arlington Hotel and assure the NMU seamen that we would get them back on their ship in spite of the SUP attempt to block us. The crew was glad to return to the ship and accepted as my credentials a telegram from Joe Curran, president of the NMU, authorizing me to act in his behalf.

Locally, our Party's organizational efforts emphasized the importance of building unions that functioned democratically. Already the Longshoremen provided a functioning model where the members actively participated in making the decisions that determined policy. Harry Bridges was an effective example of a leader carrying out the wishes of his membership, while at the same time leading them. That progressive liberal leadership style fit our political activities in the Washington Commonwealth Federation, the left-wing coalition working within the Democratic party. That left-wing CIO activity with the WCF brought us into conflict with Lewis' national policy, however. Lewis had set up Labor's Non-Partisan League with Eli Oliver at the head to help reelect Roosevelt president in 1936. I always considered that to be a part of a "gentlemen's agreement" about the CIO.

The WCF was also committed to the reelection of Roosevelt in 1936, and it seemed that the WCF and LNPL ought to have been able to unite, or to at least work together along parallel lines. It seemed logical that each could express similar ideas separately while meaning the same thing. But there was a fundamental obstacle in that situation that eventually led to our downfall. The WCF was an integral organizational part of the Washington State Democratic Party and was widely known as the progressive wing, representing about one third of the voting strength, members, and influence. Labor's Non-Partisan League, on the other hand, was completely detached from any other political alignment and intended to remain completely independent. It was really a paper organization making use of United Mine Workers Union officials scattered throughout the nation.

When the Party people learned that I had an appointment with Lewis to discuss our political problems, some of them told me to suggest to Lewis that it was time to form a labor or third party. When I talked with Lewis about it, he advised me he considered that the time was not ripe to form a third party, mainly because of the split between the AFL and the CIO. He pointed out that they disagreed on too many issues to be able to form any kind of liaison. Lewis also advised me that he intended that the LNPL would have a hand in the new political move. My report to the Party was disappointing to them, but convincing.

During the several conferences I had with Lewis over political issues, he usually referred me to Eli Oliver for answers. At first Oliver was reluctant to discuss politics with me, but when I pressed him for answers because Lewis had referred me to him, Oliver explained that it was not their policy to have parallel relations with any other political groups. They intended to remain strictly independent and nonpartisan. After Oliver left LNPL in 1940, I went back to Lewis to pursue the subject further because it was bothering us all the time. Lewis refused to give me any encouragement. Instead he referred me to Gardner (Pat) Jackson, who took over Oliver's place in LNPL. He tried to work out a solution by having Howard Costigan, head of the WCF, visit Lewis in Washington, D.C., early in 1940. Jackson later reported to me that, unfortunately, Costigan offended Lewis with his "brash" enthusiasm for expanding political programs beyond the programs' real potential, such as promoting a Western States Conference, to be led by progressives, to influence the next presidential nominating process to favor Roosevelt. All later efforts to heal the breach failed.

After that, Richard Francis, Lewis' local representative, increased his newspaper attacks against the WCF as a nest of reds inimical to the purposes of the CIO, and condemned those of us in the state CIO Council who continued to support the WCF. In spite of opposition from Richard Francis, we succeeded in getting general local public approval of the CIO organization program. There was widespread public interest in the CIO because the AFL had persisted in its high initiation fees and dues, and continued to practice jurisdictional, craft union, picket line strikes that frequently inconvenienced the general public without adequate explanation or justification.

Locally, our CIO unions could not leave the WCF without losing political influence in the Democratic party, which we felt we needed to keep. And we could not join LNPL because it was not really an organization, it did not actively support progressive programs, which we were used to doing, and Richard Francis was opposed to us as "reds." So the state CIO Council suffered nationally at the hands of Lewis, and locally at the hands of Francis. And the zig zags in the Communist party political policies in international affairs created problems for us locally that we could not truthfully justify or explain. For example, we opposed the obvious war preparations going on, while most public officials were advocating mobilization for a war that we feared was aimed against the Soviet Union. Some officials even said it was.

During the late 1930s many famous people visited me in the state CIO Council to gather information about the CIO and our many activities. Dorothy Day of the Catholic Worker organization was one of the first, and she impressed me with her devotion to the causes of the working people. But she let me know that Communists were not to be trusted and she indicated that she had me pegged.

Mary Heaton Vorse spent a short time with me in 1938, but became disinterested when she learned that we only had approximately 25,000 members, which was too small and weak to be a rival of the AFL (which outnumbered the Washington State CIO by about 2 to 1, with approximately 50,000 members). She seemed to be doubtful about the future of the CIO nationally. I think she had some inside information that John L. Lewis was going to change political alliances because the tie with Roosevelt was broken.

I had a perplexing meeting with A. Philip Randolph. When I learned that he was in the city, I wanted to meet him and discuss our problems of race relations with him. He was a vice president of the CIO as head of the Brotherhood of Sleeping Car Porters union, which at that time was exclusively black. To meet him I had to go to the Bush Hotel which was on the edge of the Chinatown district of Seattle, and occupied only by blacks.

When we met I tried to learn what his ideas were about obtaining equal rights for Negroes. But he resisted giving any indication that it could be done through integration. I got the impression that he preferred independence for all Negroes, and that he would not make any effort to change the all black composition of his organization, the Sleeping Car Porters. I also got the impression that he felt any integration in that union would endanger the security of the blacks. I further got the impression that he had no intention of attempting to do anything in the councils of the CIO because he did not trust the leaders there, especially Lewis. My meeting with him was a disappointment. He indicated that he knew I was a Communist and he didn't trust Communists or the Communist party. Further, he stated that he was opposed to the Communist program which advocated forming a separate black nation to be carved from the so-called Black Belt in the United States. He dismissed that idea as being impractical. He seemed to stick to a belief that blacks would lose their independence through integration, and he was rigidly opposed to that result. He didn't seem to have a program that could hold forth hope for a solution to our race friction.

By 1940, the political atmosphere internationally and nationally became so confusing to the Communists locally that we could not be certain from one day to the next what we were for and what we were against. When World War II broke out in 1939, we switched from advocating "Collective Security" against fascism to the slogans "The Yanks Are Not Coming." We later demanded "Open The Second Front"—with good reasons because of the changed situation after the Nazis invaded the Soviet Union on June 6, 1941.

Hitler's war in Europe caused our political perspectives to become a puzzle to the ordinary worker. The Soviet attack on Finland in September, 1939, was explained in the Communist party circles as necessary because the border under the command of the anti-red Finnish general, Mannerheim, who was allied to Hitler, was too close to Leningrad. President Roosevelt hastily condemned the Soviet Union for that move, branding it as "aggressor" as defined by the old League of Nations. Roosevelt's public criticism of the Soviet Union aroused a lot of hostility to the Soviet Union. It also created much political difficulty for those of us who had attempted to explain that the invasion was a defensive move, because at that time the Communist International, led by Stalin, was pursuing policies that seemed to be nationalistic ones deserting Marx's teachings about emancipating the working class, and that left us in a political vacuum.

Political leaders working in the Roosevelt administration, such as Washington Senator Lewis B. Schwellenbach, who later became secretary of labor, put continuous political pressure on Howard Costigan, executive secretary of the WCF. Schwellenbach persisted in urging Costigan to demonstrate the WCF's loyalty to Roosevelt and the Democratic party by denouncing Russia for its aggression against Finland. Costigan discussed this subject with us in the District Buro of the Communist party, asking for help in answering Schwellenbach's demands. But the local Communist party was unable to satisfy Costigan's attempt to work his way out of this difficult political dilemma. Unable to resolve this and a few other political problems, Costigan, at the insistence of his then-wife Isabel, went on a religious retreat in the spring of 1940. This proved to be his break with the Communist party. When he came back from that vacation he found that he could no longer work with his former Communist associates. He became isolated from and deserted by most of his friends, and his efforts in the WCF ceased to attract public attention. No one was able to take up his reigns of leadership. DeLacy assumed most of the responsibilities, but he did not generate the enthusiasm that was characteristic of Costigan. The WCF began to fade out of the political picture. Later Costigan had ambitions to run for election to Congress against Hugh DeLacy, but he was unable to mobilize enough support. He left the area in the mid-1940s, after he came to believe the Communists were responsible for him being dropped from every job he was hired to do.

The local Finnish people found our explanation of Russia's war with Finland unacceptable. A sharp rift occurred between the so-called "red" Finns and the "white" Finns in the Aberdeen area on Washington's southwest coast. The red Finn hall was virtually destroyed in Aberdeen by unknown forces. Shortly after, a staunch red Finn organizational supporter, the Luoma family, became critical of Russia's military invasion of Finland. Immediately after, on January 5, 1940, Mrs. Luoma's daughter, Laura Law, wife of Dick Law, a well known militant lumber worker union official, was hideously murdered. I heard about it on the 7:00 A.M. news broadcast by the well known reporter Johnny Forrest on radio station KOL. Immediately I made a few telephone calls to make sure this bad news was recognized by political leaders in Seattle. I urged them to get in touch with their people in Aberdeen to make certain the situation was not turned against our progressive labor leaders. I went to Aberdeen myself as soon as I could.

In the coroner's office I viewed the body of the victim. Laura's head had been split in two places so deeply that it was almost in three separate pieces. Her chest had six points that reminded me of the marks made by one kind of mole trap. It looked to me like Laura had been tortured before being killed. An axe that could have been one of the weapons used was found in the house. But no weapon to produce the cluster of six wounds on her chest was ever found that could be connected with the crime.

When I visited people in the union movement that I knew in Aberdeen, there was an unmistakable feeling that terror had descended on that city. I boldly urged everyone to overcome their fear by moving around in public instead of retreating to their homes. The major question was, "Who would do such a crime, and for what reason?" The public officials with whom I spoke seemed to be of the opinion that it must have been her husband, Dick Law, whom they hated. I strongly warned those public officials, the prosecuting attorney, the sheriff, the county commissioners and others, that the state CIO would not tolerate any frame-up of Dick Law. The remainder of the handling of civil rights in the case was left to Irwin Goodman, an attorney from Portland, Oregon, who had defended Dirk de Jonge in the early 1930s against prosecution under the criminal syndicalism statute, and John Caughlan, an attorney from Seattle, Washington, who handled many civil rights cases.

At the funeral all the prominent labor leaders eulogized Laura for her union activities. Among them was Harold Pritchett, president of the International Woodworkers of America (IWA), O. M. "Mickey" Orton, vice president of the IWA, and myself for the state CIO. When I spoke, I pledged that the labor movement would do all in its power to find and prosecute the criminal who did that dirty deed. When I said that, there was a blood-curdling rumble that swept through that crowd of about 3000 people. I never understood how to interpret that outburst. That case has never been resolved. The local public officials did not pursue the case as I believed it deserved to be, and no one has been able to give a provable answer to the question, "Who murdered Laura Law? And why?" A renowned Seattle criminologist, Luke S. May, spent many weeks studying the evidence in this case, but he was unable to report any solution.

When I attended a meeting of the national executive board of the CIO at the close of the second national convention in San Francisco, I got a clearer picture of the actual situation within the center of the CIO. I attended because I was invited by C. W. Deal, president of my union, the Inlandboatmen. That meeting was held in the Georgian Room of the Whitcomb Hotel at 10:00 A.M., October 14, 1939. I took extensive notes in longhand and transcribed them shortly after the meeting to try to retain the full nuances of what transpired. My conclusion about that meeting was that an impending attack was going to be made on the Communists in the CIO.

I read those notes to the District Buro of the Northwest Communist party when I returned from that convention. The members seemed to be reluctant to discuss the contents of my notes. Rapport, the district organizer of the Communist party, ordered me to destroy those notes, but I never did, as can be seen in the Appendix. My judgment then was—and still is—that these notes contain significant information revealing the basic political conflicts that undermined the integrity of the CIO. I thought these notes should be sent to the national office of the Communist party because of the questions they raised about our support of Lewis, but Rapport said no.

In the meeting at the convention, Lewis chided the vice presidents for arriving late, remarking that he "supposed the convention elected more of them so he would have to spend all his time waiting for them." He then stated he "had two subjects he wanted to bring to the attention of the Board."

Lewis first outlined changes in the assignments of the staff for organizational purposes. He said he made those changes to speed up and centralize the organizational drive. Then he hammered hard on the question of dues payments, insisting that all organizations pay on their full membership and stop chiseling. He demanded that the whole CIO support the organization of the Construction Workers, even if they signed contracts for lower than the prevailing wages, which I considered "scabbing." He claimed that the South could and would be organized.

The second subject was about Communists in the CIO. He made the point that he assumed there were some among the members because the employers hired them, but there were none among the leaders or in positions of control. He condemned the behavior of ex-Communists testifying before the Dies Committee. He implied he thought they were doing what the Communist party instructed them to do to promote the Communist program. He condemned it, and threatened to make a public denunciation if it was not stopped. He absolved himself of any connection with the Communist party or its policies. He instructed his staff not to hire any known Communists.

The floor was opened for discussion. Van Bittner and Philip Murray did most of the commenting, giving unqualified support to the stand taken by Lewis. Most of the leaders present who spoke pledged their support to Lewis and to what he proposed. When John Brophy spoke, it sounded as though he was apologizing for his opposition to Lewis in the past. There was one incident of conflict: Harry Bridges attempted to explain his policies and his difficulties where the farm workers were deprived of their civil rights. Lewis insisted that the new California governor, Olson, could correct that situation, and firmly advised Bridges to insist that the governor live up to his promises to protect civil rights. Lewis ridiculed the attempt to organize the movie industry. Bridges defended that effort claiming its benefits extended everywhere. A few more spoke endorsing what Lewis had said. Several did not speak. Lewis adjourned the meeting as Joe Curran promised to pay the National Maritime Union's dues.

From the beginning, Lewis controlled the purse strings of the CIO by furnishing the money from the treasury of the United Mine Workers union. He intended to get it all back from the newly organized international unions. The constitution of the CIO was drawn up parallel to that of the United Mine Workers, which gave dictatorial authority to the head of the organization to control the locals whenever he chose to do so. Although the organizers were almost a complete spectrum of all the political influences existing among the working people at that time, Lewis made it crystal clear that all of them were under personal obligation to him.

The reduction in Bridges' position from West Coast to regional director, for California only, was a clear rebuff. Then Lewis' interruption over civil rights and the role of the California governor really ridiculed Bridges' approach to organization.

Lewis' claimed ignorance about Communists in the CIO was an outright lie. He knew better, but he didn't choose to handle it at this time because he had already laid plans to drive the Communists out of the CIO. Murray's discussion was a confession that he knew all about Communists in the CIO. His discussion was an official warning that Communists had a very limited time left in CIO. The executive board members who did not speak sat silently observing, without committing themselves to anything.

I think Lewis knew who I was because he looked straight at me when he promised there would be no future for aspiring Communists in the CIO.

Lewis' declared goal of ten million members was never reached. In fact, there was never any significant growth after this meeting.

When the Soviet Union signed the Stalin-Hitler non-aggression military pact in 1939, it was an unbelievable event. Then the Soviet Union joined Hitler in occupying Poland, and it was impossible to justify anything about it. The general public was bitterly hostile to known Communists. For a time it seemed that all Communists, and labor leaders supporting the Communists, were going to be wiped off the face of the earth. Then on June 22, 1941, when Germany invaded the Soviet Union and the Allies declared their support to the defense of the Soviet Union, we were able to reestablish some respectability. But we never fully recovered in the public mind-set because of the residual antagonism to the Communist party and its followers. Our previous open loyalty to the Soviet Union was looked upon with suspicion and tolerated only for the duration of the war.

Many of us Communists felt betrayed by the top leaders of the party because of the zig zagging, sudden changes in policies. Our membership in the Party hung on a thin thread. The Allies' decision to join in the defense of the Soviet Union gave us a new lease on life. The American Communist party quickly made a sharp turn in policy, which caused us endless difficulty by declaring that "we must subordinate the class struggle to the national interest," and some of the Party officials began to express chauvinistic phrases about the "Japs," the "Huns" and the "Eyetalians." That compelled us to give up the struggle for equal rights for minorities and women, and ultimately allowed the capitalist corporations to make unconscionable war profits.

When John L. Lewis made powerful anti-fascist speeches and visited the Soviet Embassy, it flattered the Communists and encouraged them to put up with his autocratic power in the CIO and United Mine Workers union. There probably was not much they could have done about it anyway. In the United Mine Workers, Lewis had a constitutional authority to take over any local union when it suited his purpose. He could then appoint his loyal followers to office so he could control his national conventions and enforce his will by a process that became known as "provisionalism" or "receivership." The way Lewis explained it, it sounded like it was democracy in practice, because he contended he was fulfilling the needs of the miners better than they themselves could if they had the authority. By "provisionalism," the efforts of the miners were restricted to what John L. Lewis decreed. The Communists could not seriously oppose Lewis' autocratic power as such because the Communist party actually functioned in a dictatorial manner itself, through its application of a political principle known as "democratic-centralism." This was centralism in practice, with only a facade of the "democratic," and a rigid discipline was imposed on any who failed to obey and practice the "Party line." In fact all big unions have that arbitrary power.

One of Lewis' subordinates, Walter Smethurst, told me that he spent most of his time enforcing contracts that contained wage cuts that Lewis negotiated for the coal miners in Montana and the western states. That kind of administration was offensive to me and contrary to my ideas of what the CIO promised to do. But there it was.

Lewis' concealed hostility to the Communists was what I consider to have been the Achilles heel which, in the end, left the CIO as moribund as the AFL. After a promising start, Lewis and the Mine Workers left the CIO to pursue his personal grudge against Roosevelt, because Roosevelt made it clear that Lewis was no longer included in Roosevelt's political plans. Lewis was no longer invited to the White House.

Lewis conducted coal miner's strikes during the war in defiance of the orders of the War Labor Board. Lewis challenged their authority and defied them to do anything to him. There were threats of jail for Lewis, but no government agency was willing to prosecute him. The whole labor movement was embarrassed by those strikes because, although there were many defects in the union contracts that needed to be corrected, the "no-strike" pledge imposed by the War Labor Board prevented appropriate strike action. The rest of the labor movement criticized Lewis. The Communist party criticized Lewis for sabotaging the war effort. Lewis fought alone. In the end the coal operators had to give in to Lewis. No one pursued their past grievances with Lewis after the war.

At the national CIO conventions, the top officials vigorously pursued demands that the affiliates hasten the job of organizing the unorganized by offering to help with manpower and money. So I, along with other delegates from the Northwest, particularly from the IWA, arranged to have personal conferences with John L. Lewis to go over the organizing situation in the Northwest and to ask for his financial help. He was always very evasive in replying to us, and usually advised us that he intended to spend the CIO money and energy where there were masses of unorganized workers, implying that our situation in the Northwest really didn't qualify.

But in May, 1940, when Richard Francis and the right wing of the IWA requested help from the national office of the CIO, Lewis and his staff responded by assigning Adolph Germer to take charge of all organizational activities in the Northwest. Germer was an experienced, professional, factional political fighter from the old Socialist party and the United Mine Workers. I was well aware of Germer's background as a one-time secretary of the old Socialist party during the Debs era, and of his having participated in the old fight which split the Socialist party from the Western Federation of Miners and the IWW almost thirty years before. I was not aware that he had endless amounts of money with which to mobilize a powerful bloc of anti-communists to drive me and my progressive following out of the state CIO Council.

When the October, 1940, state CIO convention met in Olympia, Washington, the delegates were optimistic and enthusiastic about the possibility of growth and better organization. The famous Earl Robinson, composer of "The Ballad of Joe Hill" and "The House I Live In," sang and entertained at the pre-convention banquet with inspiring labor songs, such as "Picket-Line-Priscilla" and others. But when Richard Francis, president of the state CIO Council, called the first session to order, it was revealed that he, with Germer's help, had no intention of allowing the convention to transact its normal business.

Richard Francis presided with a dogged determination to drive all liberals, progressives, and Communists out of official positions by having the Credentials Committee refuse to seat the accredited delegates from those local unions that permitted exoneration of dues from seasonal workers. That decision adversely affected all unions that experienced seasonal work, which included the Cannery Workers, the Fishermen, and the Woodworkers. The majority of the state CIO Council Executive Board believed that the exoneration of dues of its unemployed members was proper and legitimate according to a policy statement on page 47 of the proceedings of the first CIO national convention in 1938 which declared that: "CIO international unions and local industrial unions are urged to keep on their membership rolls all their members who are on relief or WPA projects, subject to the provisions of their constitutions."

According to that declaration of policy, the majority of the state CIO Council Executive Board judged that if international and local unions provided for exoneration when the members were unemployed, those members were to be counted as continuing members. Because of this understanding, we made allowance for exoneration and representation of the seasonal workers in the call to the convention. But Francis, Germer, and Dalrymple insisted that delegates could only represent dues-paying members, which reduced the amount of representation allowed unions that had seasonal employment to contend with. These unions were my, and the Washington CIO left wing's, strongest supporters.

So Richard Francis ruled the convention call violated the CIO Constitution by allowing representation of exonerated members, and the 1940 state CIO convention was never able to transact any business. The Credentials Committee also arbitrarily reduced the number of delegates allowed from several organizations that did not provide for exoneration. So the delegates assembled refused to accept Francis' ruling or the Credentials Committee report. Adolph Germer was called upon by Francis to render his national CIO authority judgment about the validity of the convention call, and, as expected, he sided with the Credentials Committee and Richard Francis. This resulted in a deadlock, and Francis' bloc refused to attempt to work out any adjustment. After three days of uproar, the convention was in a state of suspension. Richard Francis accepted a motion that asked John L. Lewis to take over control of the council.

John L. Lewis accepted Francis' report about the convention motion and ordered my removal from the office of secretary of the state CIO Council—without the formality of ever claiming that I was guilty of any violation of the CIO Constitution. The Francis-Germer forces controlled the votes of the convention by arbitrarily disqualifying more than a third of the delegates pledged to my support. Within a few days, Francis served notice on me that John L. Lewis had ordered my removal. I was to turn over my office to Harry Tucker of the Aberdeen IWA's anti-international officers' bloc. I did so immediately. (See Appendix.)

My supporters united in a "Continuations Committee" in an effort to persuade the 1940 national convention of the CIO to reverse Lewis' decision. Conscious of the attack that undermined my strength in the CIO Council, C. W. Deal, president of the Inland-boatmen's Union and a member of the national CIO Executive Board, tried to persuade the leaders of the national CIO under the Lewis and subsequent Phil Murray administrations to correct their persecution of me, but they gave no consideration to Deal's efforts.

The upshot of it was that John L. Lewis had a statement drawn up which gave complete power to a United Mine Worker official, J. C. Lewis (reportedly no relation to John L. Lewis), to conduct the next convention. All of us who had appealed to the CIO to reverse Lewis' decision were required to sign that agreement, which gave total power to J. C. Lewis to run the convention the way he saw fit. (See Appendix.)

When the "J. C. Lewis" Washington CIO convention was convened in the spring of 1941, there was a goon squad of miners who were appointed sergeants at arms. They deliberately intimidated many delegates by challenging them in their seats without cause. J. C. Lewis did what Germer and Francis had planned: he legalized my illegal removal from the office of secretary of the state CIO

Council. Afterwards we saw UMW goons slug some of Murray's supporters in the convention hall elevators in Detroit during the 1941 National CIO convention. I recognized one of the goons as the same person who had knocked down IWA International Secretary Bertel McCarty in the doors of the hall at the earlier Washington State CIO convention, when the Lewis forces under Richard Francis stole control and ousted me as the secretary. A short time later, several groups of United Auto Workers defense squads made their presence known at the convention. That ended the violence of the United Mine Workers squads.

From that time on, most of Francis' CIO activity was devoted to administering the Washington state affairs of the United Mine Workers and publicly supporting the effort to organize the United Construction Workers by signing contracts with employers that would cut the wages and lower the conditions under which local construction workers operated. That policy was doomed to failure from the start. It ultimately fizzled out and disappeared when the AFL and CIO merged years later.

We built the CIO in spite of overwhelming odds against us. But Lewis and his subordinates destroyed us by offering financial help and then sending in their own organizers such as Germer, who devoted themselves to redbaiting, and organized anti-red blocs in local unions to drive out of office all alleged Communists or fellow travelers. They did not add to the CIO total membership. Instead they drove factionalist divisions deep into the CIO. It never really recovered from these fissures. Our own mistakes and higher Communist party political zig-zags contributed to our defeats.

During those hectic days when we were being pushed out of the CIO local leadership, the Communist party policies lost most of their validity because they were not policies to emancipate the working class from the capitalist system. In mid-1941, they were changing the "struggle on behalf of the workers" to "demanding obedience and discipline of the workers to support the war effort" because they claimed that was the best defense of the Soviet Union.

The Communist demands for civil rights for minorities and equal rights for women were suppressed when the Allies declared their defense of the Soviet Union. I found myself unable, in good conscience, to cast aside those policies so dear to the hearts of the workers who we had influenced for so many years. I therefore quickly fell into disfavor and suspicion by the changing Communist party district leaders. My old friend Morris Rapport had been replaced by Heinie Huff, Phil Frankfeld, Lou Sass, and Andy Reames. Rapport was ordered out of Party office by the national Party center because he could not become a citizen, having emigrated from Russia as a child and never having obtained citizenship. My relations with the newcomers seemed very fragile and unreliable. I had doubts that they understood our local situation. Huff was reluctant and almost unwilling to openly discuss Party policies with me as an individual. Frankfeld seemed to me to be trying to imitate the Party's general secretary, Earl Browder, when emphasizing a point, by rolling his head from side to side the way Browder did. Sass impressed me as a good follower, but not as a leader able to initiate something new. Reames seemed to fit in better than the rest. I had a lot of respect for Reames because he seemed to have a good grasp of Party policy and was willing to discuss issues with me individually. He seemed to understand the importance of Party work in the factory and gave much more attention to it than did any of the others.

It became embarrassingly evident that I did not fit with that group after I had been ousted from leadership in the CIO Council. My opinions and judgments were ignored and rejected. When the time came to consider the composition of the District Buro, the nominating committee, headed by a prominent professor from the University of Washington English department, pointedly dropped my name from the list to be proposed at the upcoming convention. I called their attention to the fact that the new list was overwhelmingly non-working class. They replied that all members of the Party had equal standing, and the Party was not following the old class rules. They ignored my observations and left me out.

ǝ◣

WORLD WAR II

ǝ◣

Although it was evident that war was imminent after Stalin and Hitler signed a "non-aggression" military pact in 1939, the American Communist party tried to keep up its anti-war policy by supporting the American League Against War and Fascism. Most Americans tried to keep some hope that war would be avoided. That caused a lot of confusion because the leaders of the major powers, England, France, Germany, Soviet Russia, and the United States, did not pursue clear-cut policies to prevent the outbreak of war. Instead each played a game of procrastination to confuse all the others. Only Hitler carried out a consistent policy, which was to encroach on Germany's neighbors and to demonstrate his skill at suppressing his opponents. In the beginning much of it was bluff, but as each bluff succeeded, Hitler became bolder, to the point where his policies propelled him to make the ultimately fatal decision to fire the weapons that killed twenty million and enslaved many more. Poland went up in flames. The big powers squared off.

To some extent a few news reporters did warn us that war was imminent, but most of our government leaders were unable to choose a course that would protect us. President Roosevelt did make concessions that led to the Lend-Lease program, which helped England endure the first blows of the war. The big powers had trouble deciding which way they would line up for this war. In the beginning most of them wanted to let Russia fall victim to Hitler. But as events unfolded, England and the United States made their decisions to help Soviet Russia resist Hitler in the hope that the Nazi expansion would fail. That decision probably saved the world from sinking into another Dark Age. At least the barbaric policies of the Nazis had to stop with the defeat of Germany. The world was not able to adopt a fool proof post-war program. (A noble effort was made with the formation of the United Nations, but it has not been able to prevent the outbreak of regional conflicts. The colonies that existed before WW II have succeeded in throwing off the control of the big powers. But hunger, disease, and want still prevail among the undeveloped nations, which conflicts with the ambitions of the big powers to expand their influence. National rivalries have kept uncertainties foremost on the agenda. So it has been with us workers.)

After my removal from the state CIO office, I had to find employment. Because for several years I had held union offices that caused me to be involved in many political activities that I wanted to continue, I tried to find work ashore instead of aboard ship so I could stay politically active and have a home life with it. I had to accept casual jobs handling cargo on the docks, sorting cargo, or loading or unloading railroad cars. Sometimes the Longshoremen's Union would ask for extra "bull" drivers (fork-lift operators), which I am qualified to be, or hand truckers. But that work was abruptly cut off for me in 1942 when the army lifted my waterfront pass, which had authorized me to work on any dock where military cargo was being processed. An officer by the name of John J. Sullivan, a Seattle attorney, told me when he lifted my pass that he was certain I was a Communist and therefore a security risk, and there was no way I could get my pass back. I had no answer then. (Many years later—Jan 6, 1969—I did get it back when United States Senator Warren G. Magnuson, who had known me well for over thirty years, prevailed on the navy to restore my unlimited pass. I was then permitted to work on any dock as a marine cargo checker under the jurisdiction of the ILWU No. 52.)

The Selective Service draft and demand for expanded production created a manpower shortage that caused many industries to advertise for workers. In a local newspaper, I saw an advertisement which solicited men to apply for work in a local steel mill operated by the Bethlehem Steel Corporation. I applied and was immediately hired and assigned to work as a laborer on October 19, 1942. I stayed there until the army drafted me on September 17, 1943. During those eleven months I established myself as a good worker. The probation period there at that time was six months; I completed it without incident. However, within a few days after I completed the first six months, the FBI ordered the company to have me fill out a detailed personal history. Nothing ever came of it, although I suspected it was an effort to trap me into some falsehood. There were some questions asking if I belonged to any organization that advocated the overthrow of the government by force and violence. The honest answer to that was no, because the Communist party had adopted a resolution about 1938 disavowing all previous doctrines and policies that had proclaimed its purpose to be the overthrow of the capitalist system. That step was taken shortly after Congress enacted the Voorhis Act, which authorized the government to prosecute any foreign or domestic agents who did advocate the violent overthrow of the government.

The Steelworkers' Organizing Committee was actively recruiting members at the time I entered the plant. I signed up immediately in the Open Hearth, where I was a helper to a first helper named James McCarthy, who was president of the local union.

Apparently my work satisfied the company. They obtained two draft deferments for me without my knowledge, since I was classed as an essential war production worker. But by August, 1943, the second deferment ran out. I was reclassified 1-A and ordered to report for induction August 23, 1943—even though I was over thirty-five years of age and married. This occurred because I was not married at the time I registered with Selective Service. I was given an immediate three-week furlough, then ordered to report for active duty on September 17, 1943.

The army processed me in Ft. Lewis after screening physicals in Seattle. While waiting for orders in Ft. Lewis, south of Tacoma, I met Basil Hoke, whom I had known as the secretary of the Northern Washington District Council of the International Woodworkers of America. I did not learn at that time what he was doing there, but assumed he was assigned to a regular unit or was waiting for assignment, which was none of my business. We did not discuss anything important because we were under direct orders not to. Later I learned that Hoke was a medic. When I was assigned to go to New Orleans, I was given the temporary rank of acting corporal and assigned to take three other men with me, to see to it that they did not communicate anything to anyone enroute that would disclose troop movement to a possible enemy spy. It was somewhat difficult to persuade them that we were under military orders and had to obey them. Two of the four wanted to phone their family from Los Angeles and tell them where we were. I had a hard time persuading them that that was out of order. The trip took five days and was very boring. We made frequent stops, and each time I had considerable difficulty keeping all three of them with me. Somehow I succeeded, and we all arrived safely in New Orleans during a hurricane. All the regularly assigned soldiers in that camp (named Hanrahan at that time, later renamed Plauche after a renowned pirate of earlier years) were ordered out that night to pack sand bags on the Mississippi levy near the Huey Long Bridge, because if the river broke over the levy it would have flooded the camp. I was not ordered to do that work because I was not yet assigned to a unit.

The next morning, at about 5:30 A.M., we were called out to line up for duty instructions. We were led around by a "buck" (three-stripe) sergeant who saw to it that everything that had been ordered was carried out; clothing was issued; barracks and work assignments were made; and meals were scheduled in the area mess. They completed our shots and checked our physical screening again. Another buck sergeant took charge of our work assignment, which turned out to be digging holes in the ground and later filling them up. That went on for a few days, until regular assignments were made.

Finally, I was assigned to help train a squad in a "mobile port battalion" to handle cargo. I had been classified as an experienced longshoreman. The work gang was practicing hooking-up empty drums to be loaded and unloaded on a "land ship" (a training platform). The most important instruction I could give the squad was to be safety conscious and careful all the time, to protect the hands and feet, to inspect the hook-up for defects such as loose or worn bolts and lines, and to watch out for the safety of everyone working in the crew. I followed that routine of training for about a month.

I was surprised to see them practicing with a "single winch" loading procedure (one man per winch). I spoke to the officer in charge of our training group and told him that on the West Coast we almost always used the "double winch" (one man operating both winches), which was more efficient and made it possible for the winch driver to maneuver a load to anywhere it was wanted and to keep constant control. The officer very firmly told me that the army was going to use the "single winch" system because it was the rule on the East Coast and Gulf, where most of the work would be done, and that eventually the army was going to have Dave Beck take over the West Coast Longshoremen from Harry Bridges. Work would run on the West Coast like it was on the East Coast and the Gulf.

I laughed at that, and told the officer the Longshoremen on the Pacific Coast would never accept Dave Beck as their leader. They had the ability to determine their own destiny because their union was democratically operated. The members decided their policies, and Harry Bridges had to carry out the wishes of the membership—which was diametrically opposed to the methods used by Beck, who told the members what they had to do. The officer did not challenge me.

One day, another buck sergeant asked for my name when I was eating in the mess hall. When I responded, he asked if I could prove that I could type sixty words a minute, which was what I had written on one of the questionnaires I had filled out. I told him I could. He ordered me to follow him to the camp headquarters office where he gave me a letter to copy. That letter was full of errors, which I corrected as I went along. When he saw the letter I typed, he told me I was to stay at headquarters and would be reassigned on special orders, to be written that day, which would take me away from the land ship assignment. It turned out they were in desperate need of a clerk-typist to replace one who had been making so many errors they couldn't catch up with him. We had to go over hundreds of service records to correct his errors. I stayed with that detachment for the duration. I was immediately sent to a two-week army administration school where we were taught the fundamentals of army regulations, War Department circulars, special orders, court martial, and military correspondence.

Our Headquarters and Headquarters (Hq & Hq) Detachment was a group of specialists who helped train units in personnel basics and inspected units when they were ordered to embark for overseas duty. Our camp was a training and staging area. We had to make certain the units were qualified for shipment overseas. These units were port battalions and railroad battalions. They were sent to the Persian Gulf, Italy, Africa, and to the South Pacific. Many times we were stunned by reports that filtered back to us that whole battalions had been wiped out in Italy and in the South Pacific. We knew they were good units and we wept over their destruction. Sometimes we heard that the enemy bombers wiped them out before the Allied fighter planes could come to their defense. We became bitter at the use of the phrase "They were expendable."

Being in an Hq & Hq Detachment, we kept irregular hours on duty, and enjoyed some privileges out of the ordinary. We were advised that the area commanding general insisted that all members in his command had to sign up for GI insurance; failure to do so could result in immediate transfer to overseas units. Everyone signed up.

Because we kept such long hours on duty, sometimes as much as twelve to fourteen hours, we couldn't follow the usual routines of units in training. We did not stand regular formations or guard duty, did not have KP duty, and ate in the officer's mess at irregular hours when we could get relieved. We got our basic training at irregular schedulings. At one of these we were advised that every soldier was serving the orders of the President of the United States. We did go through the infiltration course and fired the M-1 for record on the target range at Slidell, Louisiana. We did swim in Lake Ponchartrain to qualify for our own lifesaving requirements. We got auxiliary MP training. We had bayonet training. We did a little squad marching. We were given anti-riot training. I told the training officers that I could never serve in that duty against unions on strike because I had organized on the workers' side all my life. (I think that was recorded in my physical-mental profile because there is a "4" at the beginning of my number and a "3" next to the end, both of which classified me as generally unfit for any more duty.)

None of our combat training was ever called into use. We were confined to camp only once, to be available if needed for auxiliary MP duty. During the Battle of the Bulge in Europe, the senior German officer with the prisoners of war in our camp served an ultimatum on our camp commander to surrender to him, fully believing that Germany was making the final push to win the war. That group of 500 German POW's was from the Afrika Corps and consisted of conceited, tough, and disciplined soldiers who kept their loyalty to the Nazis to the very end. They had open contempt for the 500 Italians who were also POW's in our camp.

The Italians came to our camp first. They asked for and received a well groomed soccer field on which to play and exercise, under the provisions of the Geneva Convention pertaining to the treatment of prisoners of war. When the German POW's arrived for internment, they insisted on having a better soccer field and better accommodations than the Italians, because the Germans insisted that they were superior to any other race or nationality. Our camp commander complied with their demands to avoid any extra trouble with them.

Our MP's who guarded them were authorized to carry loaded rifles with live ammunition at all times. The MP's never did have to fire those weapons in our camp. We had reports that the Nazis killed two of their own members when those members showed too much interest in learning how our democratic political system worked. To the best of my knowledge, the Nazi officers could not be tried or punished for enforcing Nazi discipline on their own soldiers while all of them were POW's.

Race relations between whites and Negroes became a critical issue when black units from the Virgin Islands came to Camp Plauche for training. Several incidents occurred in New Orleans where the Virgin Island blacks refused to obey the streetcar conductors' Jim Crow orders that the blacks had to sit in the back of the car only. We received reports that the Virgin Island blacks got out of cars a few times and tipped them over in the street. Soon we were advised to try to help the white officers as much as possible to maintain discipline and respect for authority among those black troops. There really wasn't very much we could do to stem the rising tide of rebellion among the blacks.

We were called to a special meeting where the whole issue was discussed by white officers and we were encouraged to join in the discussion. When I got a chance to speak, I suggested that a partial solution would be to install black officers to reassure the black enlisted men that they would receive fair and equal treatment. Some of the black enlisted men waiting outside for their time to discuss their situation overheard my remarks and applauded. That caused our meeting to be adjourned immediately.

Not too long after that we were advised that orders for partial integration were being prepared by the War Department, mixing black and white enlisted men as far as practical. We saw some of that, but friction continued no matter how much we tried to overcome it.

During this time I got acquainted with Ralph Metcalf, who was running mate with Jessie Owens in the 1936 Olympics. Metcalf had the rank of a first lieutenant, but he did not have a real duty assignment. He worked out of Special Services. His presence was an attempt to calm the fears of the black soldiers. He was thoroughly dissatisfied with his somewhat inferior assignments. I talked to him about his efforts in the 1936 Olympics. I specifically asked if he and Owens had an agreement on how the races were to be run, because that was a rumor that had circulated. He told me they did have such an understanding: he was to lead Owens at a fast pace in the first part of the race, which would compel Owens to break records to pass him. And that was how they won for America. Recently (1984) I read with sadness that he had died. His passing is a heavy loss, although little is generally known about him except that his cooperation made it possible for Jessie Owens' great victory in

1936—which so embarrassed Hitler that he left the platform to avoid acknowledging the achievement of a black man.

After a kidney stone attack in May, 1944, I was classified as "ineligible for overseas assignment." When I wrote that to my wife Harriette, she decided to come to New Orleans. She stayed until I was discharged. She got work as a stenographer in the local office of the National Maritime Union, which enabled her to pay her own expenses. My rank of corporal did not allow me to live off the base, so we were able to be together only when it was my turn for an overnight or weekend pass. She, however, did bring me up to date on what had been happening in the Communist party in both Seattle and New Orleans. She related that our previous policies in the Rainier Valley branch of the Party, advocating equal rights for minorities and women in war work, had been stopped. She had been removed from leadership in our Party unit for that reason. Ultimately (in May, 1944) the Communist party had actually dissolved and replaced itself with a Communist Political Association, completely dedicated to supporting the war effort because the Allies were joining the policy of defending the Soviet Union.

Through her employment in the National Maritime Union office, Harriette became acquainted with many sea-faring Communist Party members who expressed confusion over the political turn of events. Then, without advance warning, *The Daily Worker,* spokesman for the Communists, published a letter from a French Communist leader named Jacques Duclos, which condemned the American Communist party for dissolving. Soon after that, in July, 1945, came a call for a special convention for the purpose of reconstituting the Party. At that convention, William Z. Foster was reported to have thoroughly condemned Browder for his "liquidationist" policies. The overwhelming majority of delegates reportedly supported Foster's position and voted for Browder's expulsion from the Party. *The Daily Worker* reported that very few delegates supported Browder, and most of them dropped by the wayside within a short time. Browder, who had earlier commanded almost total obedience from all Party leaders and members, ceased to be of any influence in political matters in the United States after that.

This series of events caused me to question many of our formerly sacred beliefs. We used to be taught that the Party political leadership was the wisest, and was almost infallible. I found that could no longer be upheld. The zig zag policies pursued by the Party from 1939 to 1945 revealed an uncertain course that could not be explained away and a willingness to sacrifice principle for expediency. And, if they were construed as changes in policies, it then had to be admitted that some of the earlier policies were wrong. Yet there was no assurance that the new policies were sound or correct. That situation left the members uncertain that the policies they were pursuing would last and be justified. There was no longer any stability on which to depend. Many individuals in the ranks felt that they were being sacrificed for the security and advancement of those at the top.

Obviously, I could not participate in Party discussions as long as I was in the army. But I could think, and did think for myself. I realized there was no longer any real justification to consider the Party and its leaders infallible. It was so obvious that the Party must have made major mistakes in recent years, that any thinking person was justified in questioning the reasoning behind many efforts we had made, where we either failed or were defeated because of pursuing wrong policies. This led me to think that the Party had too many incompetent leaders. My own local experiences confirmed that judgment.

After I was discharged from the army, October 11, 1945, I studied all the literature I could find explaining what had happened to the Party during the war. Nothing forthrightly explained the sudden changes in policy, especially the liquidation of the Party. Nothing satisfied me that we could rely on any improvement in the way the Party functioned. The single consistent explanation made by Party literature and Party leaders was that the changes in policy were to aid in the defense of the Soviet Union. But my thinking revolved around the question, "What about the policies affecting the American working class?"

My experience with the Party representatives after the army was very unsettling. After my army discharge, while I was still in New Orleans and getting ready to drive home, a top Party functionary arrived from New York. He had meetings with every former Party member in New Orleans to instruct them how to get back into the Party. He instructed me to send a telegram to Heinie Huff, the Party district organizer in Seattle, advising him when I would be back in Seattle and ready for a Party assignment. Needless to say, I did not send such a wire because I thought it stupid to flaunt Communist party activity in the face of the United States government intelligence authorities, which I thought such a telegram would do. Besides, I had planned to take some time to tour the eastern United

States with my family. Before making the trip home, we worked around New Orleans for about a month to help solicit funds for the community chest there. Then we bade adieu to Manny Levin, the lovable Communist leader who resumed his position as district organizer of the Party in New Orleans.

My experience in the army taught me to appreciate the efficiency and the inefficiency that existed. I was surprised to learn that commissioned officers in the lower ranks practiced a form of democracy when they filled out efficiency and character-rating reports on each other. Those forms were kept in permanent personnel files and were used to determine eligibility for promotions. Of course, the higher echelon ranks of officers obtained their promotions through political influence in Congress, and if passed over too many times and frozen in grade, their only out was to resign.

When the army considered it necessary to make changes, it could do so expeditiously. But most of the time it allowed the established wheels to grind in their own deliberate ways. Early in my army experience I tried to volunteer for paratroop duty, but I was rejected because they said that at just under five feet six inches, I was too short. I also applied for OCS, Officer Candidate School, but was rejected because I did not have enough actual army experience. I did not know how to give the proper commands for squad marching. When the war was over I applied for duty overseas in the Army of Occupation. I was rejected, probably because by the time the war was almost over, the intelligence officers had reviewed practically every soldier's record to make certain of his political loyalty. Although I was very loyal, the intelligence officers would not think so because of my long record of Communist party and union activity.

When discharged, I had a Military Occupation Specialty of 502, which means Administrative NCO (noncommissioned officer). All NCO ratings are appointed by the commanding officer of the unit to which one belonged. My 502 specialty entitled me to at least a buck sergeant rating (three stripes), but it could never be given to me because our company was also a "holding" company—it was always overloaded with more higher grades than the Table of Organization allowed. We had instructions to make no promotions until the excess in grade had been absorbed by "normal attrition"—that is, transferred out—so we were frozen in grade while an effort was made to find some place for those excess officers.

I took my discharge in New Orleans because my wife and her son were there, and I wanted them to see as much of the eastern part of the United States as possible on our return home to Seattle. We bought a car (Packard eight-cylinder) that turned out to be a lemon because the crankshaft was out of balance from retooling burned-out bearings. Although some mechanical work made it possible to drive the car, we took a big risk attempting to drive across the nation. But we did, and we made it.

Our greatest difficulty was with tire rationing. I was eligible for and applied for three coupons, but I never received them. The New Orleans Post Office advised me that coupons for rationed goods were always lost and there was no hope of replacing them. The tires held up conveniently most of the time, except they had a habit of going flat just as we stopped near a service station. Each repair seemed to be a hopeless gamble, but we made it with "boots" and patches.

After Chattanooga, Tennessee, we got on a long road that wound around the mountains endlessly. We were impressed with the many monuments to the Confederacy in Chattanooga.

As commonly happens with young people when travelling, my wife's son Hugh had to go to the toilet when we were winding around the mountains on a narrow road. One time, we finally came to a one-pump service station. Hugh dashed into the station and asked for their bathroom. He came back telling us we had to drive on because that service station did not have a restroom. So I walked over to the attendant and asked how they could operate a service station without having a toilet. The attendant said, "We got a toilet, but we don't have a bathroom." That crisis was met, and gave us a refreshing lesson on the importance of using precise words.

Washington, D.C., was beautiful and impressive with all the monuments and federal buildings surrounded by lush green grass and flowers. The Washington Monument, the Lincoln Memorial, and Arlington Cemetery made a lasting impression on me because of what they stood for—human sacrifices made for a free nation promising liberty to all. We obtained a room across from the White House and were impressed with the calm that prevailed in that area. Everything seemed to be functioning without interruptions.

Because I knew Congressman Hugh DeLacy quite well, we made a special effort to look him up and found him in a jovial mood. He entertained us with a meal in the Capitol dining room. He pointed out several important people, including Vice President Henry Wallace, who happened to be there at that time. Also present was Victor Hicks, whom we knew in the Teacher's Union in

Seattle and who had given us enormous help dispatching units in the 1936 Seattle Labor Day Parade. Hicks was there to get DeLacy to lend his name for endorsement of some campaign. DeLacy commented that he thought his name had been used for too many different things. Hicks promised not to burden DeLacy again. When I asked Hicks what he was so busy doing, he told us that he was soliciting machine tools for shipment to China.

That opened up a discussion that raised the question of what was going to happen in China. Hicks assured us that his information was that China was going to press forward to complete a revolution. I expressed doubts that China could lift itself out of the ruins of the Japanese occupation. Hicks reiterated his opinion that the Chinese were not only able to go forward, but would do so no matter what else happened. That difference of opinion was a warning to me that some political events had passed by without my attention and knowledge. Before we left Washington, D.C., DeLacy did obtain a tire ration coupon which made it possible for us to continue on our way.

Our journey through Baltimore and Philadelphia into New York City was very depressing. The streets were filthy, the houses were unpainted and looked run-down, and the monotony of miles and miles of uniform tenements looked like hopeless places for anyone to live.

While in New York City, we made a point of visiting the Statue of Liberty. It was showing deterioration and the public was restricted on how far up the arm we could go. We went as far as allowed. Even restricted as it was it was inspiring and impressive. We did stop to read the inscription: "Give me your tired, your poor, Your huddled masses yearning to breathe free . . ."

One evening Harriette and I went to Tommy Dorsey's dinner dance. His music was everything everyone boasted it was. Even though the dance floor was only about ten-feet-by-ten-feet in size, the crowd thoroughly enjoyed the melody of that beautiful trombone. We walked through Central Park and were surprised to find it in almost perfect condition. We visited an RCA exhibit that demonstrated how television would work. It forewarned us that it was the big new medium of information and entertainment. It was getting into the middle of November and we began to get worried about the weather forecasts, which indicated that the winter cold and snow were on their way, so we headed west.

ટ**ઢ**

BACK HOME IN SEATTLE

ટ**ઢ**

It was December before we were able to get back home to Seattle, and I became quite ill from the strain of driving long hours at night. I spent my first couple of weeks in Seattle in the Firlands Naval Hospital. I was treated for general debility, and prostatitis from the passage of my kidney stone, until they were satisfied they had done all that was possible for me at that time. The burden of getting a place to stay and settling down fell unfairly on Harriette, because I was not able to help.

After I got out of the hospital, H. J., the then-Communist party section organizer in Kirkland, Washington, registered me in the Party under my given name for the first time. All previous registrations had been under my Party name of Victor Haines. I did not protest against this because I felt that my identity in the Party was probably indisputable; it could no longer be denied or concealed.

I wanted to take some time to get reoriented to everything. I read Party literature extensively, and made a point of talking to every person I could find who had any knowledge of what had happened politically during my absence. I was disturbed because there were no remains of the Party unit I had led in Rainier Valley before joining the army. (Rainier Valley was and is a working-class district in the south end of Seattle). The people who used to be active in it seemed to no longer have any ties to our equal rights efforts for Negroes and women. When I tried to enter into political discussions with Party members I had known before the war, I found them reluctant to attempt to explain the changes that I observed. Later I came to believe they couldn't explain it.

Before I left for the army, our Party unit had recruited about 150 members around the issues of equal rights for women and the many minorities that had deep roots in the Rainier Valley area. When we began to study these problems, we found that each group had suffered from discrimination at one time or another, and there were long-standing prejudices existing from offensive experiences long ago. We had been conducting many discussions among these different nationalities advocating an anti-chauvinist attitude, for each group to accept the members of every other group the way they were. My then-wife, Harriette, grew up in that area and had known many people there personally for most of her life. She became enthused about the possibility of overcoming many frictions that bothered all the groups. Our Party program seemed to stir new hopes among the downtrodden. We put out many leaflets in the neighborhood condemning chauvinism wherever it reared its ugly head. Many individual cases of discrimination were protested with demonstrations against the offenders, usually a tavern or neighborhood store. People were beginning to believe that something could be done.

Our Party unit was inspired by the public response to our efforts to stop discrimination against any minority. We had large numbers of Italians, Jews, Negroes, Slavs, Poles, and others, all eager to break out of the traditional restraints imposed on them. We made many stores and taverns take down their signs that declared, "We reserve the right to refuse service to anyone."

The Negroes bore the worst brunt of that discrimination. Some of them developed a tactic wherein groups entered a tavern together and occupied the stools at the bar. They refused to move when the owners tried to get them to leave. In some instances, the Negroes pressed so hard that a backlash developed, and some of the owners prevailed on the police to intervene.

In the year before my induction into the Army, I had fallen into disrepute in higher Party district circles because I disagreed with certain policies adopted after Earl Browder's *Victory and After* was published late in 1942. Browder wrote that workers should seek to avoid labor-management economic strain and labor-government political strains by submitting disputes to arbitration and participating in government war agencies rather than engaging in strikes. He opposed the concept of "equality of sacrifice" by labor and capital, contending that the most important point for workers was to ensure that their basic needs were met, regardless of their dollar wages.

I argued that this book's ideas were a tactical line adapted to the war situation, and therefore our basic program remained and should be advanced. During a class on *Victory and After,* one of the District leaders engaged in a sharp polemic against my contention that Browder's book was not a programmatic solution to our political problems. I did not then realize how deep my disagreement was, but apparently the district leaders did. They blocked the further development of the broad struggle of Negroes fighting on their own behalf that I was attempting to organize within the framework of the Party. I was dropped from the Party District Buro. Because I anticipated induction into the Army and knew it would be impossible to engage in any sustained efforts to clarify my differences with the leadership, I dropped the issue and confined myself to attempting to root our basic Party policies among the Negro people and the workers at the mill. My interpretation of *Victory and After* as not being a principled programmatic statement regarding a fundamental change in Party policy precluded my seeing it as a revisionist document outlining policies which would later result in Browder's expulsion from the Party.

In September, 1943, I was inducted into the service and had to give up my efforts. While I was in the army, one of our black Rainier Valley Party members, Eugene Mozee, was shot to death by the police at a gas station he was operating. He had refused to give up the fight for his civil rights.

Shortly after I was drafted, my wife wrote that most of what I had attempted to do had been wiped out and that she had been disciplined along with almost all the rest of the branch leadership who had attempted to carry on the line I had pursued. My counsel to her was that she must accept the discipline and be alert not to allow anti-Party forces to take advantage of the situation. The Party leadership reorganized the unit, diverting it from our course. I never was satisfied with the explanations a few Party people gave me for the Party's liquidation of that unit.

On my return from the Army, I attempted to get political information from the Washington district organizer, Heinie Huff. He flatly told me that the Party had changed; the line was already established; there was no longer any time to discuss policies because they had been established by higher authority; and now the Party was a party of action. I reminded him that I had been away for over two years and that enormous changes had taken place during that time that I did not participate in or understand. I reminded him that we used to have elaborate discussions in the Buro to make certain that everyone fully understood the reasons for our policies. Huff advised me that that was no longer possible, and he didn't have time for that procedure.

I tried to talk with several others with almost the same result. Bill Dobbins did advise me that the Buro had decided they didn't

want Phil Frankfeld around Seattle any more, and when Phil returned from the army he was told to go back to New York. Dobbins
also said most of the others who had come out to Washington State
from the East were advised to go back because they were not
wanted in Washington.

Andy Reames seemed to be a different case because he did stay
here for a while. He invited me to attend a meeting of returned
veterans to discuss a Party policy regarding us. But I was shocked
when W. C. took charge of the meeting and reported that the Party
line was to take over the existing veteran's posts. He insisted it
would be fairly easy to do. I protested that was an unsound policy
because the American Legion and Veterans of Foreign Wars were
chartered by Congress precisely for the purpose of preventing the
Communists from obtaining any political power. I explained that it
was done at the close of the First World War and was the continuing policy of both organizations. I further pointed out that if the
Party people did succeed in taking over any of the veteran's posts,
the higher-ups in them would remove every Communist as soon as
he was found out. W. C. scoffed at my discussion and remarked
that I was too far behind the times. He persuaded the group to
adopt the policy he proposed. Later I heard that Party people did
succeed in taking over a few posts, but as soon as they were found
out, the higher-ups moved in, took over the posts, and kicked the
Communists out. I had urged that we devote our efforts to obtaining better health care for veterans, but that was ignored and a beautiful opportunity to get on the correct path was lost.

Soon after my return to Seattle, attorney John Caughlan, who
had handled many civil rights cases before the war, invited me
to his home one evening. There my wife and I met Carl Marzani,
who was the first Communist to be kicked out of the State Department for having Communist connections. Also present was Bill
Pennock of the Washington Pension Union (later a Smith Act defendant) and his wife Louise. The discussion focused on the necessity
of arousing public support to defend the victims of civil rights
violations. Marzani informed us that in Detroit he had met with
considerable success among the Auto Workers, but that people at
most other places seemed unable or unwilling to stir up any organizing on behalf of civil rights. All of us had been very active in this
work before the war, and it seemed natural that we would pick
up where we left off. At one point Marzani contended that during the war he had carried out the Party policy, which was to coop-

erate with the government activities to win the war. He went on to say that he was more than a hundred percent loyal to the United States government, and as proof stated that he was the one who picked the targets (Hiroshima and Nagasaki) on which the atom bombs were dropped in Japan. Later I saw that statement quoted in the *New World* for October 9, 1947, and in *Newsweek*, June 2, 1947, p. 22.

Marzani's reasoning and claim astounded me; it seemed to be overreaching for credit and involved approving of the use of atomic weapons on civilian targets, which was a position not generally approved of except by the military. Shortly after that claim I excused myself to leave. I had to go to work, and I was turned off by that conversation. Later I tried to discuss these problems with Andy Reames. He advised me that the Communist party could not allow itself to become burdened fighting for the civil rights of any other than the Communists themselves; a broad policy in civil rights was out of the question. Those two shocks, one from Marzani, and the other from Reames, steered me away from those activities.

As I was trying to chart my course for the future, Heinie Huff approached me to become the district trade union secretary, suggesting that my experience fitted me for that assignment and that they needed someone right away. I declined on the ground that I was in poor and uncertain health. I did not feel that I really qualified because I did not understand Party policy well enough at that time. Huff scolded me for that answer, and belligerently asserted that he would ask me only once because he didn't have time to beg me.

The obstacles in the way of resolving what course to follow caused me to explore going back to school and resuming teaching. But here also I was dissuaded, this time by the registrar at the University of Washington, who argued that it would be impossible for me to get enough financial assistance from either the Veterans Administration or the university's student loan funds. He also discouraged me from attempting to re-enter the scholastic world after my long absence. He expressed some hostility to my experience in the labor movement—something to the effect that it disqualified me for academic activity. So I had to return to the roots previously established in the work-a-day world.

Being unable to find any suitable alternative, I decided to return to work in the Bethlehem Steel Mill in Seattle. But just as I was ready to apply for a return to work there, the Steel Workers' union went out on a national strike. I joined them on the picket line. They welcomed me back with open arms. I returned to the job on April 12, 1946, when the strike was over.

The company personnel officer, Tommy Sanford, welcomed me back warmly, noting my army "good conduct" medal. He saw to it that I was assigned the proper position, respecting my time in the army. I was stunned when Sanford died soon after in a hunting accident. LaVerne Crossen replaced him a short time later, and he pursued a hostile attitude toward me for as long as I worked there.

In respecting my seniority the company had to have me broken-in on the next-higher rated job. I continued on this line of progression for the reheating furnaces in the 22" mill until my retirement, by mutual agreement, on June 30, 1966.

The Seattle plant of the Bethlehem Steel Corporation produced all the small and medium sizes of flats, angles, I beams, structural reinforcing bars, and rounds for the local market and some for export. Although it was an old mill, it had been kept up to modern efficiency and had the record of lowest unit cost of production in the whole Bethlehem system.

When I returned to work in the steel mill, I sensed that the Communist party members I had known there before going into the army were reluctant to talk about Party policies with me and resisted attempting to get together to resume Party activity. Nevertheless, I insisted that we try. At one of our first group meetings, Alex Harding questioned the soundness of the Party policy about race relations with Negroes, and asked for a full political discussion about it. (Alex Harding was no relation to A. E. Harding, a former Seattle CIO leader.) So I asked the county section to send someone to meet with us to discuss that subject. The county sent Eddie Alexander, who got into a hopeless argument with Harding (which, I later learned, did not satisfy him at all). Harding contended that the problems of race relations had to be straightened out before anything else could be done. Alexander contended that the Party view was that race relations could not be resolved until capitalism was overturned and a socialist society was established. Harding accepted the idea that it was the capitalist system itself that promoted friction in race relations, but he contended that it was necessary to wage a consistent fight for equal rights. Alexander admitted that would be ideal but said it was impossible in reality. Shortly after that discussion we were advised that Alexander's explanations were incorrect and his positions about many other Party policies were also wrong. Soon after that Alexander disappeared from Seattle and was either expelled or dropped out of the Party.

When I got back on the job I observed that the complaints the workers had before I went into the army had grown to include:

1) Violation of seniority rights;

2) Poor safety conditions, and no confidence that anything could be done to improve them;

3) Lack of information about pay rates;

4) Great fear that the World War II "Adjustment of Inequities" (later known as the "Job Description and Job Evaluation Program") ordered by the War Labor Board would somehow work to the advantage of the company and to the disadvantage of the workers;

5) Disappearance of conditions which the workers had fought for and won in previous years (by the old Amalgamated Association of Iron, Steel, and Tin Workers, which predated the United Steelworkers of America), such as

a) extra help when jobs became exhausting,

b) special allowances on pay when production conditions were especially out of the ordinary,

c) seven-hour instead of eight-hour shifts on Saturdays and before holidays,

d) the "sliding-scale" (tonnage pay tied to the market price of steel) in the 16" mill;

6) A belief that the government's weight was always on the side of the company during World War II; and

7) A growing feeling that whenever wages were increased during negotiations for new contracts, the company managed to take something else away so the unit cost of production continued exactly the same as before and the workers did not actually gain financially from being organized in the Steelworkers.

A general result of all this was that many workers had an increased skepticism about the relationship between the company and the higher-ups in the union.

These feelings, which I learned from the men on the job, constituted a real challenge to me. I felt it my duty to point the way to a course of action that would make it possible for those workers, through their organized action in the union, to acquire a new hope that their lives were worthwhile, and that they could do something on their own behalf by becoming active in the union instead of neglecting it. I propagandized to the effect that the union was created to provide the workers their own organization, through which the democratic processes could be brought into operation. Thus the rights and privileges of full citizenship could be brought to every worker.

Charles Legg and Jim Bourne had been assigned by the county Party section to be the liaison with our steel branch. I took up these problems with them, and asked for some help in sorting out a Party policy to pursue in the union. Struggle by the workers to defend their positions was on our agenda. But the Party never did give us any help to analyze our problems at the steel mill, let alone point to solutions. Their failure to help us made me conclude they did not have any real understanding of our problems, nor of their impor- tance to the workers. All the Party wanted to do was collect dues and sell Party literature that had virtually nothing to do with our local union situation and problems.

Gradually I became aware of the fact that the Soviet Union used an incentive system borrowed from the big corporations of the United States. I began to suspect that the incentive system being extended to us was similar to that which existed in the Soviet Union. That was what we were facing. The imminent question be- came, "What shall the Party attitude be toward the installation of an exploitive incentive plan here which compares favorably with such a plan in the Soviet Union?" I never could get any declaration that answered that issue from local Party leaders. I had to formulate my own policy along the lines of protecting what we had and pre- venting anything worse.

ર્જ

A COMMUNIST PARTY FRAME-UP

ર્જ

In early March, 1947, Jim Bourne, one of the liaison connections between the county section of the Party and the Bethlehem Steel Party branch, visited me at my home and told me that he had heard a rumor that I was an FBI agent. He said it came from a discussion that occurred in the steel mill scrap yard, where some of our Party members were talking about me and my activities in the union. Some of the black members were expressing a belief that they couldn't trust the whites because they could be working for the FBI, and that went for me along with the rest of them (meaning the union officers).

That report stunned me. I tried to think out how such a story could actually occur among members of the Party who had known me for so many years. I told Bourne it was a hideous lie, but I was afraid it might be based on something that was partly true. Then I recounted how Harriette, my wife, had been approached during the war by a "Mr. Smith," who asked her to help him do some work on behalf of winning the war by reporting any production bottlenecks in industry she heard about. I had told her to "clear it" with Heinie Huff, the Communist party district organizer. She had and Heinie told her to go ahead and find out what it was all about.

So I suggested to Bourne that he talk to Heinie about it. I thought it could be cleared up right away. It was widely known that the Party gave more than one hundred percent support to the war effort and had instructed its members to give total support to every effort to win the war against the fascists and to aid the Soviet Union.

Bourne seemed to understand that situation and told me to just sit tight and he would get in touch with me later. I waited from March to June without hearing from Bourne. In fact, I have never heard from or about Bourne to this day (1988). I knew that he had been living with Barbara Hartle, the highest ranking woman in the district leadership, and assumed that he must have close contact with the top district Party leaders.

About that time the Washington State legislature's Canwell Committee investigating "reds" was beginning to make headlines in the newspapers. I became apprehensive that I might be caught up in that political witch-hunt unprepared, so when I met Party leader Andy Reames, I asked what the developments were in that situation. He informed me that the Party was having a meeting of all persons who might be involved one way or another and invited me to attend. I did go to that meeting even though there had been no indication that I would become involved, and I never was.

Attorneys John Caughlan and C. T. (Berry) Hatten outlined the legal problems involved and cautioned everyone that there were many potential traps to avoid in any appearance before the committee. They advised everyone to be prepared to invoke the Fifth Amendment of the United States Constitution, which protects witnesses from self-incrimination. They also mentioned other provisions of the Constitution that were appropriate, but they emphasized the Fifth as the most reliable protection against having to name friends with whom we were politically active. They explained that generally government committees aimed to trap hostile witnesses into committing perjury, which is hard to defend against in later court trials.

Most of the discussion by those present supported the plan of relying on the Fifth Amendment to avoid any unforeseen risks and to avoid being compelled to name others whom they knew in the Communist party. I was the only one to express a different opinion. I raised the idea that someone ought to use that opportunity to actually outline Party policies and let the public know what the Party stood for. I called attention to Lenin's instructions to the old Bolsheviks to make use of every opportunity to express the Party program, and I suggested using the hearings to challenge the authorities who were attacking the Party.

The lawyers argued against me, claiming that no one would be allowed to do what I advocated and that that would open the opportunity for the committee to crucify whomever attempted to speak that way. I did not get an opportunity to counter that argument. But my thoughts after that were that the Party was attempting to hide behind "legalism" instead of promoting politics. And the public would be led to believe that the Party had something sinister to hide—something the Party feared could be used in criminal prosecution. At that time the problem facing the Party was that the Smith Act declared that membership in the Communist party was itself a crime. That law was later declared to be unconstitutional by the Supreme Court.

(It has to be recorded that when the hearings were held, many University of Washington teachers were crucified by accusations made against them to which they did not or possibly could not answer. They were hopelessly victimized by their silent behavior. The testimony of detectives who had been assigned to teachers' branches intimidated many, and it convinced the public that the Communist party was a real threat to our democracy and especially to an educational institution, namely the University of Washington.)

As the meeting ended, Andy Reames made a special effort to invite me to a meeting of the district committee to be held a day or two later. So I asked Andy what was being done about the rumor that I was an FBI agent. Andy said he did not know of any decision on that, but he knew that I was not an FBI agent and he wanted me to come to that district committee meeting. He said the FBI question was entirely in the hands of Heinie Huff.

I told Andy that the rumor had existed since March, and here it was June with no resolution. Because of that, I felt it would be highly improper for me to attend a confidential meeting of Party members. Andy still insisted that he wanted me to come to that meeting and went so far as to inform me where it would be.

I did not go to that district meeting and told Andy that I wouldn't until my status was cleared. Heinie Huff was standing next to Andy when we were talking and must have heard our conversation. I turned to Heinie and demanded that something be done to resolve my status because the workers at the steel mill were prodding me to get at the job of resolving their long-standing problems. Heinie suggested they would call a meeting of the Control Commission if that was what I wanted. I answered, "Do anything to get it cleared up." He said they would call a meeting for me soon. They did.

The Canwell Committee made sensational headlines in the newspapers. I read about many persons I knew in the Party who were being destroyed by this publicity, and I felt there must be something wrong with the Party policies which allowed this sacrifice to happen.

I was surprised that I was never called or approached to be called. It was my intention, if called, to try to outline Party policy as best I could. I wouldn't have hidden any of our weaknesses but would have promoted our intention to emancipate the working class to save modern civilization from the rot and decay setting into the capitalist system. But it did not happen. Instead I spent all of the summer of 1947 disheartened to find that after years of total devoted effort to serve the Party, I was being wasted in a cloud of suspicion that made it impossible for me to accomplish much needed union activities on the job.

As a result of my demand on Heinie Huff that the Party settle the issue of the rumor that I was an FBI agent, I was called to two different meetings of the Party Control Commission. Huff went to great lengths to avoid any hint that there was any involvement with disciplinary considerations. But I knew there was always something of that involved whenever a member met with the Control Commission. I thought the facts were so clear in my case that there was nothing to worry about.

At the first meeting (held June 14, 1947), Huff, Clayton van Lydegraff (the Party's district organization secretary), John Laurie (Chairman of the Control Commission), and Carl Brooks asked me all kinds of irrelevant questions for about three hours. Huff admitted that he had a dim memory of discussing with Harriette the problem of reporting bottlenecks in war production, and he had told her to go ahead and find out what it was all about. At the end, I was ordered to submit a written statement giving all the details involved. I agreed to write the statement, but refused to sign it or name other Party members because I feared that it might fall into the wrong hands and be misused. (At the time, I was suspicious that both the erratic course the Party had taken since 1940 and my own growing alienation from the Party leadership were the result of penetration of the Party by anti-working class agents and were also a symptom of late capitalist decadence.)

I did prepare and submit the requested statement. The statement included what I knew about Harriette's work reporting bottlenecks, the disagreements I had with the Party in 1941 and later regarding Earl Browder's line in *Victory and After*, and what I took as my ostracism by the District leadership after World War II while I attempted to earn back a leadership position. I agreed that I was too subjective, but pointed out that I had come into disrepute over specific policy issues and that I had become suspicious of newcomers in the Party leadership.

At my second meeting with the District Control Commission, August 29, 1947, Huff opened by stating his general opinion of my case, which was that my written statement was partly satisfactory but still reflected a basically "subjective" attitude, which he contended was the cause of all the complications the Control Commission faced with me. He stated that my "subjective" attitude had to be examined and conclusions reached about it. Huff went on to state that my differences with the leadership were evidently of long standing and hung over from the pre-war days and asked me to discuss them in detail.

I described some of my differences with the leadership from the "Revisionist" days (i.e., the Browder era), and concluded with the declaration that there was something about the whole situation that I was unable to come to any conclusions about. I felt there was something hidden from view that I could not account for which resulted in my feeling that I was not welcome in the Party, that I was excluded and isolated from the Party, that there did not seem to be any channel through which policies were transmitted from the District Bureau to our branch, and that our branch's problems did not seem to find their way to the leadership. The whole situation was so nebulous that I could not put my finger on any specific cause or condition.

Van Lydegraff then suggested that either there was some fault in me as an individual which caused me to have some differences (possibly subjective) with the leadership, or the leadership had some differences with me, or that there might not have been any real differences at all. He asked for my explanation of the problem. I responded that the whole condition was so intangible at that point that I could not answer the first two alternatives affirmatively. I knew I had certain subjective weaknesses, but they did not seem to me to account for what had happened. I was inclined to believe that there were no real differences at issue.

At that point, Carl Brooks observed that my written statement seemed to be a good account of what had happened, but it did not place the correct emphasis on my subjective weaknesses. It should have contained a more positive approach, including a determined statement that I would work to overcome my weaknesses.

Huff then reasserted that I was subjective and charged that my weaknesses had caused me to become anti-leadership. He added that the district leadership generally agreed that they did not have time to discuss matters with me because it took too long, and said that, if I really wanted to do anything, I could go ahead and do it without taking up their time in discussions.

I took vigorous exception to this last series of statements. Never in my life had I heard Party leaders assert that they would not spend any time working out policies with anyone working in a key industry, regardless of that individual's personal weaknesses. I rejected the proposal that I should go ahead and organize outside of the leadership to get something done. To me, that was advocating nihilism and had nothing in common with the party policies on organization.

I said that I could now see what the barrier was between the leadership and myself. It had been erected unknown to me. It accounted for the difficulties in mobilizing our party forces to engage in and participate in the struggles of the steel workers. I could only conclude that they regarded me as an obstacle. If that was the case, I told them, they should take action against me. Regardless of their attitudes toward me, they should undertake to get things moving in steel. I cited recent instances when we had wide-open opportunities to win substantial positions of leadership by default but failed to do so. The accumulation of these missed opportunities was doing great damage to the Party and to the workers in steel.

Huff reemphasized his contention that the whole trouble was my subjectiveness and anti-leadership attitude, and further asserted that if the District concentrated on mobilizing our forces in steel it could probably get half of them to participate in union affairs. I charged that this statement proved the leadership had not been concentrating on steel, and that that was contrary to our Party's approach to its tasks. Huff responded that the Party was engaged in a fight for its very existence and could not find time for everything. I contended that this was not a valid explanation. It did not account for the fact that the people in steel were willing to work with the District. There were many months prior to the attacks on the Party in which time was available for concentrating on steel, but Huff was unwilling to do so.

Huff then claimed that my position was all wrong because I was the only one with whom the District found it impossible to work. I called his statement a lie and told Huff he knew it was not true. I knew of more than one that the District had great difficulty mobilizing for anything, and that the fault could not all be in our people in the various industries and unions.

At this point, Laurie, the chairman of the meeting, attempted to stop the cross-fire between myself and Huff. Huff stated that the meeting might as well adjourn because it was clear to him that it would be impossible to resolve or conclude anything at the meeting.

I said that I, too, considered that nothing more could be accomplished at the meeting, mainly because the commission was allowing new variations of charges to be made against me without pursuing any one thing to a conclusion. It appeared to me that Huff was introducing new charges in order to expel me when he thought he could get enough on me. I refused to take the line of organizing outside the leadership because I had seen such courses in the past lead to factionalism, and I was determined not to pursue that course. All I could do was to continue to fully participate in the union's affairs alone, using the best of my own abilities and judgement until the commission came to some decision about me. I would not discuss the questions before the commission with the Branch members or any other members until I was either cleared or expelled.

Laurie then adjourned the meeting. As he did so, I stated that I considered the heated discussions of the meeting to be entirely political. I did not hold any personal feelings against anyone because of our arguments, but I had been taught long ago to fight vigorously for a political principal when it was the subject of controversy. I had attempted to do this. The group was standing around without speaking, so I said, "Since you have adjourned the meeting, I'll adjourn too," and left. The meeting had lasted about three hours.

It struck me as very strange that it had taken so long for the District Control Commission to come to grips with my problem. I could not help but feel that the leadership was engaging in false struggles with many of our forces who had long records of devoted Party work and that this was dissipating our strength unwisely. I was astounded to hear from the lips of Heinie Huff, the district chairman, the confession that I was deliberately avoided, boycotted if you please, and then advised to try to do my work without bothering them. It seemed to me that, since the leadership admitted it wanted nothing to do with me, it was absurd to claim that I was anti-leadership. If the way they were dealing with me was leadership, I was against it. But I contended that their approach was basically anti-Party, and I would fight against it.

Very outstanding in this whole situation was the diversion from the original incident (Harriet's reporting production bottlenecks during World War II), and, in particular, the slurring over of Huff's part in it. In the course of the June 14 meeting, Huff did admit that he had some recollection of discussing the matter with Harriet. I could understand how human frailties could cause an ordinary person to dismiss such a loss of memory without a second thought, but it was inconceivable to me that a Party district chairman could do so. Ever since my return from the service I expected he would make some move to follow up on Harriet's work. But instead my cooperation was turned into persecution.

Indeed, Harriet and I were expelled by the Party district committee on October 5 or 6. On October 15, John Laurie came to our house and requested that Harriette and I return our Party membership books to him. My first inclination was to decline to surrender the books. But in discussing this with Laurie, I became convinced that this was the usual procedure in cases wherein the security of the Party was involved. Laurie told me that a statement regarding our expulsions would be issued the following week. We would be given a copy and we could appeal if we wanted to. I assured him that I had no intention of surrendering my membership, and would make every effort to be restored. I later changed my mind.

On October 20, we received our notice of expulsion, which had been postmarked October 18 (see appendix). The notice pertained to me, Harriette, and Claude Smith, a Party member who had helped Harriette prepare her reports on production bottlenecks. The notice distorted my statements regarding our relations with the FBI, ignored my refusal to work with the FBI against the Party, and concluded that I was an unprincipled factionalist who posed as "the one and only guardian and defender of a correct Party policy."

The notice was intended to remove us from all working-class or Party-related positions we held. I was a member of the Board of Control of the *New World*, the northwestern Communist newspaper. Nothing was done against me there because the editor, Terry Pettus, considered the expulsion notice to be libelous and feared that I would sue if he published it as requested by the Party. Smith resigned his position as editor of the Washington State *CIO News*. Harriet was at the time the president of her local of the United Office and Professional Workers, where ninety percent of the members belonged to the Party. Eight Party members filed charges against Harriet claiming that, because the Communist party had expelled her, she must be an enemy of the working class and in violation of her union's constitution. The non-members of the Party were bitter to have to fight that battle and rose up vigorously in defense of Harriet. Harriet's fight was drawn out over several weeks but the accusers finally had to withdraw their charges. Harriet chose not to run for reelection and gave up trying to set the record straight.

Although the notice of expulsion was distributed at the Bethlehem Steel plant gate, the steel union ignored it. The men I worked with in the 22″ Mill Department accepted my version of what had happened.

Later, when I was called by the Immigration Department to be interrogated about my life in the Communist party, I was told by the local director, Mr. John R. Boyd, that I could be restored to membership in the Party if I would work for them. I answered, "No thanks."

The Communist Party Constitution adopted July 28, 1945, provided in its Article IX, pertaining to disciplinary procedures:

Section 1. Conduct or action detrimental to the working class and the nation as well as to the interests of the Party, violation of the decisions of its leading committees or of this constitution, financial irregularities, or other conduct unbecoming a member of the Party may be punished by censure, removal from posts of leadership, or by expulsion from membership. Such conduct or action by any committee may be punished by the State or National Committee, which shall then order new elections for said committee.

Section 2. Adherence to or participation in the activities of any clique, group, faction or party which conspires or acts to subvert, undermine, weaken, or overthrow any or all institutions of American democracy, whereby the majority of the American people can maintain their right to determine their destinies in any degree, shall be punished by immediate expulsion.

Section 3. Personal or political relations with enemies of the working class and nation are incompatible with membership in the Communist Party.

The attempt to tie me to the FBI was a contrived lie distorted from the facts which I submitted in good faith. Heinie Huff admitted he authorized Harriette's activities in regard to reporting production bottle-necks to her mysterious visitor. That was his responsibility, not mine. In the charges against Harriette, the Party praised the FBI for its operations against criminals, as seen in this extract:

Let us examine the role of the FBI. Organized labor recognizes that law enforcing agencies are absolutely necessary in the protection of public and private property, prevention of crime, and safeguarding our welfare.

It would seem to be significant that the Party's constitution does not identify the FBI as an enemy of the working class, although the expulsion notice refers to the FBI that way. All the other Party allegations against Harriette and me were falsehoods.

I did question the wisdom of the Party policies before, during and immediately after World War II because they departed from our long established positions such as:

1. Workers' right to strike.
2. Equal rights for women.
3. Civil rights for everyone.
4. Opposition to chauvinism.
5. Appealing to the masses in city elections.
6. Emancipation of the working class.

As stated previously, I had also opposed specific policies such as taking over veterans' organization posts, refusing to testify before the Canwell Committee, and decreasing the numbers of production workers in the state Party leadership.

For quite a long time I had been seriously thinking of resigning my membership in the Party because its changes in policy and program seemed to me to be deserting the working class. But when the Control Commission charges were made against me, I felt it was necessary to try to disprove those vicious claims. In that I failed. The expulsions were frauds, and the reasons were lies.

ह&

STEEL UNION MEMBER

ह&

During the period of uncertainty about Communist party union policy I felt it was inadvisable for me to commit myself to any office-holding responsibilities in the Steelworkers union. So I attended union meetings, took part in the discussions, and helped indicate suitable action on the various problems which arose.

Because of that regular participation I was frequently elected to represent the union at local CIO council meetings, State CIO conventions, and district steelworkers conferences. At all those meetings I tried to actively promote policies that I thought favored the working class. I pushed hard to prevail on the union negotiating committee, through adoption of appropriate resolutions, to obtain the many changes in the union's contract with the company which would better our conditions.

It soon developed that many of my ideas were at cross purposes with those of the international union's district representatives, and they started sniping sharply against me in union meetings and had their followers try to undermine my efforts among the workers in the plant. But the workers in the 22″ Mill Department where I worked stood by me all the time. It became a constant struggle to articulate a policy which would benefit the workers on the job, in spite of sabotage from the international representatives.

Other workers in the steel plant told me that there was a long list of problems that were not being attended to by the officers of the Steelworkers union. When I asked for specific information along that line I was amazed to learn that:

1) Scheduling of workers for the jobs was irregular in all departments causing friction and dissatisfaction all around;

2) Pay rates were a mystery. Nobody could find out what each job paid. The company maintained that information was confidential between the man on the job and the company;

3) The "Little Steel Formula" imposed during World War II was not understood and the international representatives did not explain it satisfactorily although its principle was that pay increases during the war would be allowed only in cases where it was necessary to adjust inequitable existing pay scales;

4) Most of the incentive plans were mysteries. In the 22" Mill Department, the incentive plan was known as the "Premium," which had been handed down for many years but was never understood among the employees. When the industrial engineers were asked to explain it, they claimed they did not know when nor how it was established; it was completely different from anything they did.

Another problem arose later when President Truman seized the steel industry during the 1952 strike. The settlement granted certain increases in pay to all employees but the companies were not "allowed" to pay them until the worker left the employ of a given company or retired. This postponed wage payment was referred to as a "vested" interest all employees had in a company.

In spite of my reluctance to accept any position because of the cross currents promoted in the union against me, I was elected by the workers to the Plant Safety Committee to represent the 22" Mill Department. The company prepared the minutes of the Safety Committee meetings in a manner that provided little real substance about the subjects we discussed. In fact, the company made one set of minutes for local circulation, but a much different set which was sent to the State as required by law. Existing State legislation did not require more information and there was no disposition on the part of the official in charge (Mr. Ed. Sorger) to obtain legislation to make the changes I had requested and suggested. I pressed hard to get the company to adopt a policy of trying to prevent accidents. But they resisted with the contention that everything was already safe and could not be considered unsafe unless an accident occurred. Then they would fix it.

The main contention of the company was that most accidents were the result of human failure and that the individual worker must have been at fault. I contended that where any burden was excessively heavy on an individual person he should have relief help before he got worn out or excessively fatigued. The company maintained that they had been doing the same things for years and everything was okay until I made a fuss about it. At one time the company threatened to have the company guard come into the Safety Committee meeting and escort me out of the meeting because I had become too much of a nuisance. I dared them to attempt that move to intimidate the Safety Committee members, and the company dropped the threat. I did win one major issue over pollution. The ingots to be charged in a reheating furnace had to have trimming around the butt ends with an oxygen torch. Frequently that burning created clouds of polluted fumes that enveloped those of us working on the reheating furnace. It took quite a lot of pushing to budge the company on that issue. They claimed that they were in compliance with the standards established by the Bureau of Mines. I contended we needed a test from the Environmental Department of the University of Washington. Under the Safety Committee pressure the company finally authorized the test I requested. It proved that the polluted air was hazardous; it contained elements from several different alloys used to establish ordered specifications in various items of ingot steel. The result was the company had to move that operation to another location where it did not interfere with the workers' health.

From that experience and all other issues that came in conflict, the company developed a very open hostility to me. The union members on the Safety Committee gave me full support all the time, and that worried the company because, by tradition, the company could handle any individual when isolated to himself, but it is quite another matter when he has the support of his associates.

My Safety Committee term was limited to six months by the provisions of the union contract, but because I had stirred up a lot of activity the workers wanted me to get into another union position. Our efforts along that line were interrupted by another strike.

At midnight beginning October 1, 1949, the Steelworkers union struck for paid pensions. A wage increase and better provisions for Social Security were supplemental issues which the national leaders of the Steelworkers union contended for. The strike lasted from October 1 to 31. The Local Union made no preparations for conducting the strike or for picketing. I organized a crew from the 22" Mill Department to do voluntary picket duty the first night. They stood duty all that night. With them, I helped preserve sobriety, sending home a few persons, including James McCarthy, a past president of the local union, because they were obviously under the influence of liquor and making a nuisance of themselves and placing the picket line in some jeopardy because the Seattle police were patrolling the area. The next day, when the picket headquarters had been established by the officers of the local union, Sub-District Director Hugh Mathews was reported to have given high praise to everyone there about the good job I had done the night before.

Within a short time after the 1949 strike started quite a few union members were hard pressed and suffering from lack of income. The union's international office had made no provisions for helping members in distress. We went to the Community Chest, stated our predicament—involuntarily out of work—and asked for help. Our members had no say in calling the strike. It was done by the national union leaders without our approval. After an extensive conference with the Community Chest executives we were advised that they would not help any workers who were on strike even if involuntarily. That embittered nearly all workers because in the past they had liberally and generously contributed to the Community Chest thinking it would help everyone when in distress. We found out it was not so. During the strike the steel companies were able to use up their surplus stockpiles supplying their customers, so they profited from the strike while the workers suffered a huge cut in earnings.

Walter Bloxam, the president of Local Union 1208, appointed me chairman of the local union publicity committee for the duration of the strike. That committee kept active reporting regularly with mimeographed bulletins to all the members, and reported regularly to the local newspapers any developments made known to us from the national office.

On November 5th, Carl Jones, Wage-Policy Committee member from San Francisco, reported to the 1208 Executive Board at a meeting in the old Frye Hotel on the terms of the strike settlement which became effective October 31, 1949. Jones' report was very incomplete. He expressed dissatisfaction with some of the terms of that settlement. Members of 1208 Executive Board, including myself, also expressed dissatisfaction with some of the terms of the settlement. The concerns were that too many matters were not being dealt with such as protecting our rights under established past practices. Our follow-up discussions on the job aroused strong sentiment to press the international union to work to improve the union contract with the company during the next negotiations.

When it became widely known that I had much experience as a union official and was previously the secretary of the State CIO council the members expressed a belief that I should run for office in the local union, specifically for local union Recording Secretary and department Grievance Committeeman. When nominated I was unopposed for election to those two offices, so I was unanimously elected.

The Steelworkers Sub-District international union representatives were very disturbed over my election to local union office because they knew my past reputation was that of a radical and that I had already established a solid reputation of upholding the workers in every dispute with the company. And I had already asked the district union representatives to help us defend our positions in the face of the company's plans to reduce our wage rates.

I immediately made it a practice to keep very substantial accounts of our discussions in the Local 1208 minutes. That way, if anyone wanted to look up required information, the minutes would provide the answers. I also kept notes and various memoranda about everything in which there was a conflict between the company and the union. I made it my policy to do the best possible job for the members of the union.

I kept extensive notes because there were so many instances of bad administration left over from the previous records of employer/employee relations. One glaring example was the company's adherence to a statement on seniority in the 22" Mill Department which excluded those who worked on the graveyard shift, identified as the third turn. This old statement assumed that the 22" Mill Department was a two-turn mill, so the third turn did not really count. Along with that statement was an explanation that it was not signed by either the company or the union because it did not comply with the provisions of the union contract or the minimum wage law. So I proceeded to insist that all parties had to get within the provisions of the law and the contract which would protect all workers. Some of the old timers resented my efforts because it disturbed their illegal position of seniority, and destroyed the private arrangements the company secretly had with some of them. That illegal statement was a hangover from earlier years when the Amalgamated Association of Iron, Steel, and Tin Workers of America had a small membership among the top skilled workers for whom they bargained long before the United Steelworkers of America was organized.

Shortly before I was elected grievance committeeman, a very serious dispute arose between Assistant Mill Superintendent Malcolm M. Mosley and Furnace Heater Claude E. Long involving "combining jobs". This dispute became a grievance and was written up because Mr. Mosley had firmly declared it was the company's contention that under the terms of the contract's Article XIII the company had the right to do whatever it wanted to do and all the union could do about it was file a grievance. We, in the union, contended that the rights set forth in Article XIII were limited within the same article with the admonition "Provided that the Company did not violate any other provisions of the Contract." Therefore, Mr. Mosley's interpretation on behalf of the company was, in effect, a company declaration that the company would violate the contract any time they wanted to, and all the union could do was file a grievance and the company would take its chances on the outcome of an arbitration decision that might be against them. Mr. Mosley agreed that was the company's position and he was carrying out that policy upon instructions. The grievance was never resolved. It was deadlocked in the 3rd step. It was ultimately withdrawn without prejudice at the firm insistence of the international union representative, Chris Gellepis, acting for, and on behalf of, the Sub-District Director, Hugh Mathews. The international union was unwilling to fight that issue out.

Upon assuming my duties as grievance committeeman, I was immediately confronted with another problem of even more alarming concern. One night, on the graveyard shift, 11 P.M. to 7 A.M., I was working as a second Helper on #2 re-heating furnace with Heater Fernando Thornton when an old problem arose. The problem was that the operating schedule called for operating #2 re-heating furnace alone while making 2–^{11}/₁₆ by 2–^{11}/₁₆ billets. This was a slow mill order for a Friday night, the end of the week, when the hearth of the furnace was built up very high. It was therefore much more difficult to work with the bar, so the first helper of that furnace had to wrestle with the ingots on that hearth, and had to work all that time very close to an open door of the furnace where the temperature was in excess of 2000 degrees. And further, the past practice and custom had been when such a condition prevailed, TWO first helpers would be assigned to that job.

On that particular night, Heater Thornton called this problem to the foreman's attention. Thornton told him that a first helper could not stand to do that job for any length of time without help, and it was senseless for anyone to attempt to do so unless he was assured that he would have relief within a very short time. That particular night it took the mill crew over a half-hour to "set up the mill and adjust the rolls." (But still there was no second helper or relief first helper sent over or assigned to #2 Re-Heating Furnace.) When Heater Thornton spoke to the foreman about it again, the foreman said that he mentioned it to the night superintendent, Mr. Lee Heinzinger, but that Lee left without saying anything, so he could not do anything until he had authority to do it, which would not be until after Heinzinger would either return or call in. The foreman did not know when that would be or whether it would happen at all that night.

After about three-quarters of an hour had elapsed, during which time the crew was considering going home, Mr. Heinzinger came over to the furnace and started talking to Heater Thornton. Upon seeing this, the furnace crew and the mill crew gathered around Heinzinger who was bawling out Heater Thornton for not getting started. Thornton told him that he had left word with the foreman, asking Heinzinger to authorize furnishing a relief first helper in accordance with past practice, and that he was waiting for Heinzinger to do so. Thornton advised Heinzinger that although the furnace was not putting out any steel for the mill during the period they were down, the furnace crew had been busy "making bottom" and with the furnace in such bad condition it took a lot of time and effort. In fact the crew was already worn out from that work and could not go on without a relief first helper. Because of this, Thornton left word with the foreman. He said they could not start until they had a relief first helper, but the foreman said he had to wait for authority to assign a relief first helper from Heinzinger. Everyone was, in fact, waiting on Heinzinger.

Heinzinger got very angry and turned on the crew which had gathered around to see and hear what the decision was going to be. He told me that I was not invited to this discussion, it was between the heater and the night superintendent, and it was of a personal nature and had nothing to do with me or any of the others. I contradicted Heinzinger on the basis of what had been heard and suggested to him that the best way to get the mill rolling steel was to get the relief first helper assigned to the job right away, instead of running off trying to duck his responsibility so that somehow or other by that evasion they could put over a fast one on the crew. Heinzinger became very abusive to everyone present. Everyone on the furnace crew was ready to go home, and told Heinzinger they would not work that job that night without help. Heinzinger left in a huff. The crew stood around for a while. Then the foreman assigned a second first helper, and left word that Heater Thornton was to stop in the mill superintendent's office to see Mr. Heinzinger on the way out in the morning. Thornton told me about it and asked me to go with him to see Heinzinger, expressing the belief that Heinzinger was going to attempt to discipline him for standing up for the rights of the men according to past practice. I agreed to go with Thornton.

Shortly after 7 A.M. I did go with Thornton to Heinzinger's office. As soon as I stepped inside the door with Thornton, Heinzinger told me to leave, that I was not invited, was not wanted, and would not be tolerated. I told Heinzinger that Thornton had asked me to accompany him because he anticipated the subject-matter of the conference involved discipline which was clearly within the jurisdiction of a union representative. Heinzinger declared that he would not recognize me as a union representative and would refuse to discuss anything with me. I advised Heinzinger that under the law he must recognize the duly elected union spokesman and that I was present in that capacity.

Heinzinger attempted to discuss some irrelevant matters with Thornton ignoring my presence. Thornton made it clear he considered that he acted clearly within his rights as the heater, since by tradition and custom of very long standing the heater is in charge of the crew on the furnace and is responsible for everything that happens there. The meeting ended without taking up any important matter, and settled exactly nothing. That incident was never referred to again.

Soon another bitter controversy broke out in what became the Berieault arbitration case. One day when I arrived at work some of the fellows in the locker room vaguely told me about a noisy outbreak between the foreman and Heater Claude Long over a foreman taking a conveyorman, Berieault, from his position on the furnace and assigning him to do clean up work on the mill during a break-down.

When this was called to Long's attention he complained to the foreman that no one had the right to take members of his furnace crew away without his permission, and that in this case the company was clearly violating the rights of Berieault by making him do work which was not part of his assigned job, therefore not in his job description, so it was a violation of the contract. During this controversy between Long and the foreman, tempers flared quite high. The foreman told Long that if he did not stop arguing about this matter, he, the foreman, would call the company guard and have Long thrown out.

When I saw the foreman, I told him that it was very much out of order to attempt to settle any dispute by threatening to call the guard and have an old timer like Long thrown out of the place simply because he was sticking up for the rights of the men. This dispute went through all the grievance steps after being written up by me. Before it reached arbitration, Berieault was laid off, found another job, and never returned to the plant to work. He did return to appear as a witness during the arbitration proceedings. The decision of the arbitrator was against the union and for the company, but limited its application to the specific case, and thus the matter did not become one of precedent making application.

Before I was elected to union office, the company had carried out a new system of job classification and pay rates following the conclusion of a national agreement between the company and the union. This grew out of the Little Steel Formula ordered by the War Labor Board during the Second World War, presuming to settle "inequities" claimed by the union.

By 1948, the company had progressed a long way toward establishing the new rates and job descriptions. When I studied what was taking place, I found the job descriptions had changed many job classes resulting in a lower standard which ultimately would cut the wages of those jobs. By mutual agreement the company and union had classified those lower job classifications as "red circle" jobs, which meant that those on that job before the re-classification would continue their previous rate of pay, but any new person promoted to that job would have to accept the lower classification which meant lower pay.

The agreement governing these changes contained provisions which limited the time during which the union could present protests of grievances. By the time I came along the time for filing protests had expired. Nevertheless, I found some errors and asked that admitted errors be corrected. The company refused, and the international union claimed it had already done all it could, so both parties refused to do anything to correct admitted errors.

When we went back to work after the 1949 strike, my department foremen began to harass me by leaving me off the work schedule at times, which cut my earnings. The union contract with the company provided that thirty-two hours should be the normal minimum schedule for regular workers. But on Wednesday, November 30, 1949, the foremen told me there would be no work for me the rest of that week. I argued with the foremen, stating that if younger men were going to be scheduled for four days that I was entitled to four days and would come out to work the fourth day which would be Friday.

When I did come out and reported for work on that Friday, the clerk in the foreman's office claimed he did not know anything about the matter and did not assign me to a job for that day. So I decided to wait for the foreman to iron it out. Having seen him go past his office earlier, I waited from 6:30 A.M. until after 11:30 A.M. feeling certain that the foreman was around and would sooner or later return to his office. Finally, tired of waiting, I told the clerk that I would go to the washroom and change clothes.

Taking a little longer than usual to change clothes, I heard the foreman ask someone else in there if I had left. Before anyone could answer, I came out from behind the row of lockers and told him that his behavior was certainly deceitful and cowardly to make a man wait all day while he attempted to dodge his responsibilities. It was especially reprehensible for him to act like a child and hide in the ingot yard, especially since younger men than myself were working a full week, thus violating my seniority rights. The foreman claimed he was sick and could not discuss the matter with anyone now and he was going home.

I don't know whether he went home. I believed he was putting on an act to divert me from my objective. I told him I was going to take the matter up with his boss the mill superintendent, Mr. R. P. Herr, better known as "Curley." The foreman, Dominic Orcucci, better known as "Shorty," said "go ahead". At that moment Curley Herr came walking around the corner so I spoke to him about my schedule problem and he readily agreed that I was entitled to thirty-two hours of work and advised me to come out Saturday and that I would be put to work somewhere. I did come out on Saturday, December 3, 1949, and worked on clean-up in the 16" Mill department. Herr's orders did allow me to make up for some of the lost time, but it didn't restore all the lost wages because my assigned job was at a much lower rate of pay. It helped to serve notice that I was going to insist on exercising my rights, no matter what obstacles were put in my path.

On January 27, 1950, as a local union official, I was invited to a post-war meeting of most of the labor officials in Seattle with Cyrus Ching, then Secretary of Labor. During that meeting he made a strong plea for organized labor to continue to cooperate with the government to avoid work stoppages and keep the "no-strike" pledge that had been in effect during the war.

I had to tell him that our members did not favor that because they had too many unsolved local problems. Also, I asked if it was true the Social Security trust fund had been used to pay for the war, as had been alleged recently by some newspaperman, so the money was gone. Ching explained that when one department of government borrows money from another the debt of one becomes a credit of the other. Since both are in the government that bond is a promise to pay. The government still had the credit of that money. In this case it was used to finance the Lend-Lease war program which made it possible to send munitions and other war material to help England and Russia, so he considered that money was still an asset of the government because it was to be paid back some time. Nobody in that meeting believed his assumptions, but we didn't get a chance to pursue the question because Ching's assistants hurried him out of that meeting to another without giving us a chance to ask further questions.

Just as I was becoming weighted down in union problems, my wife, Harriette, launched herself on a career in the lumber brokerage business which took her first to Oregon, then on to California, thereby separating us. Soon she decided that she didn't want to try to live through all the struggles that appeared before me, so we agreed to a divorce after over 10 years of marriage. It became final in a year.

That divorce required me to obtain a new mortgage on my home so I could pay off Harriette's equity. The existing mortgage holder was Carroll-Hedland. But they refused to write a new mortgage for me at that time, without explanation. I then went to Washington Mutual and was again turned down when they learned that Carroll-Hedland had refused me. I began to think I was being discriminated against because of my union activities or my previous Communist party activity. But a friend suggested that I try Sparkman-McLean, which I did, and they quickly granted me a new mortgage. Later I learned the reason for the turn-down by Carroll-Hedland was because they were using their "mortgage" money to invest on the stock market instead of in mortgages. That information became public during the McClelland Senate Committee hearings about Dave Beck, head of the Teamsters' union. One of the executives of the Carroll-Hedland mortgage company was testifying in an attempt to help Beck and had to reveal how he was manipulating mortgage money funds on the stock market.

On September 20, 1951, a person who identified himself as R. McNamara and a partner by the name of Nelson from the FBI visited me at my home to ask me to become a professional witness for the FBI against the Communist party. My reply was that I really had nothing significant to testify about. McNamara told me the FBI would furnish me with all the information and material I needed to become a star witness. I told him that I couldn't testify about anything that wasn't within my own experience and I doubted that I had anything significant or worthwhile to bother about, so I declined his offer. At that time I really didn't think my experiences had any special value. My ideas have changed quite a lot since then.

By 1952 the Socialist Workers Party (Trotskyist) had invited me to hear their speakers outline their criticisms of the Communist party and Stalin. I found some of their contentions to be quite valid within my Communist party expulsion experience. But I knew that the Trotskyist movement was a split from the Communist party over very complex political issues that bothered me because I could not see any way of resolving those old conflicts which were a diversion from the course I was pursuing in the union. I knew from reading Communist literature that Stalin had pursued a deliberate policy of destroying possible rivals for his position of control and that he had used every possible method to accomplish his purpose of establishing himself as the final authority after Lenin.

Stalin's book on Leninism clearly outlines his tactics of splitting his opposition and destroying them, one-by-one. Trotsky was one of those victims. He was pursued to his refuge in Mexico where he was murdered by a Spaniard carrying out Stalin's policies. Krushchev's 1956 revelations provided some evidence that the various Moscow trials were conspiracies and frame-ups against Stalin's rivals. Because I had been publicly expelled from the Communist party, the Socialist Workers party tried to recruit me. I did respect their criticisms of the Communist party's bureaucracy and zigzag policies and forsaking the teachings of Marx in behalf of the working class. But I was never able to accept their contention that the teachings of Trotsky would emancipate the working class because they had a long history of opposition to nearly everything I had been involved in.

I concluded that the whole issue was really moot (dead) as far as I was concerned. I did accept the Socialist Workers' party right to engage in political elections and signed one of their Independent Party nominating petitions on September 9, 1952. That was later used against me in the union by the International office, who based their judgment on the Attorney General's designation of subversive organizations.

During 1950 I was elected a delegate to several CIO Political Action Committee (PAC) meetings; to the State CIO convention, and to a Steelworkers union school in Pullman, Washington, September 16th and 17th, at Washington State College. The main value of that institute was intended to be a class conducted by an international union representative named Kessler. The class explained the history and method of the job classification and evaluation agreement reached by the companies and the union. Kessler advised us that it was the culmination of the decision of the War Labor Board to eliminate the inequities in Steelworkers' compensation. He reviewed that development as a great advance for the workers. I disagreed with him.

I questioned him extensively about how to deal with the difficulties the companies caused the local unions by lowering the job classifications, creating "Red Circle" pay rates and refusing to correct admitted errors that had crept in. Kessler admitted that those things did occur but contended it was necessary for the local unions to learn to live with them because it brought order out of chaos. Everyone from the local unions was flabbergasted to find the union authority did not offer any way to correct the errors. Kessler's point was that time had run out according to the terms of the agreement made at the national level. Sub-District Director Mathews openly revealed that he was bitterly upset with me for raising such problems which embarrassed the international. I attempted to show that the problem existed. The issue was not raised to embarrass anyone, but to attempt to find a solution. No one in his right mind could accept the answer that it was unsolvable. Mathews had to suppress his anger at that time because all the rank and file thoroughly agreed with me.

Near the end of 1951 the company announced that it was going to make more pay rate changes, because of some production methods changes. Under the contract, the company could make changes in the pay rates whenever they changed the production process or equipment. There was also provision in the contract for a trial period to evaluate the changes and a stipulation that new changes should not work to reduce the worker's earnings. But the union had no way of determining what the total effect of any new changes would be.

I began to receive repeated requests from members for information on the actual rates of pay on the various jobs. As recording secretary and keeper of the union records, I searched for and inquired of every possible source to obtain that information. To my surprise, and everyone else's, no such records were to be found in the possession of the local union or in the Sub-District Director's office of the international union, and in fact the company refused to let any worker know what the pay rate was for any other workers. No information on that problem was obtained at the Washington State College in Pullman, Washington. In the proceedings of the Sixth Constitutional Convention of the United Steelworkers of America (May 13–17, 1952, p. 81) appears the following paragraph:

EMPLOYER'S DUTY TO SUPPLY DATA
    During the last 2 years the Labor Board has continued to hold that employers are guilty of a refusal to bargain if they refuse to furnish the union with the information reasonable (sic) necessary in conducting intelligent bargaining negotiations. The employer's obligation to supply information exists if the information is necessary for negotiating a new contract or for policing an existing one . . . This doctrine was relied upon by the Steelworkers over the past few months in order to obtain certain economic data from the steel companies for use in negotiations. These data, which will enable us to determine more accurately the cost of various wage, fringe, and other adjustments were available only from the companies. Certain companies, including U.S. Steel, furnished only some of the requested data and refused other data. Other companies furnished all of the data requested.

On the strength of that official information I went to the local National Labor Relations Board (NLRB) and explained our situation. I asked if we could file a complaint against the local company for refusal to furnish us the pay rate information referred to by the National union. When the local NLRB informed me that we had that right, I filed such a complaint.

In spite of this knowledge being available to everyone in the upper echelons of the United Steelworkers union, a Mr. Phil Curran from the international union office in Pittsburgh, Pennsylvania, came to Seattle twice to confer with the NLRB after we filed that case. Mr. Curran never did get in touch with us in the local union.

The NLRB later told us that Mr. Curran tried to get the NLRB to throw our case out because he contended that all the bargaining was done on a national scale and that the local union really had nothing to do with it. But the NLRB answered that they had to act on the basis of the complaint before it which asked that the information be furnished to the local union and by law that was the local union's right.

Instead of trying to help the local union get the information it was entitled to, the international union actually did everything it could to try to prevent us from obtaining all the pay rates we needed to police the contract. They also stirred up more criticism among the members of the local union, implying that we local officers had overstepped our bounds and would probably cause the company to try to get even with us some way.

By April, 1953, the company called me and stated that it would furnish all the pay rates as asked for in the NLRB case. The case was scheduled for its first hearing before a field examiner. I accepted the company promise to deliver the pay rates, and they did within a few days. So, on behalf of the local union, I advised the NLRB that the company had agreed to voluntarily furnish the pay rates to us in the local union, so the complaint we had filed was withdrawn.

ða

CONFLICTS, COMPANY AND UNION, 1951–1953

ða

On June 4, 1951, a special meeting of the local union executive board was held at the Frye Hotel to meet with Carl Jones, our wage policy man. The reason for the meeting was not made very clear at the time. And, although he was not a member of the local union executive board, James McCarthy, a past president of the local union and past wage policy committeeman, defeated by Carl Jones in a previous election, was present at some unknown person's invitation. But no one raised any objection to his presence because there was a chance that he might be able to give us the benefit of some of his previous experience on the Wage Policy Committee.

The meeting was chaotic. No one seemed to be able to establish any sort of order. Jones did not make any cohesive report to the meeting as a whole. He did speak to individuals who raised isolated questions, but for the most part waited for anyone to prod him into letting us know what he knew about the Wage Policy Committee actions. Several were drinking. McCarthy became drunk rather early and more or less dropped out of the discussion after he made a raucous demand on Jones "to lay his cards on the table," which Jones ignored.

I had to leave the meeting at 9:45 P.M. to go to work on the graveyard shift. Harry Nelson, vice president of Local Union 1208, left at the same time with me for the same reason.

A day or two later, John Stariha and Scotty McCulloch, Open Hearth Department leaders, came to my house and talked to me about grievances pending. Stariha wound up by suggesting that because I was so "hot" with a known background of a Communist party affiliation it would be better for me not to take such a prominent part in controversies with the company. They suggested, however, that since I had the knowledge and experience needed by the local union, that I should do my work through other people and stay in the background. I replied that I thought that proposal was unsound because it imposed two conditions which were false; one was an attempt to impose second-class membership on me, the second was to attempt to speak through someone else which was impossible because I could not advise anyone in advance as to what to say before the subject was known.

Stariha and McCulloch both advised that they did not believe the members would tolerate my leadership if they knew I had a "red" background. I replied that I was perfectly willing to put that up to the members to find out, and that as department grievance-man I would call a special meeting of the department and report this matter fully to them and let them decide. Stariha and McCulloch drove away smiling and shaking their heads.

I called that meeting on June 9, 1951, and won a unanimous endorsement. Later, David Adams, president of Local Union 1208, told me the rest of the time at the Frye Hotel meeting was spent discussing how they could get rid of me. Adams stated that he disagreed with that group and told them so.

On June 16, 1951, I was among the delegates elected to attend the State CIO convention in Spokane, Washington. USWA Sub-District Director Hugh Mathews was a pre-convention appointed member of the Rules Committee. But before the convention could be called to order he was already drunk and disoriented.

When the Rules Committee report was made there was a peculiar twist in the rules which required a vote on the majority report of a committee before a minority report could be voted on which is the reverse of Robert's Rules of Order. Arvid Swenson, Harry Tucker, and I spoke against that portion of the report and caused it to be sent back to the committee for correction. That correction was made, reported back to the convention and adopted.

During the argument in the convention over this, Mathews expressed his anger at me for objecting to the rules. He said they were the verbatim rules always used by the Steelworkers union at its conventions and I, a member of the Steelworkers union, had no right to go contrary to the rules used by the Steelworkers. In his illogical thinking he also accused Swenson and Tucker of being a part of my "Red" plot to obstruct the convention. Both of them laughed that off because Swenson was a conservative insurance agent and Tucker was a leader of the "right" wing of the convention, had a long record of being an anti-communist in the IWA, and had been appointed by John L. Lewis to take my place as Secretary of the State CIO when Lewis ordered me removed ten years earlier.

On September 14, 1951, I was elected by L.U. 1208 as a delegate to the District Conference of Steelworkers in Spokane, Washington. In preparation for this conference, the local union executive board held several meetings to work out our ideas for resolutions to submit to the conference, mainly about changes we wanted in the union contract. The Executive Board directed me as Recording Secretary to write up their ideas into resolutions for the conference. The rules of the conference call provided that all resolutions had to be signed by the president and recording secretary of each Local Union. We had more than 20 such resolutions from L.U. 1208.

I made it a point to meet with District Director Charles Smith before the conference officially opened and conversed with him about the contents of the resolutions, asking what he thought about them. His comment was, "My God, you want to rewrite the whole contract." I answered that our members were very unhappy with the Bethlehem contract because it did not give the workers the protection they expected from a labor contract. He walked off without commenting further. Most of those resolutions were adopted without opposition.

The Bethlehem Fabricating Plant in Seattle had just been organized into the United Steelworkers union with the cooperation of the Bethlehem Steel Company, which gave a list of the names of its workers to the USWOC organizers. A bitter dispute arose between the workers in the plant and the union because the members wanted to negotiate their own agreement with the company based on area wage standards. According to the fabricating workers, led by Joe Gamba, a local shop steward, the union officials wanted to blanket cover the fabricating members under the existing nationwide general agreement, whose ready-made job classifications and standards were below area standards.

The district conference was a "touch and go" proposition with the international union representatives spending large amounts of money pouring liquor down the fabricating delegates' throats, especially Joe Gamba's. Because of this, Gamba was not able to take much part on the floor. When I observed this, I advised our delegates from 1208 to be very careful to not fall into the same pitfall, because our members gave us a responsibility that was very great and required that we do our best to adequately represent their wishes.

Soon after the Conference got under way it became clear that the major objective of the International Staff Representatives present was to bring about adoption of a resolution endorsing a raise in dues, which would help them get a raise in salary. When that resolution came on the floor I criticized it, stating that our members felt they were entitled to a raise in wages first and there were other contract changes which had been previously neglected which should also be taken care of before raising dues. My statement was deliberately mis-construed by Sub-District Director Hugh Mathews, who accused me of saying that the union had done nothing for the members. I invoked my right of "personal privilege" to contradict Mathews' misconstruction of what I actually said. But that subject touched the most sensitive spot the international staff representatives had. Many of them spoke vigorously against me, with Mathews cursing me from the floor and deliberately calling me a "God-damned-liar". I had to ask Chairman Smith for a second time to make my point that they should reverse the order of things—get some new benefits for the dues of the past 10 years, then consider raising the dues to meet the raise in salaries the staff desired.

After the session adjourned for the day, fellow delegate Claude Long and I were leaving the convention from the center aisle. Mathews started shouting from a side aisle, cursing and approaching me with arms waving violently. Mathews had another staff member with him. Both were obviously intoxicated. While Mathews was shaking a menacing fist in my face calling me a "God-Damned, and Dirty God-Damned Liar", Mathews' fellow staff man, Jerry Conway, gave me a big shove into another staff man who had come up when he saw trouble brewing. Long's wife saw the storm and came rushing up to join her husband. Long and I placed ourselves back to back to prevent any surprise from the rear. Then Long, who towered over the Staff men, talked to them advising them not to start any rough stuff.

When the staff men dispersed, Long and I conferred briefly over what was the best thing to do about this matter. We concluded that District Director Smith should be advised about it. We did so and urged him to put a stop to this nonsense before it got out of hand. Director Smith promised that he would handle it. Later, Long and I learned that Director Smith held a staff meeting where he reprimanded both Mathews and Conway and ordered them to apologize to me. Jerry Conway did apologize to me but Mathews never did. Later, at the national Steelworkers convention, the leaders found this issue of raising dues was so hot that President Murray ordered that the resolution would not be put into effect until after the new contract was negotiated with long overdue wage increases.

For many years before the Bethlehem Steel Corporation took over the Seattle plant (it used to be owned by an independent company), segregation of nationalities into different departments was the established practice. The open hearth was Irish and Slav. The pouring pit was Italian. The 16″ Mill was Swede. The 22″ Mill was the elite white Americans. The Scrap yard was Negro and unclassified workers. Negroes did the clean-up. Each department maintained its own exclusiveness. Racial discrimination and separation was a sort of "Gentleman's Agreement" type of thing—subtle, not

openly expressed usually, but silently practiced and using deroga-
tory terms of identification such as: "Mick," "Wop," "Dago," "Nig-
ger," "Hunyak," "Greaser," "Foreigner," and many others.

The most critical discrimination constantly irritating everyone
was that against the Negroes. And to make it more complicated,
most Negroes, while smarting under such obvious injustice, felt restrained from attempting to do anything about it, believing that all
that could possibly happen would be more "trouble" for themselves. The company fed this idea while at the same time contending that the reason Negroes were held back was because of the
union rule of seniority, and that the Negroes lacked the ability to do
the higher paid work.

I recognized these situations were pernicious and had divisive
consequences. So I embarked on an effort to offset the company
propaganda blaming the union for the lowly condition of most Negroes, but I came into collision with all the entrenched whites who
feared that giving Negroes equal rights would in fact result in lowering the positions some of the whites held. This problem became
more complex the further one got into it. I was confronted with rising opposition from the other departments of the company, the
union, and some of the workers in the plant. I saw the problem as
so acute that the very life of the union depended on finding a solution. We found that the international officials contented themselves
with pious declarations that "it was in the Constitution of the
Union that there shall be no discrimination because of race or color,
etc." It was very clear that few were willing to tackle the problem. It
became necessary to do something substantial in addition to utter-
ing the good words. So I proposed to the local executive board that
we push hard to get the company to agree on lines of progression
and establish seniority rosters for all jobs, and that these be posted
on the bulletin board where all could examine them whenever they
had reason to do so. Where we found problems of dislocation we
would then negotiate settlements with the company.

We found many rank and file workers willing to support such a
program because we were able to cite violations of the seniority
rights of more than ten black workers. In the face of specific examples it was no longer possible for anyone to contend that discrimination did not exist. The dates of their initial employment and the
position they held on the job ladder proved that something was way
out of line. Then the excuses became, "They don't have the ability."
But everyone knew better because the blacks often had to relieve

workers on higher jobs. This proved they could do the job, but they were never allowed to be promoted to hold the job on their own.

Most Negroes were unwilling to trust the union and its white leadership. Then one of the Steelworkers' district conferences set up a committee to promote equal rights through establishing Local Union Civil Rights Committees. Mr. Gill Anya, on the staff of District 38, deserves recognition for the work he did to get that resolution adopted and implemented at the conference. Local Union 1208 seized upon this instrument to come to grips with all forms of discrimination.

There began to be some evidence that the local plant management was becoming somewhat amenable to the idea of negotiating lines of progression and job seniority rosters because these promised to eliminate many uncertainties and sources of disputes. But, when local management attempted to get clearance from higher company authority, such approval was denied. This resulted in the local plant management offering to work out the problem "unofficially". I contended that would be unsatisfactory unless it was official.

In October, 1953, the Company locally changed its attitude and declared for the "nth" time that seniority was void in the Seattle plant. I spearheaded the local union effort to take the matter to the NLRB. Then the international union became alarmed over the situation and instructed Sub-District Director Mathews to file a complaint with the NLRB before the local union could do so. When the company saw this turn of events, it reached Mathews at the NLRB office before the case could actually be filed, and advised that the company would furnish plant and department seniority rosters to the international union. This they did within a few days, and the international, through Mathews, furnished a copy to Local Union 1208. We still had to negotiate the local lines of progression and job rosters. This was accomplished after many company delays, but it did solve many problems of scheduling by an orderly method.

In the spring of 1952, the national leaders of the United Steelworkers made a strong push to strengthen their bond with the rank and file by demanding substantial wage increases and a few other benefits. The newspapers were becoming a little more critical of the Steelworkers because of the frequency of strikes. So, when I was invited to a class taught by a Professor Hopkins at the University of Washington, I accepted and took the opportunity to explain that the Steelworkers were lagging way behind others who had progressed since the war. In answer to some of the students' questions about the economics of wage increases, I replied that I believed Karl Marx was correct in his analysis of the capitalist system and that it was necessary for the workers to constantly attempt to raise their standard of living. All the evidence indicated that the present demands of the union could be met by the companies without any difficulty because they had amassed enormous profits during and since the War.

On June 2, 1952, we were ordered out on strike again; it did not end until July 24, 1952. It was the same situation as in previous strikes. They were called and settled without the local members having anything to say about them. Also, there was an interesting comment about it made in *Life* magazine, October 22, 1956, where Benjamin Fairless, President of U.S. Steel, relates that he and Phil Murray, President of the Steelworkers, reached an agreement to settle the strike "within 5 minutes" but Murray would not let him make the announcement right away, because they had to make it look tough to the newspaper reporters who were waiting for the announcement.

On July 16, 1953, the international sub-district office advised us that a new international representative by the name of William Jacko, an expert in pay rates, was coming to help us on the pay rate grievances. When he found out how complicated our grievances were he proposed that the best procedure at this point would be for the company to reach local agreement with the union on a "trial period." This would afford everyone adequate opportunity to observe just how the plan operated, with particular concern over the questions of whether it was equitable to the plan it replaced and whether it would provide equitable compensation. This was the procedure outlined in the contract between the union and the company.

But the company rejected Jacko's suggestion. We never made any real progress along that line after that. Also, it soon appeared that Jacko was in very poor health. He had a retching cough that made everyone fear he would choke to death from strangulation. When Jacko saw that the company had no intention of paying any attention to his suggestions he arranged to get transferred from Seattle. Before he left, he privately told me that he was sent here to get rid of me, and he found that I was doing such a good job that he couldn't in good conscience do the dirty job on me that had been ordered. He would not identify the source of that order, but left the inference that it was from the Western District. We never heard anything more about Jacko after he left.

On August 9, 1953, I was again elected to attend a CIO school, this time in Portland, Oregon, for a week. It was run by several leaders who had participated in the organization of the rubber workers and the flat glass workers. They taught several catchy folk songs and dances that were used by them in those organization drives. They seemed somewhat childish to those of us used to the rough and ready climate in which we lived. But they were recreational and did give us a lot of relaxation that most of us needed.

One sour note there was the prejudicial attitude of some of those easterners. They went out of their way to condemn Harry Bridges as a red, even though he was still the CIO Director for the State of California. I challenged them to come to Seattle and try to run down Bridges in the Longshoremen's meeting. I contended that Bridges represented what the members of the ILWU wanted and we should support them and him for the best interests of the CIO. The telephone worker delegates from the Communications Workers Union agreed with me and told that easterner to go back East, that we didn't need his kind in the West.

I was one of five delegates from L.U. 1208 elected to attend the October 2nd, 1953, District Conference of Steelworkers in Pueblo, Colorado. Violence flared during a pre-conference caucus of Bethlehem delegates before the conference actually got under way. I insisted that the conference should deal with the new problems of incentive pay. Joseph Angelo, the chairman of the caucus, disagreed to such an extent that he arose from his seat at the head of the table, knocked over a pitcher of water, and rushed at me threatening to "shut me up." Angelo doubled up his fists and made signs that he was going to strike me. But I remained seated, refusing to become embroiled in a physical combat. L.U. 1208 President Adams, a codelegate with me, rose to his feet, met Angelo and warned him that if he struck me, Angelo would have to fight Adams, too. With some brief exchange of opinions against threatened violence, Angelo returned to his seat and the caucus proceeded to finish its business.

After that Bethlehem caucus I had a talk with International Vice President Jim Thimmes, explaining our pay rate and job classification problems along with the current violation of seniority in the Seattle Bethlehem plant. I gave him a detailed report of how we had obtained the pay rates for all jobs by going to the NLRB, and told him we were resisting the wage cuts involved in the revised pay rates and job classifications.

Thimmes told me that we as a local union couldn't do those things. I told him that we already had. He insisted that the local union had no bargaining power, that all bargaining power rested in the hands of the international. I told him again that we had already done it. He threw up his hands and walked away, and never talked to us again.

Among the many resolutions Local 1208 submitted to the conference was one proposing that the conference be reconstituted as a convention. Our thinking was that it would have more influence and help guide the locals in carrying out their decisions. Other CIO unions we knew, such as the Woodworkers, held regional conventions. But the officers and staff leaders pounced on our resolution, condemning it as divisive and injurious to the conference. After I had attempted to defend the resolution I was declared "out of order," the resolution was declared "out of order" and Chairman Smith made a direct threat from the chair to the effect that they had had others like me before but they were no longer with them.

I thought that was a personal threat, and since it was near the close of the conference, Adams and I decided to get out of there before anything more could be done to us. We left quickly, before menacing gestures could be translated into action. I interpreted this experience as a signal for a general attack on me. Later events were thoroughly convincing.

Probably the most important issue in the 22" Mill Department had been the revision of incentive pay rates. The rates seemed to be very complicated and technical when first presented to us in writing. As we came to understand them better we found that they were cutting into our total earning. So, on behalf of the Union and the workers in the 22" Mill Department, I prepared thirty-three grievances which covered every section of the new plan, and one that covered the whole plan.

Five of these grievances dealt with the principles and fundamental points in the union contract which implied that any new plan must provide equal earnings compared to the plan being replaced. Some of these points were argued all the way up to the fourth step in the grievance procedure (the next and last step was arbitration). These grievances were held there by the International for many months, and were practically outdated at any later date because the Company had been almost constantly revising its production procedure, and each revision permitted them to revise the rates.

Among the principles at issue were Union challenge of the Company's right (1) to arbitrarily lower the hourly portion of the rates of pay; (2) to arbitrarily cut the actual earnings by as much as forty-four cents per hour as the new tonnage rate plan provided; (3) to "Red Circle" or "Two Tier" any job classification because of changes the Company made in the tonnage and/or incentive rates. We made many other complaints, but these illustrate why the local union challenged the right of the company to wipe out all "past—practice—conditions" by the expedient of revising pay rates.

Because I carefully analyzed each rate and each class of rates and formulated specific grievances based on the provisions of the agreement with the company, the company made four revisions in its master plan after it was in effect. One of those revisions resulted in back pay in excess of $2000 for distribution among sixty workers, some of whom got as much as $50.

With each revision the Company gave more expression to its hatred of me. It became clear that they, with the assistance of the union's international representatives, were going to attempt to use me as the "whipping boy" and try to make a "horrible example" of me to deter all others who might entertain the hope that something could be done through the union with courage and persistence.

When the company was working out new job classifications and pay rates from 1947 onward, they were compelled to modernize their incentive system. The modern industrial engineers attempted to completely overhaul the systems that had been operating for many years and were consequently outdated. Because we realized this was going to be a big change we asked the international representatives to help us understand what was going on. Their answer was that everything was being worked out on a national level. But we could see that the company was doing something on a local level. We concluded that the only avenue on which we could protect ourselves was to actually make our own study of what was going on.

When the industrial engineers were making wholesale time studies preparing to put into effect new classifications and pay rates, I kept detailed records of everything that happened when I was on the job. It was my understanding that the union contract had language in it promising the new contract would maintain the same level of benefits as existed in the old contracts. So the main thrust of my challenge was that the company was violating the contract. That stirred up a holocaust. No one in the district or international union, it seemed to me, wanted to stick his neck out about it.

They had some very confusing correspondence among themselves about this but they never did respond to our calls for help.

₰

STEEL UNION EXPULSION, 1953–1955

₰

The several CIO schools and Steelworkers conferences I had attended stimulated my thinking and activities in pursuit of efforts on the job to benefit my fellow workers. That required me to obtain a broad conception of what was going on everywhere. I continually asked the union's international representatives to help us defend ourselves from the attacks the company kept making against us. They did not respond. In the end I had to do most of the work myself. A major problem was to determine what would be a "fair" incentive.

There was provision for a time study and trial period to determine a normal average production. Then, a standard hourly rate of pay would be established at seventy-five percent of the normal average. That should have worked out to allow an incentive of about twenty-five percent above the standard hourly wage rate when one hundred percent of normal average capacity was produced by the workers' average effort. With that type of plan, the company obtained a standard unit cost of production for administrative purposes, which was more important to the company than the cost of the incentive plan.

Converting the above percentages, I argued that the normal average became one hundred percent which in turn made possible above average earnings of fifty percent more. I determined that raising the average during the trial period would result in obtaining a higher average earning with this incentive system. That was opposite to the average thinking and it worked out as I thought it would. We did increase our earnings.

To obtain some figures that we could use to keep our incentive earnings as high as possible, I spent many days working up calculations on every order size we rolled in the 22″ Mill so I would know how many pieces of every order size we had to roll to get the maximum pay. My target was usually one hundred fifty percent of the standard hourly wage rate which resulted in increased earnings for the whole 22″ Mill crew. I was in the driver's seat because my job as the First Helper on the furnace gave me the responsibility to set the pace of taking the hot steel from the furnace and sending it to the mill for rolling. I was the "pace setter", and as long as I was on that job, the pay for everyone of us in that crew made the maximum amount of money instead of the minimum. No one else seemed to understand how I could do it even though I showed them my figures. I tried to help the other crews by telling the other furnace helpers the pace that would pay the maximum on the order they were running. Sometimes they were successful at keeping that pace but most of the time they were not. I used a stop watch to keep on target speed, and it worked. The crew I worked with were quite pleased with our above average earnings.

Then one day in September, 1953, I noticed something in a syndicated Alsop newspaper column which referred to the political dispute between the Soviet Union and Tito's Yugoslavia over their conflicting theories about production incentives. I interpreted the Alsop references to be a criticism of something Lenin had written in a pamphlet entitled "What Is To Be Done". There, Lenin analyzed "economism", which refers to depending on the economic condition to develop a socialist political philosophy. My impression of the article was that Alsop had misunderstood what Lenin had written, so I wanted to look it up to confirm or contradict my memory about that subject. I couldn't readily find my old copy so when I was downtown one day a short time later I went to the Communist Frontier Bookstore, where I bought a copy; I had it with me when I went to work that afternoon. As I changed into my work clothes, I laid the pamphlet down on the bench by my locker. When I went to pick it up it wasn't there. There were several workers standing nearby so I asked if any of them saw what happened to my book. No one admitted knowing anything. A day or so later I asked another group standing around my locker if they knew anything about who took my book. Rolland Gilland, nicknamed "Gabby", was among the group. His locker was near mine. He had a sheepish grin on his face when he said he didn't have the book but he thought he could get it for me. I told him I would appreciate it if he would get it.

I believe it was another day, or more, later that he did bring the book back to me and said he had looked at it and thought it would be interesting to read and he would like to do that. I told him it was written in a very polemical political style that I thought he would find difficult to understand unless he had already studied some other books of that type. He insisted that he wanted to read it. So, reluctantly, I let him take it. I made him promise that he would return it soon because there was something in it I wanted to read. He promised to bring it back soon.

Although I had some misgivings about loaning that book to a person like Gilland who could hardly read at all, I had no idea it would ultimately be used to drive me out of the union. The company and the international representatives of the union both imposed hardships on me throughout the fall months of 1953. By January of 1954, I became apprehensive about Gilland not returning my book so I made three attempts to get him to return it. But he tried to avoid meeting me and instead of returning it he took the book to the company.

The previous month had been a continuation of sniping and carping against me from members who were seen frequently with international district representatives Furman and Mathews. It was plain to see that something was being hatched to "get me."

Then on Saturday, January 30, 1954, a special executive board meeting of L.U. 1208 was called by international representative Furman. Furman presented an affidavit prepared by Gilland on January 29, 1954, with the help of the international's lawyer, Joseph Kane, alleging that I had forced Lenin's book, "What Is To Be Done", on him and that it contained, on page 131, threats to him and his family that scared him so much he made a report of it to the FBI. (See Appendix.) The executive board members discussed the subject very extensively. Most members ridiculed the idea that reading any book could scare anyone the way Gilland claimed. Hoy, Adams, and I explained that Gilland had been trying to violate the seniority of other members working on the better paying jobs at the mill. Gilland's true job was lower paid labor.

International representative Furman insisted that, when charges such as these were made, the union had to put the accused on trial. I insisted that the charges were false, that Gilland's story was false and that the international representatives were pushing the local union on a wrong path. But on February 1, 1954, Gilland, at the prompting and counselling of Furman and with the assistance of attorney Kane, presented formal charges against me specifying my violation of the Constitution of the United Steelworkers of America in Article III, Section 4 and Article XII, Sections one (a) (d) (e) (f) (g) (j) and (l) and asked that I be expelled from membership or prohibited from holding office or serving on committee, either elective or appointive, in the United Steelworkers of America CIO. (See appendix.)

On February 6, 1954, the executive board of L.U. 1208, under demand from international sub-district director Mathews, voted to hold a trial with a committee of three to be appointed by the local union president, which was done.

The trial was held February 20, 1954, with a trial board of James Giggans, Ole M. Johnson, and Robert Petris as chairman. The chairman read the charges. I pleaded "not guilty" and acted as my own defense counsel. Gilland was represented by James McCarthy, former president of L.U. 1208. He was constantly coached by international representative Furman, who, in turn, was advised by lawyer Joseph Kane.

At no time was any evidence submitted substantiating any of the charges listed in the complaint. McCarthy praised Gilland's patriotism in bringing these charges against me and took advantage of the hysteria of that time promoted by U.S. Senator Joe McCarthy, and expressed alarm at my presence. I defended myself by claiming the right to think and deal with our working class problems as best I was able. I recounted the many bad experiences I had with the Communist Party, that I had been expelled in 1947 because I would no longer obey their arbitrary orders and that I had an honorable discharge and a commendation for excellent service from the U.S. Army, which I had served proudly. None of my opponents could duplicate my record.

During the period when the trial board was trying to make a decision, one of the executive board members, William Hawkins, without my knowledge or consent, tried to quash the whole matter by getting Gilland to agree to withdraw the charges. When the international learned about that, they persuaded Gilland to sign another affidavit re-instituting the charges and repudiating his statement withdrawing the charges.

So the trial board proceeded to try to make a decision. I was recalled twice during which appearances they suggested that everything would be better if I voluntarily stepped aside. I informed them that I would like to get out from under the union burdens but felt that under the circumstances it would injure the union to do it as they proposed.

On March 21, 1954, the trial board made a report which did not find me guilty of any charges. They used an expression that I was "guilty of imposing (my) political views in the mind of Rolland L. Gilland" without identifying what those political views were, or how it could be done. They recommended specifically that I "not be expelled from the Union, but be removed from office." (See Appendix.)

The vote on accepting the trial board report was: for acceptance 149; for rejection 70. (The total membership was about 600). I immediately submitted my resignation from all union positions. Some of my friends attempted to also resign at that time but the meeting refused to accept any resignations other than mine.

At the April 3, 1954, meeting of the union, James McCarthy, who had acted as counsel for Gilland, presented a petition demanding a plant gate vote to expel me from the union. He claimed to have about 220 names signed to that petition. The trial committee chairman, Bob Petris, informed the meeting that the trial committee did not find me guilty of subversive activities as claimed in the petition and there was no evidence of that kind submitted to the trial. After considerable discussion Petris moved to close the case completely. The motion was duly seconded and carried. I asked international representative Furman where he stood in this matter. Furman answered that he did help draw up the petition. Later several members from other departments in the plant told me that LaVerne Crossen, the company industrial relations man, was seen in various departments with members circulating that petition.

When I later studied the names on that petition I found four names of workers who were members of the Communist party before my expulsion. Significantly, two late-comer party members whom I knew did not sign it. Only one person from the 22" Mill Department (where I worked) signed the petition; he did this when visiting another department.

On April 22, 1954, there were evidences that international representative Furman and his followers were continuing their efforts to bring about my expulsion in violation of the local union's decision to close the case against me completely. My friends told me they heard that Furman was cooking up some dirty scheme with attorney Joseph Kane, and for that reason I had better get a good lawyer. Other friends suggested Kenneth A. MacDonald as the up-and-coming young civil rights lawyer, so I consulted him. He submitted my problem to two new young lawyers, one of whom is now a Superior Court Judge here in King County, Washington. They studied the facts in the case a few days and came back to MacDonald with a recommendation that we prepare to fight with a libel case because it was obvious the opposition was intent on destroying my right to work and to exist.

On May 13, 1954, I signed a libel complaint against the company industrial relations manager, the local international representatives of the United Steelworkers of America and several of the local union members opposing me. That first complaint did not stand up in court so another one was filed. Each time, my opponents were quite nervous about being sued, although their lawyer, Joe Kane, assured them they were in no danger. My lawyer assured me we had a strong case and piled up a lot of pretrial depositions with admissions of prejudice against me. I had to wait until 1956 to have my day in court.

Meanwhile, in June, 1954, the House UnAmerican Activities Committee came to Seattle with a star witness who was serving time in a women's prison after having been convicted of violating the Smith Act. Barbara Hartle was personally qualified to name every member of the Communist party because she had been the district membership director, and when testifying, did exactly that. I was among those she named by reading from the Party expulsion notices that had been circulated far and wide. Previously, I had made a point of explaining to the workers in the Steelworkers union that I expected to be called and that I intended to testify to the best of my knowledge because I had a clean record in every respect. I also explained that I knew a person by the name of Karley Larson who was expected to be called and I believed that he would not be able to use the Fifth Amendment to avoid testifying, because he had already been tried and was acquitted of violating the Smith Act, so he could not self-incriminate himself by testifying again.

I also explained that I had known Karley many years earlier when he was a progressive leader in the International Woodworkers of America. He had given me solid support when I was Secretary of the State CIO Council and under fire. I wanted to talk with Karley before our appearances before the UnAmerican Committee, but never got a chance. I was also disappointed with Karley's testimony because he allowed his attorney to make it appear that he did not follow the policies agreed upon in the Communist party. I always thought Karley's successes in his union were because he was a faithful follower of the Communist party line there.

Most of the witnesses called before the HUAC invoked the 5th Amendment of the U.S. Constitution, which provides that no person may be forced to testify against themselves. My lawyer, Kenneth A. MacDonald, had informed me that since I had been out of the Communist party for over seven years the statute of limitations had expired as it applied to me, so I was in no danger of self incrimination. Because I was free to speak as I wished, I planned not to invoke the Fifth Amendment. But when I was called to the witness stand, MacDonald informed me that he had a phone call from attorney John Caughlan just before the hearing opened. Caughlan strongly urged MacDonald to have all his clients invoke the Fifth Amendment to avoid possible entrapment in perjury as well as to avoid giving names of Communist members when demanded by the Committee which was their regular practice. So during the first day of my interrogation by the HUAC, MacDonald counseled me to invoke the Fifth Amendment whenever the question was one of substance which could lead to waiving my rights under the Fifth. Once a witness begins to answer substantive questions he is then compelled to continue to answer. At that point any refusal to answer can be prosecuted as contempt of Congress. The situation that developed completely upset my plans to testify freely.

When I returned to work the next day, the men I worked with told me that the only way I would be able to stay on the job would be to testify without hiding behind the Fifth. I tried to explain that it was every witness's legal right to decline to testify under the provisions of the Fifth Amendment, and my lawyer had advised me to do so. But they insisted that I would appear to be guilty of something if I did not testify, and that this would worsen my problems with the Steelworkers union.

So I went back to MacDonald and told him that the men I worked with demanded that I testify regardless of what it did to the Communist party. MacDonald arranged with HUAC for me to return to the witness stand. I did this on June 17. I began my testimony, promising to testify fully later at a later date because the Committee was running out of time scheduled for Seattle.

It was March, 1955, before the UnAmerican Committee returned to Seattle. When HUAC investigator William Wheeler was interrogating me in preparation for the public hearings, I asked him why I was subpoenaed when it was publicly known that I had been out of the Party for over seven years. He replied that the Steelworkers union and Bethlehem Steel both requested it. I testified fully for several sessions, at the conclusion of which the Committee declared they were satisfied with my testimony as that of an intelligent and truthful witness.

Most of my testimony dealt with official Communist party policies. I tried to explain the main shifts in Party policy which occurred during the time I was in the Party, and explain that we Communists had tried to do something for the hungry victims of the Depression. The Committee demanded that I name others with whom I had worked in the Party. I did so under protest, reluctantly and apologetically. I had to confirm Barbara Hartle's testimony regarding the Party's policies and the names of members. I think I named a few that she did not, but they probably were not outside the top echelons of the Party with whom I had worked and who had already been named. I believe my testimony did not, for the most part, hurt anyone more than they had been already hurt. The one exception I remember was that of O. H., a Finnish-American machinist who had served in Spain with the Abraham Lincoln Brigade. I had records of the Pioneer (CP youth organization) school that he had attended in the early 1930s. I had completely forgotten about it and was embarrassed when Bill Wheeler pulled that out of my files. He already had O. H.'s name from his FBI records.

It was always obvious that HUAC intended to destroy the public influence of the Communist Party. I think the Committee succeeded to a large extent because the Party tried to conceal its program rather than using the hearings as a forum to present its views.

My agreeing to testify did not improve my situation with the Steelworkers. On July 6, 1954, I received a notice from the union International Secretary, I. W. Abel, that the International Executive Board would act on Gilland's petition demanding my expulsion. The petition was prepared in legal form which was beyond Gilland's ability.

On July 16, 1954, my aunt Pearl Formick in Salem, Oregon sent me a letter advising that my father was critically ill. So I went to see him and his doctor, who told me there was nothing they could do for him except try to keep him comfortable and free of pain. He was 84 years old, was hemorrhaging from his kidney which was probably cancerous, and he would be unable to stand corrective surgery. Dad died a month later on August 25, 1954, in a nursing home. I was not able to give him the time he needed. I have always regretted that. Only one act of compassion occurred. Harry Nelson, chairman of the sick committee for Local Union 1208, did send flowers to Dad's funeral. I am grateful that some human kindness survived.

August 30, 1954, I received a special delivery letter from the Steelworker's District office ordering me to attend a meeting of their trial committee on Friday, September 3, 1954. On September 1, 1954, there was a local union executive board meeting and a local union meeting to consider a possible strike, but I was excluded from the meetings which was an illegal act because I was still a member in good standing.

On Friday, September 3, 1954, I went to the international trial committee at the Smith Tower, Room 406. I asked that my attorney, Kenneth MacDonald, be present. That was refused with the explanation that the union constitution did not allow outside counsel to be present. That was the Burke-Doherty Commission which accepted the claims my opponents and rejected my claims. On September 8, 1954, they recommended my expulsion. I. W. Abel notified me by letter, dated September 9, that the International Executive Board would hear my case on September 15, 1954, and that I could attend at my own expense. I couldn't because I didn't have any money to spare. On October 4, 1954, Abel notified me that I had been expelled from the Union.

Since failure to pay dues under the "maintenance of membership" provision in the union contract is the only excuse a company can use for discharging anyone expelled from the steel union, my problem now was how to pay dues when the contract has a "check-off." The local union does not collect the dues. The company sends the dues to the international union office and the international remits to the local union. I knew that the union would notify the company not to collect "check-off" dues after I had been expelled and that could result in my dismissal from the job if the company so desired.

So, I conferred with Kenneth McClaskey, a field examiner of the NLRB, as to what to do. He advised that I try to pay the dues by

sending them to the international office each month with a demand
of a signature on a return receipt. I did that for two years without
receiving any cancelled checks or acknowledgment about the
money. Then I wrote to the international asking why my checks
were not being cancelled and returned to me. The international
sent me a letter expressing total ignorance about the checks. Then
within two weeks all the checks arrived in the mail without having
been cancelled. I took that bundle to the NLRB to show them what
had happened. McClaskey advised me that I had done everything
possible and that they would stand behind me if the company or
union made any further attempt to force me off the job. A relatively
short time later I learned that McClaskey committed suicide because
he had been harassed endlessly over a short affiliation he allegedly
had with the Communist party in England when he was a Rhodes
scholar there.

November 5, 1954, foreman Orcucci allowed me to have a conference with him about my job status. I advised him that the NLRB
had told me that under Section 9–A, I was protected on the job, so
I wanted the company to provide me with an individual seniority
line. He did not satisfy my request. In fact there was no answer.

Throughout the remainder of 1954 and 1955 the company imposed special restrictions on me. The orders were that I was not
allowed to use my calculator to figure tonnage rates, I was not to
read, I was not to take my bag of personal items to the job. I was
not allowed to visit workers in other departments.

It became obvious that there was a coordinated and thoroughly
planned attack being made on me in spite of the fact that for years it
was a standard custom throughout the plant for workers to read or
rest when their labors were completed for a brief period. In the 22″
Mill Department we usually busied ourselves with mending tools
such as bars, squaring up hearths in old furnaces, and adjusting
supplies so that when the mill started up we would be able to furnish the hot steel as the mill could use it. Then, when those routine
chores were taken care of, we relaxed, and some did read. I often
used that time to do a lot of calculating on the incentive pay from
the tonnage reports. I also knitted sometimes because it helped to
keep me awake and was a useful hobby that permitted me to make
mittens for children, stoles for women, socks for men, and other
useful items.

Finally I became exasperated at the special harassment being
imposed on me and sought help from the U.S. Department of La-

bor. I understood that there was some provision in the labor laws that required unions to have on record with the department the rules of its procedure about expelling members. I had a suspicion that something was out of order or illegal in the way the Union expelled me. So on November 21, 1955, I wrote to Secretary of Labor James Mitchell, recounting the experience I had gone through with the Steelworkers union and asked if that procedure complied with the law, and asked what the law did provide. Stuart Rothman, Solicitor of Labor, answered my request with an elaborate explanation that the information I asked for could not be furnished to a person who was not a member of that union. I repeated my request to Mitchell, and got another answer from Rothman which closed the door on me. I found out that the Taft-Hartley Act protected the international union officials against the lowly individual union member. I felt there was a broad conspiracy operating against me.

ᏉᎧ

LIBEL SUIT AND AFTER

ᏉᎧ

After exhausting all other courses open to protect my job, I spent endless amounts of time with my attorney, Kenneth A. MacDonald, in an effort to accumulate persuasive evidence for the libel trial. We obtained pretrial depositions from all the defendents in which many expressions of hatred and disagreement with me were obtained. MacDonald told me they constituted good evidence with which to press my case.

The trial started on October 29, 1956, before Judge William J. Wilkins, who had served in the Nuremberg trials of the Nazis, which made me think he would be fair. But now I think I was wrong about that.

The Defense insisted on a jury trial. After the jury was selected my counsel made an opening statement briefly outlining how I had been injured by the actions of those I was suing. The defense counsel, John Spellman, a Republican who was later elected Washington's Governor, made an opening statement denying all claims made by my counsel. Then the witnesses testified. Robert Petris, chairman of the union trial board, confirmed the findings of the board that I should step out of union office but not be expelled. Ole Johnson corroborated Petris. International representative Furman testified that it was his job to enforce the union constitution on the local. International representative Mathews claimed he had nothing to do with the case.

Robert Ferguson, the local union treasurer, reported that he had discussed my possible expulsion with Mathews, Thimmes, and international attorney Arthur Goldberg in 1953 and with Charles Smith, Chris Gellepis, and Mr. Shewmake, and other international representatives. He stated that he disagreed with me over: relations with international union representatives; material in the union bulletins; endorsement of political candidates like Hugh Mitchell (I had opposed contributing union money to him because I thought he was too weak as a candidate); politics of organized labor; grievance procedures; and using the NLRB. Ferguson said he always doubted that my expulsion from the Communist party was genuine.

Walter Bloxam testified that I was very active in the union and was doing good work. Phil Miller testified that he knew me, but not much about me. Harry Nelson declared that the Burke-Doherty Commission failed to take its record under oath. Former local president James McCarthy testified that he solicited signatures from members for the petition demanding my expulsion from the union.

David H. Adams, president of the local union, testified that I had been doing a job for the union like it had never been done before. He reported having had a conference with Mathews, who warned him that if he didn't run the local union the way the international wanted it, Mathews would "get" him. After the expulsion petition was circulated many members were afraid that association with me would hurt them, too.

Joe Candido, a mechanic, reported that he saw Gilland attempt to destroy the calculations I was making on the new incentive pay rates. Jack Hoy declared that I served the local union faithfully. La-Verne Crossen, the local industrial relations official for the Bethlehem Steel Corporation, admitted that he saw the petition being circulated in the Open Hearth Department and other departments and made no objection to it. He also testified that before the petition was circulated, he had discussions with Mathews on how to get rid of me.

The witnesses for my side of the case faithfully supported me. The witnesses for the defense faithfully supported their side.

On November 1, 1956, Judge Wilkins interrupted the trial to render an oral opinion dismissing the suit. The judge dismissed the case on the ground that the expulsion was consistent with Gilland's claim that I was acting subversively in the union and that I had indeed acted in a subversive manner; furthermore, the claims of my subversive activity were an internal affair of the union and that I had not been maligned before a third party. That reasoning seems incredible because it twists the facts beyond recognition.

Attorney MacDonald always said I was entitled to my day in court. The way it turned out, I did not have my day. In the first place, the Judge accepted as a fact Gilland's claim that I forced Lenin's book "What Is To Be Done" on him. In the second place, I do not think my attorney made much of an effort to show Gilland's story to be transparent lies. Then, in his decision to dismiss my case, the Judge quoted some decisions which stated that "On certain occasions one is qualifiedly or conditionally privileged to publish false and defamatory matter of another and is not libel therefore, provided such privilege is not abused." So the judge contradicted all the logic of the facts. The case's dismissal left me without further recourse. I did not have the money to make an appeal and had to drop the legal route.

I summarize the results of this libel case in the following way. The major purpose of the case was to obtain redress through legal means to correct the injustice meted out by the international union in collaboration with the company. A side value was to challenge the "class angle" contention about the role of the courts against the working class. Being in court did save my job. The company had to restrain it harassment of me. The trial did fulfill a promise to carry the case to my ultimate ability. It did obtain under oath testimony revealing the international union's persecution of local union officers. We failed to show affirmatively my constructive achievements and good reputation in the union. The relations between my counsel and myself deteriorated during the course of the trail. My counsel failed to present enough facts favorable to me in the court or to expose Gilland's initial lie about the book. By dismissing the case before it could be considered by the jury, this court denied me the redress initially sought. My counsel had many conferences with the judge, in chambers, whose substance was never reported to me. During the trial, I saw my counsel walk down the stairs in the Court House several times with Tyler Hull of Bogle, Bogle, and Gates, the counsel for Bethlehem Steel, having animated discussions. Nothing was ever reported to me about those side conferences.

There were significant dangers to civil rights in the judge's decision such as: the notions that the plaintiff, me, was in fact subversive as the petition claims; and that use of privilege allows a lie and malice to be accepted as a legal fact.

So the union and the collusion of the United States Department of Labor thwarted all my efforts to get my union membership restored. My efforts revealed that there is a heavy hand in the Department of Labor working against the efforts of individual workers to clear their name after they have been framed like I was.

On December 31, 1956, I was invited by Jim Woodside, a fellow steelworker, to attend a peculiar New Year's Eve Party at the University of Washington. Jim was a fellow steelworker in the fabricating plant who maintained active consultation relations with some University of Washington metal researchers. Several high officials of the U. of W. were there and singled me out to make an emphatic point. They advised me that they did not like the House UnAmerican Activities Committee investigation of the University faculty because it upset the University's program of keeping track of, and thereby controlling, their own campus radicals. They insistently urged me not to testify anymore about the Communist party and its inroads on the campus. I answered that it was out of my hands.

Defeated by the international union, refused help from the U.S. Department of Labor, and finally denied justice by the court, I turned to new and different avenues to try to live a full life.

I saw an advertising circular which urged workers to take a study course from the Lincoln Extension Institute, which trained foremen. I thought it a good idea to get a better understanding of the subject so I signed up for the course and obtained a certificate of graduation. At the end of the course, a Mr. Hagen from the Lincoln Institute visited me and urged me to apply for a job as a foreman with Bethlehem Steel Corporation. When I explained to him that I had a long struggle with the company and had been defeated, he agreed with me that I was not a suitable candidate to move in that direction; besides, I was nearing retirement age.

I got curious about the financial condition of the company and bought a couple shares of stock, one common, one preferred. The Company sent me lots of information about stockholders meetings to which I was invited. But I could not attend because they were always in Delaware.

I played golf with an operations department man in the Seattle-First National Bank, a good friend who urged me to invest in that bank. So I bought several shares in it. That caused me to be invited and I did attend several meetings of the bank stockholders. There I observed that the meetings were controlled by blocs of proxy votes held by a few people who limited any discussion to increasing the capital growth of the bank. Everything was promotion to expand. A few years later I sold all my stock at a good profit.

I received an invitation to join the American Management Association and did for a few years, but dropped out when they began to double their membership fees. There I learned that the primary goal of business was to "maximize profits" regardless of the social consequences. They stressed the necessity for all businesses to make long range plans on their profit schedules and stressed the requirement to modernize with the most advanced equipment. The use of computers was bound to completely change the qualifications of human employees. All this management discussion was consistent with the practical experience of the working class under capitalism.

After one of the AMA seminar sessions I spoke to the leader about having attended district conventions of the Communist party and a district conference of the American Legion and found that they conducted their meetings almost identically. In each organization a leader reviewed the previously adopted program, criticized their failures, adopted new objectives and promised to do better in the future. The AMA leader nodded an understanding of what I was stating and commented that what I said simply proved an AMA principle that there are constant principles that apply to the success of all organizations. Only their purposes are different.

From May 23, 1964, to July 1, 1966, I had the following medical record:

—Bleeding hemorrhoids and bleeding urinary ulcer, 1964.

—104 visits and consultations with doctors.

—1 Systoscopic examination which caused a ruptured bladder. Following emergency surgery at midnight, my body was paralyzed. It took 12 days to recover in West Seattle Hospital.

—1 Pylogram, negative (looking for kidney stones).

—1 Gall Bladder X-ray (negative).

—1 Lactose test (negative, no apparent diabetes).

—1 Monilia test (negative).

—1 Twelve-hour gastric flow test, excessive.

—6 Bursitis X-Rays, resulting diagnosis permanent partial bilateral disability (both shoulders).

Dr. Ed. Speir's surgery in 1965 removed a crater in my duodenum, removed the appendix, severed the Vagus nerve, and enlarged the outlet of my stomach which had been puckered from numerous ulcers which healed. He rearranged the intestines to a normal configuration (a birth defect placed the appendix high under the ribs). He reported that he examined the entire length of the intestines but found no abnormalities such as tumors, polyps or cancers.

During that two-year period, May, 1964, through June, 1966, my health problems interrupted my work so much that when I had a defensive argument with the Company supervision it was clear I had reached the end of my physical ability to adequately defend myself and protect my employment at Bethlehem Steel.

Malcom M. Mosley, the mill superintendent, stepped into the middle of an argument I was having with the foremen. My argument was over their abuse of scheduling so that we had long delays which wiped out the earnings we had made working at the incentive pace. I contended they were incompetent and deliberately destroying our efforts to earn more money. There were bitter exchanges between the foremen and myself which could not be resolved.

Mosley ordered me suspended with intent to discharge. I filed a grievance which the union processed to the fourth step, just a step from arbitration. Though I had been expelled from the union, I was still working in the plant, and by law, the union was the only legal bargaining agent for all the workers there, including me. I had to follow the union procedure, and the union had to represent me, which they did. When the company representative from back East came to process the fourth step I asked the union fourth step man, Carl Jones, to obtain my retirement by mutual consent as provided in the union contract. Jones made that proposal and the company readily agreed. Both sides preferred the mutual agreement, and it was a necessity for me because my health was broken and I could no longer stand any strain of conflict.

June 30, 1966, was my last day with Bethlehem Steel Corporation. Financially, I could not make a go of it with the minimum pension from Bethlehem which was $100 a month at that time. So by July 8th, 1966, I decided I would have to find other work to survive. I went to the Unemployment Compensation office and explained my situation to a Mrs. Scales who re-classified me from a furnace helper to a materials handler and a clerk for a job search. I advised her that I had longshore experience, had taught school, and had Army administration experience.

On July 11, 1966, I saw an advertisement in the newspapers soliciting clerks to check cargo on the waterfront. I made the rounds meeting various longshore union officials and applying for a clerk's job. By August 2nd, I took the checkers test, passed, and began working right away. I was ordered to apply for Navy and Coast Guard passes. The Coast Guard issued the pass upon application, but the Navy held back until I asked Senator Warren Magnuson, who had known me for over thirty years, for help. His influence got the Navy pass for me after over a year's delay.

In the meantime I encountered many old Communists who knew me. Most of them avoided being around me or working with me. But total avoidance was impossible. Some of them tried to ignore my directions for sorting freight, but the foremen stepped in and directed them to carry out their duties. One person whom I did not know did try to intimidate me by taking a couple of swings at me because of my testifying before the House UnAmerican Committee. His swings did not reach me, and his threats to get me later never materialized. He threatened that he would get me outside the gate and "cut my heart out". I replied that I'd protect myself and it would be to his disadvantage. By that time a guard and the foreman came over to see what was happening. The foreman ordered the longshoremen watching to get to work sorting the freight. I later submitted an affidavit regarding this incident to the Seattle Police and the County Prosecutor, and a copy to the FBI. The County Prosecutor's assistant advised me that it would not serve a good purpose to attempt to prosecute my attacker and that I could not bring a suit without the risk of a counter suit which I'd probably lose considering the general political attitudes prevailing at that time.

By the end of 1971, my health broke down so far that I could no longer do even the light physical work of a checker, so I applied for my retirement at age 63 and retired from work in January, 1972.

My first efforts in retirement were to relax, play lots of golf and hope to recover my strength. I took in many symphonies and traveling road shows that filled in the gaps left from being so tied to the union work. Because of my union work, I had no recreation over a long period of time. But as I tried to make up for that gap my health problems overwhelmed me. Doctors found my heart beat to be very irregular and was slowing down below forty, so they installed a pacemaker. But that did not solve the general deterioration. Two arteriograms showed severe coronary artery disease, with blockages tight against the heart muscle. Against the advice of six of his associates, Dr. Lester R. Sauvage reluctantly did a three by-pass open-heart surgery on me January 26, 1976. For five years after that there was no angina. Since 1981 the angina has reappeared. This condition caused me to use increasing amounts of nitroglycerine paste and tablets.

At the end of 1982, my supplemental Medicare contract was cancelled because the carrier claimed that Medicare imposed restrictions on them that made it impossible for them to continue the extensive service I had been getting from them. I had to apply to the Veterans Administration in January, 1983, to take over my medical care. I was entitled to this because of "service incurred disability". By then my accumulated medical problems included: nephritis (kidney stones); gout; dry alcoholic; arthritis, hands and back; fourth heart pacer; hemorrhoids; enlarged prostate; prostate cancer; coronary artery disease; diabetes; peripheral vascular disease; and a T.I.A. (Transient Ischemic Attack, which is next door to a stroke, probably from a restriction in the arteries in the back of the neck). I had metastasized cancer which showed on a bone scan and CAT scan in 1986, but after taking massive doses of vitamin C and undergoing an orkiectomy (castration) it seems to be arrested and partly receded according to a recent bone scan. There is diabetic degeneration in my left eye which has been treated with laser beams with some success. In 1987, I received a "whip-lash" and back injury from an automobile rear-end collision. My health seems stable at this time, so I know from experience that the human body has miraculous powers of recovery.

In 1979, I received an invitation to join a group to tour the People's Republic of China because I was on the mailing list of the *Peking Review* for many years. At the last moment, I decided to join that tour with the China Booksellers of San Francisco, California. I had just enough savings to pay for that trip, about $2800.

I was in the second group allowed inside China after the fall of the "Gang of Four." The tour guides and leaders did speak of the almost total chaos that prevailed during the ten year reign of that Gang; we tourists could see for ourselves that mainland China had suffered extensive destruction. Most of us were very favorably impressed with the efforts the Chinese were making to overcome the losses. Schools had been destroyed, many valuable activities had been stopped and there were reports that probably a million people had lost their lives during those ten years of chaos at the hands of the Gang of Four. In spite of it all we were entertained lavishly, were escorted to numerous sites of historical importance, and met with some Communist Party Central Committee members who discussed their domestic and foreign policy with us, explaining that they would overcome the mistakes that had been made. Near the end of our visit some of the leaders admitted that Mao was responsible for the errors of judgment that caused the Cultural Revolution.

One of the leaders I met told me it was his judgment that there was no prospect for a proletarian revolution within the foreseeable future in the United States. For that reason, among others, China was determined to work to keep world peace so they could modernize their nation and exert a positive influence throughout the world. He said no geopolitical influence would be allowed to trap China on the side of either Soviet Russia or the United States.

I came away from China feeling assured that the Chinese leaders knew what they were doing and were determined to keep on doing it. They frequently declared their intent to build socialism by experimenting as they go along. They expressed rejection of the methods being used in the Soviet Union. They admitted they did not know any exact sure-fire route to socialism, but contended they would find the way in spite of all obstacles. They made it plain the "open door" was permanent. They insisted that China will apply scientific methods by testing ideas in practice, and that is a fundamental part of the road to socialism!

ે**

CONCLUSIONS

ે**

During my life, I have tried to function with a social conscience. My academic learning in schools supported my efforts to correct existing injustices in a class society. My purpose was to serve humanity as a whole through emancipating the working class. My studies were to search for answers to the many problems that I became acquainted with. This chapter gives my judgment about my experiences.

My background provided the foundation for a social conscience because early on in life I became aware of the deprivations imposed on most working people. Born into poverty, most workers could not satisfy their basic requirements for a full life. Health, nourishment, and culture were lacking. As I observed the lives of my mother and father I heard them question the worth of their existences. Their religious beliefs did not give satisfactory answers to their needs. That bothered me as a child because there didn't seem to be any answer for anyone.

There came a time when experience and education promised that things could be better, and ought to be. But then the great depression revealed hunger, disease, poverty, and war had encroached upon us in spite of knowledge that we should have enough intelligence to be able to avoid those disasters.

My active participation in the Communist party extended from November, 1931, to October 1947, with two interruptions—one when in the CCC from April 1933 to July 1935; the second when in the Army of the United States from August, 1943 to October, 1945. And from March, 1947, until my expulsion October, 1947, I was under a cloud of suspicion which inactivated me. There were a couple of other minor periods when I was in disfavor because of policy disagreements with some of the top District party leaders.

The Communist party and the theories of Marxism projected a new hope for solving the problems of mankind. My experience with

Communist party policies seemed to be consistent with theory during the early years of my membership. Then I began to observe what seemed to be sound theories fail in spite of our best efforts. Their failures gave me growing concern. As party organizer in Bellingham I found out that there were no sure methods by which to overcome adversity. I did experiment in the application of party theories and found they worked when applied flexibly and realistically. I soon learned that all political movements have similarities which depend for their successes on the integrity of their leaders.

The CCC was an experience in rehabilitation. I was demoralized before I went in, and inspired with new hopes when I came out. The outdoor life and necessarily clean habits restored my vitality. As a waterfront worker I learned about the reality of hard work when academic knowledge was applied consciously. The mobilization which produced the 1936 Labor Day Parade proved the class conscious union movement could make a mass show of power when it tried. The P-I strike proved that white collar workers could organize and win. After the P-I strike, the west coast maritime workers struck to preserve their unions and won. The Seattle unions entered the city political campaign in 1937 and won with candidate DeLacy. The McCleary Lumber Mill workers fought off the violent attack of the State Patrol by maintaining solidarity within their ranks and persuading the rest of the labor movement to back them up. Ultimately, the NLRB ordered McCleary to bargain with the union.

The CIO movement came on with a great promise but was undercut because of what I think was deception by the leaders who diverted the stirrings for working class emancipation into obedience and acceptance of the capitalist system through industrial unionism.

My libel suit succeeded in protecting my job when I was under attack by the company and the international union. But it did not help my fellow workers solve their problems. I did not find justice in "my day in court".

My various expulsions were revealing because they showed how established institutions enforce their discipline to oppose a challenge. The most consistent element in all these confrontations was my resistence to being bound or committed to something I did not believe or accept. I found out that when an individual becomes "organized" it means that he or she has given up certain individual rights to help strengthen some group. As long as the group adds to the strength of the individual that organization is beneficial. But when it deprives the individual of his benefits that condition should be challenged. I was in that predicament many times.

I firmly believe that the various government intelligence agencies intervened on the side of the employers many times to suppress my (and my family's) efforts on behalf of our fellow workers. Some of them are fully known to me. Others seem to be disguised so I cannot prove them. But I can relate some of these incidents.

I begin with my grandfather Dennett, who was restricted to the borders of his farm during the First World War because he had been arrested earlier for participating in the 1912 Socialist and IWW free speech fight in Portland, Oregon. I have already reported my father's and grandfather's fights with the Ku Klux Klan in the 1890s. When I was in Bellingham, 1932–33, I was informed by some friends (who were being solicited for membership to the Klan) that a newly organized KKK Klavern was devising a plan to drive me physically out of the city. My friends later advised me that the Klan was unable to get anyone to agree to do the dirty job, so the plan was abandoned.

My administrative discharge (expulsion) from the CCC resulted from an officer's panic because the military was ignorant of how to handle anything except what was ordered from above. New ideas were forbidden, especially anything studying political movements.

The FBI pursued me when Bethlehem Steel Corporation hired me in 1942. They required the company to obtain answers from me to a very long questionaire. I still have a copy of it. No one else at the plant was ever scrutinized like I was. During the national CIO attack on me in the State CIO council, one of John L. Lewis' Regional Directors, Richard Francis, hired an assistant, Slavo Brozovitch, who was a deputy sheriff who frequently conferred with the FBI. (I have been told these discussions were about me.) Attorney James J. Molthan, who did some legal work for Richard Francis regarding the Cannery Workers with whom I was concerned, stopped an NLRB hearing one time because I was in the room when they got to some questions which he identified as relating to national security. He prevailed on the hearing officer to delay the proceedings until I left the room. Seattle FBI Agent McFarland frequently conferred with Richard Francis advising him about my Communist party activities and meetings I had held with other Communists. (McFarland had legitimately pried into the affairs of the State CIO when investigating our complaint to the Justice Department, in a resolution adopted at one of our conventions, about monopoly practices of the Teamsters union with some employers which obstructed the organization of the International Woodworkers of America log haulers.)

The AFL expelled my union, the Inlandboatmen, because it voted to go CIO, which was not a crime, and we were not "dual" to any other AFL union.

The national CIO removed me from the State CIO Council office, without preferring charges or conducting a trial. No violations of CIO constitution or policies were ever claimed.

The United Steelworkers union expelled me on a false claim that I was a Communist subversive even though there was a public record proving that I had been expelled from the Communist party seven years earlier.

The Communist party itself out-did all the others by constructing a LIE, claiming that I was an enemy FBI agent, something which was not even listed as a violation of the Communist Constitution. Some of the local FBI agents did spread word around that they thought my expulsion was a fake to allow me to get in the Party "underground" apparatus. That was absurd idle speculation and very confusing to everyone.

Those many experiences demonstrate how organizations impose their will on individuals to control them. Most professional organizations call that a discipline. They compel the individual to follow a prescribed path or suffer penalties. The system has merit when used intelligently. But it is disastrous when abused. My experience convinces me that some times, if not at all times, I was a victim of overworked intelligence elements too ignorant to comprehend the validity of a social conscience attempting to improve the condition of humanity.

The conditions that caused me to adopt a belief in socialism still exist. Capitalism's social organization is controlled by a class conscious element who operate behind the scenes controlling the wealth, the property and the government power. They call this a democracy but in most instances the election process is so controlled that the "uncrowned" ruling class prevail in most decisions which render a profit for the rich. I served on the Community Chest Board and observed how the "invisible" government was manipulated by professionals who used "charity" to perpetuate the private control of the capitalist system. While it is true that the capitalist system has increased our material comforts by producing various surpluses from which it made a profit, it has not provided economic security or educational and cultural progress for the "masses". In the United States of America we still lack a national health care program to protect everyone. And a very large proportion of this nation's people are still below the economic poverty level that President Franklin Roosevelt condemned fifty years ago. The politicians in power have failed to fulfill the promise of addressing the issues that affect the second, third, and now a fourth generation who depend on welfare.

Domestic American political activity, securing the power to govern, is predominantly class struggle in which an open or concealed ruling class keeps the working class in subjection. Some minorities are stirring. But the women majority segment are still held back unfairly. It is still "a man's world". That must and will change.

War, preparing for it, conducting it, winning it, and now losing it are the major activities of capitalist nations. We have reached a place where it is now necessary to make world peace our primary objective. That will require a revision of the rival policies in socialist as well as capitalist nations. Disarmament activities must come to the fore and continue until all nations and people are safe in their homes.

I believe the Communist party's many successes in the northwest and on the Pacific coast were achieved because there was a large reservoir of workers in this area who had at some time been influenced ideologically by the propaganda and teachings of the old Industrial Workers of the World, the old Socialist party of Debs, and the honest teachings attempted by the early Communist party. I had the privilege to be an activist who was often free to get in the center of working class action at the "right" time and was somewhat ready for it from previous experience and extensive study.

I think it is appropriate here to remind the present beneficiaries of public assistance and social legislation that what they benefit from now was won after enormous sacrificies made through sit-ins, hunger marches, and strikes during the 1930s, led mainly by the Communist party activists. It was a most patriotic effort to save America.

My experience in the CIO convinces me that the whole movement was a political fraud, and the Communist party pursued a fatal opportunistic policy in it. The purpose of organizing the CIO was to *get control of the workers, not to emancipate them.* The method was to organize industrial unions and keep the workers tied to the capitalist system without revealing this fact.

Later experience demonstrated to me that the entire labor movement is at the mercy of the United States government because most
of the existing labor legislation is administered by the Department
of Labor to control the workers for the employers.

I found that the Steelworkers' union was concealing its policy of
controlling the workers for the employers by claiming that the Local
Union had no bargaining rights; that the union contract belonged to
the international union, not to the local union. Everything the international representatives did was restrictive of Local Union #1208.
And to this day the "old timers" don't accept this policy because
it grossly violates the original CIO promise to organize and
strengthen the workers. In practice to organize "from the top
down," as in the Steelworkers case, operated to deprive the worker
of his original individual bargaining rights without making com-
pensating improvements in the working conditions.

When Judge Wilkins dismissed my libel suit he made a decision
that overrode the union trial board. Wilkins asserted the trial board
"would have been justified in finding (me) guilty of subversion
which it did not." At no time did the Judge define what he meant
by "subversion." No evidence proving it existed, or was presented,
except the reference Gilland made to a pamphlet written in 1902,
Lenin's "What Is To Be Done". The judge also recorded that my
counsel did not develop evidence about malice, and left an inference that the libel claim had not been adequately presented to the
court. When he rendered his decision it sounded to me as if his
decision was based on the evidence in the precedent citation he was
quoting, not on the facts in my case. Because Judge Wilkins participated in the Nuremberg trials of the Nazis I thought he would
have been objective in my case. Therefore, I did not advise my
counsel to seek a change of judges. It appears to me now that was a
mistake. I think Wilkins also knew that we were not able to make
any appeal because we did not have any money with which to
proceed.

I believe there are those in the United States who want to govern by naked military methods that would promote a fascist terror
here against all learning and freedom of thought. They know they
are not ruling for the working people and really rely on force to
govern. There is need for an alert to halt the efforts at "thought-
control" in violation of the guarantees in the First Amendment to
the U.S. Constitution which guarantees freedom and democracy.
We must restore and promote the "unalienable" right to advocate

economic and political change as a necessary freedom of citizenship in the United States of America. The Declaration of Independence proclaims that those rights are ours, and President Lincoln expanded on those ideals in his Second Inaugural Address which has been chiseled in stone on the Lincoln Memorial in Washington, D.C. And the Constitution's Preamble declares:

> We the people of the United States, in order to form a more perfect union, establish justice, insure domestic tranquility, provide for the common defense, promote the general welfare, and secure the blessings of liberty to ourselves and our posterity, do ordain and establish this Constitution for the United States of America.

I believe we are duty bound to do everything necessary to protect and preserve these freedoms established by our forebears.

The Communist party of the United States of America was organized to "Defend the Soviet Union". The reason for that is found in the history of the Bolshevik Socialist revolution of 1917 in Russia, when the military intervention by the Allies tried to crush the first workers' socialist government by organizing and supporting "white-Russian" armies who conducted several civil war expeditions against the Soviets. Although the Red army beat back the counter-revolution within its borders, it had to sacrifice its party-soldier resources which weakened its internal political structure, and on the borders there remained hostile military forces which appeared to be attempting to make further efforts to overthrow the Bolshevik-Soviet government. One reason that opportunity did not occur was the success of Communist parties throughout the world latently challenging their capitalist governments not to make war on the Soviet Union. Lenin appealed to workers throughout the world to prevent their capitalist governments from making war by threatening to turn such a war into a civil war with the object of overturning capitalism and establishing socialism in its place. That threat was very real. The capitalist governments were militarily strong but they had to fear that the workers would revolt against the government and do what Lenin advocated. Nevertheless *Lenin expressed a belief that it was inevitable that the capitalist world would eventually attack the socialist world. And that belief was the foundation of Soviet foreign policy* until the present time (1988). But, "as of 1986, China's leadership made it clear that relations between nations transcend differences in ideology and social systems and abandoned the belief

that a war between capitalism and Communism is inevitable."
(Quote Zi Zhongyun, a professor at Beijing's Chinese Academy of
Social Sciences' Institute of American Studies, *Beijing Review*, May
9–15, 1988)

Lenin's theory and policy had deep roots in the socialist movement organized in the Second International, which spread throughout the world. For many years Lenin had fought against the old
socialist leaders who permitted their organizations to support their
own nations when at war against others. Lenin demanded that
workers not be victimized by fighting each other for capitalist profits. That way Lenin opposed the capitalist wars. The old socialists
allowed themselves to submit to the patriotic wishes of their capitalist governments which resulted in the useless slaughter of victims
who lost everything with nothing to gain.

Lenin's doctrines were adopted by the world wide organization
of Communist parties known as the Comintern, or Third International. Inherent in this doctrine was the requirement to make the
"defense of the Soviet Union" the foremost part of the Communist
program. Then in the process of attempting to follow the dictates of
the Comintern the various Communist parties urged the members
and leaders to intensely study the teachings of Lenin and Marx.
When we did that we became inspired with the revolutionary ideas
of Marx and the revolutionary practices of Lenin.

When the Great Depression of the 1930s overwhelmed the
world, workers looked to the successes of the Soviet Union as a new
hope. We believed it was our duty to bring about a Soviet revolution in the United States. We worked tirelessly to win the workers
to support the ideals of socialism and particularly to support the
policies of the Soviet Union, especially our belief that the Soviets
had solved the unemployment problem and almost all the other
problems of capitalism. Then when we studied the writings of
Marx, Engels, Lenin, and Stalin, most of us activists were inspired
with a conviction that our efforts could result in replacing capitalism
with socialism in the United States.

But history now reveals that our efforts were thwarted by international events and the changing world situation which diverted
our efforts from a revolutionary upsurge to supporting Soviet alliances which at times contradicted all our previous socialist theories.
So between the First and Second World Wars, thousands of devoted
activists in the Communist party spent their best efforts in behalf of
the ideals of Socialism and the emancipation of the working class as

projected in the Communist Manifesto, only to see the top party leaders divert us from that course because when the "crunch" occurred with World War II, most of the old sacred principles expounded by the Communist movement were sacrificed on the altar of "expediency". Faithful, loyal, self-sacrificing supporters were arbitrarily ordered to forsake all previous socialist ideals to give one hundred percent and over to the winning of the war against the Fascists. The monstrous changes in party policy, such as the Stalin-Hitler military pact, were too irrational for most of us. How could we change from hating and fighting against Hitler and Fascism to an attitude of approval of Hitler and support of the alliance made by the Soviet Union? It could not be genuinely done. The Soviet invasion of Finland violated international law and was justified as military necessity. But that act fell into the classification of "aggression" which had been previously condemned by Soviet Ambassador Maxim Litvinoff. So when President Roosevelt expressed his condemnation of that aggression the United States Communist party position was a mass of contradictions.

Then when Hitler made the military attack on the Soviet Union it was possible for the Communist party of the U.S. to order all its members to "subordinate the class-struggle" for the "national interests". Civil rights, equal rights for women, the right to strike, democratic rights for all workers; all these principles were removed from the Communist party programs as soon as the western Allies announced they would aid the Soviet Union to defeat the Hitler invasion. At a meeting of the N.W. District Buro of the Communist Party with Earl Browder, General Secretary of the CPUSA, and Wm. Z. Foster, I asked questions about sacrificing these old party policies and was told directly by Browder that we had to give up our old policies and I was personally ordered to do so.

Another event which seemed to me to be a monstrous betrayal was reported by Winston Churchill in his memoirs. In his meetings with Stalin they mutually agreed at the close of the war to give the Balkan oil fields to Russia, Greece back to England, and to share 50–50 the control of Yugoslavia, where neither had any existing military power. Fortunately, Tito and his partisans intervened to prevent that decision from being carried out.

Such Soviet Communist behavior, on top of the earlier deals with Hitler, exemplified everything we had been taught to consider as forbidden imperialism. The old humanitarian ideals of socialism seemed to have been abandoned. The "purge" trials of the 1930s

came back to our attention causing us to challenge their validity.
And later when Krushchev revealed his information about how Stalin persecuted and prosecuted his enemies within the Soviet party
many of us had second thoughts about those old claims that justified the earlier purges.

Through its affiliation with the Communist International the
American Communist party maintained connection with the Soviet
Communist party and obeyed its direction. But when Congress enacted the Voorhis Act making it illegal to maintain affiliation with
foreign organizations, the Communist party at an Emergency National Convention in New York, on November 16, 1940, took the following action:

> "That the Communist Party U.S.A., in Convention as-
> sembled does hereby cancel and dissolve its organizational
> affiliation to the Communist International, as well as any
> and all other bodies of any kind outside the boundaries
> of the United States of America, for the specific purpose of
> removing itself from the terms of the so-called Voorhis
> Act, which originated in the House of Representatives as
> H.R. 10094, which has been enacted and goes into effect
> January 1941, which law would otherwise tend to destroy,
> and would destroy, the position of the Communist Party as
> a legal and open political party of the American Working
> class;
>
> That the Convention reaffirms the unshakable adher-
> ence of our Party of the principles of proletarian interna-
> tionalism, in the spirit of its greatest leaders, and teachers,
> Marx, Engels, Lenin and Stalin, which offer the only road to
> the future for suffering humanity;
>
> That the Convention formally and officially, declares
> that the Communist Party of the United States is responsi-
> ble for no political document, policy, book, article, or other
> expression of political opinion, except such as are issued by
> itself, through its regularly constituted leadership on the ba-
> sis of the Eleventh National Convention deliberations and
> decisions, and of this present Special Convention; . . ."
> (Quoted from Earl Browder, *The Way Out* [NY: International
> Publishers, 1941] page 191–192.)

Since 1940 the classic literature containing the teachings of Marx, Engels, Lenin, Stalin, and all others from which Communist ideas were developed have not been binding on the party. So no one can logically prosecute the party for any of its old "revolutionary" ideas. This situation leaves the Communist party existing in something like a vacuum without clear cut declared revolutionary purposes or methods. It is forced to pursue an ordinary reformist role without clearly defined objectives. The political situation in the world clearly warns that conflicts and problems between nations can no longer be risked for settlement by war, because it could lead to an exchange of nuclear weapons. So this change compels all thinking leaders to exercise a reasoning process to cope with reality.

My experience compels me to conclude that the Communist party in the United States has failed to fulfill their earlier promise of being the main hope for the emancipation of the working class. Fifty years later I must express a judgment that the Communist party, USA, cannot fulfill that promise because there are fundamental flaws in the Marxist theories they hold. In the first place, Marx did not devise solutions to all existing economic problems. And the practice of "Democratic Centralism" is destructive of democracy and sound logic. A compulsion to accept a policy one does not approve is self–defeating. By tradition and practice the Communist party, USA, is tied to the tail of the Soviet Union, applauding it generously and uncritically. I think the unsound policies and methods pursued by the CPUSA have so corrupted it that it no longer serves a constructive purpose. Vivid in my memory is the fact that when I was engaged in struggles for the workers against Bethlehem Steel, not once did the Communist party express any views in support of the workers. Not once did the Communist party support my efforts on behalf of the workers in steel. My expulsion from the Party was used to help the company and the union to remove me from spearheading the cause of the workers in the bargaining process.

My experiences make me believe that new and different efforts need to be made to formulate realistic progress to overcome the suffering of the "one third of the nation" still existing below the economic poverty income level. I now believe that adversial confrontations are the wrong methods for resolving conflicts. I think they are in fact a disguised form of the class struggle where those in power inflict their will on the opponent regardless of justice to all.

What is needed is an objective view of society, not just one section at the disadvantage of all the others.

I think that will require a wider coalition of political forces committed to enhancing the progress of the lowest among us to rise to our best. As of now, I don't see the outlines of that group, but I am confident that it will have to develop because the "top" cannot survive without including the "bottom" among the beneficiaries of the economic and social system.

The traditional goal of business and management in the United States is to get ahead of the competitors to stay in business and where possible to "maximize" the profit. The basic weakness of that formulation is that it leaves out responsibility for the welfare of all the people. We are approaching a situation where it will become necessary to plan for the survival of all human beings under conditions which make it possible for them to develop their maximum potential where the social conscience is the prevailing behavior pattern. We must all become contributors to the welfare of humanity and the whole ecological environment. The facts of science already warn us to stop "fouling the nest" with overexploitation and disregard of the consequences of allowing any section of humanity to wastefully use up the resources of this planet which must be available for everybody's benefit. We must not imitate the lemmings, who blindly mass self-destruct. Alexis de Tocqueville, a French social science authority, studied the early American effort to develop Democracy and rendered a strong warning to us to protect the rights of dissidents and not allow the tyranny of the majority to suppress and destroy minority opponents and ideas. In one place he says, "A new science of politics is needed for a new world." That was written in the 1830s. I think it is still a valid goal.

I feel certain that it can be done and will be done when enough of the responsible leaders in positions of power exert their influence in a rational direction. Class-struggle politics seems to miss the mark because the combatants are consumed in the conflict. The major objective of an army is to destroy the other side's ability to fight. In that process the participants on both, or all, sides, also lose their ability to survive.

I think China's current experience is changing the time perspective in which huge political and social change, like from capitalism to socialism, can be accomplished. It requires a much longer period of time than we have been in the habit of considering. For example, history demonstrates that it took the capitalist system over a thousand years to replace feudalism. This process lasted roughly from the decline of the Roman empire to the Industrial Revolution. An endless string of legal decisions and government changes were required in many feudal states before the capitalist system was allowed to function in place of feudal kingdoms. (See *Law and The Rise of Capitalism* by Michael E. Tiger and Madeline R. Levi, 1977, Monthly Review Press.) Remember "usury", interest on loans, was not allowed to gentiles during the Middle Ages. And Shakespeare's "Merchant of Venice", written during the late Renaissance period, relates a serious problem over "usury". I think there is need to take a deeper look at China and Russia which are contemporary living examples of the difficulties and successes of attempts to make major economic, social, and political changes. It is going to be necessary for the whole world to carefully monitor their experiences objectively.

Capitalism socialized production. The next logical development will be to find a means by which to socialize distribution. That will overcome the misery of those who do the work but do not share equitably in the profits which accrue with efficient socially controlled management. I think that change will occur when the socialized production systems advance to the perfection of automation, computerization, and robots, or something more advanced and as yet unseen which I think is inevitable.

After all its efforts to defeat me, the Bethlehem Steel Corporation disposed of its Seattle plant (after I retired), by claiming to sell it to a private operator who forced the union to accept severe wage cuts and reductions in health and retirement provisions in a new contract with the local union. The international union representatives urged the local workers to accept the new cuts in pay and fringe benefits the company offered, and that is what happened.

The concept of emancipating the working class from exploitation is still a necessary worthy objective of civilization. This emancipation has to be re-analyzed to determine the actual components involved such as education, cultural composition, health care, societal integration, government participation, creative development, and recreation. These elements need to be studied to ascertain their impact on the working class. Most likely there are more elements which belong in this mosaic. They will make their existence known as other studies progress. Present working conditions in the mass production industries impose injurious health conditions on too many workers. Hours of work and excessive commuting distances from work deprive workers of the social benefits they require for a full life such as participating in the family life they all deserve.

As I near the end of my life and look back on what I did, I am proud to have participated in the living struggles to the fullest extent possible. I did the best I knew.

APPENDIXES

APPENDIX 1

The following was in the Agitprop files when I arrived in 1932. It was used to initiate new members before I came. I did not use it because I thought it was too severe and would scare members away.

Revolutionary Greetings

DEAR COMRADE:

Today you have become a full-fledged member of the Communist party of the United States and of the Communist International. We welcome you in our ranks as a new recruit to the international army of millions, who, under the banner of Leninism, is fighting for the emancipation of mankind from the yoke of capitalism.

We greet you in the name of those proletarian fighters whom capitalist "justice" has thrown into its jails and prisons.

We greet you in the name of those comrades whom the murderously brutal capitalist police have killed on the picket line and in workers' demonstrations. We greet you as one who steps into the ranks of revolutionists to finish with us what they died for, Proletarian Revolution.

We greet you in the name of the millions of Communists the world over, with whom we are joined in our World Party. The Communist International.

We greet you in the name of the Russian Bolsheviks, whose example you are obliged to follow.

We remind you that through your voluntary entrance into our Party you have pledged yourself to carry by all means the struggle for the overthrow of bourgeois rule in accordance with the decisions of the Party. From now on, the decisions of the Party and the decisions of the Communist International are your highest command. The duties of solidarity and discipline in struggle are not easy and you must take them seriously. You have not merely come to us to manifest your approval of us and to pay dues. If you want to be a Communist then your whole life and all your activities must be devoted to Communism. You cannot be a Party member only in Party meetings. You must be a Communist in your work, in your shop, in your home and in every organization to which you belong. You must fulfill your Communist duty at every post the Party assigns you. If you want to do your duty as a Communist, then you must disregard all taunts and sarcasm, all insults and hate to which all of us are subjected.

You must tirelessly devote yourself to the task of absorbing the tremendous experience which the international proletariat has gained in its struggle for emancipation, and whose expression is Marxism-Leninism. The Proletarian Revolution, the Dictatorship of the Proletariat, demands of each member of the Party that leads the revolution the development of extraordinary abilities, sacrifices and assurance. Think of what the 500,000 Bolsheviks did when under the leadership of Lenin, they led a nation of 160,000,000 people through four years of the sharpest Civil War. For all these great duties, we can offer you only the right as a comrade, with us to decide the role and fate of our Party, the Party which in the visible future will decide over the fate of this country.

Your coming into our Party is our guarantee that you are fully prepared to carry the consequences of membership in the Party—to carry on revolutionary activities under the direction of the Party, and to submit to revolutionary discipline. Without this your membership would not be a sign of your devotion to the revolutionary interests of the working class but a sign of indifference or worse.

If you have decided to march with the Communist Party to the very end, to victory, despite all persecution, despite disappointment, despite hardships and hatred, then comrade be welcome. You may then from today on, call yourself the proud fighting comrade of Ruthenberg, Bill Haywood, John Reed and Lenin, and bear the honored name of Communist, of Bolshevik!

Prove yourself worthy of the Party of Lenin!

With Communist greetings,
COMMUNIST PARTY OF THE U.S.A. CENTRAL COMMITTEE

APPENDIX 2

Following is part of a Party Section Resolution I sent to the Party national office which outlined our situation with the People's Councils in Bellingham. I thought the Party national office approved what I had sent to them when they published this portion.

PARTY ORGANIZER, November-December, 1932

In Struggle Workers Recognize Their Leaders

The People's Council in Whatcom County represents another form of rising radicalization of the workers and also the turning of the small shopkeeper and home owner towards the revolutionary movement. The People's Council was planned and organized by a non-Party worker who attempted to set up an organization modeled after the Soviets, applied to local conditions. He received his greatest assistance from an expelled member of the Party. This expelled member of the Party was used as the face of the new organization and it grew from its inception.

From the outset the name "People's Council" appealed to the workers and farmers here, more so than the Unemployed Council. The hostility of the expelled member to the Party deepened the suspicion among the Party members that the People's Council was an organization in the hands of the Capitalist class. A policy of isolation ensued. With the rapid development of this organization to over 3000 members, it was decided that the policy of ignoring the organization was incorrect. The comrades joined the organization and began to carry on work in the various councils.

As a result of systematic work, the August First demonstration was endorsed by the organization. Because the leaders directly participated in the demonstration, some reactionary elements waged a struggle against the leaders and called a special meeting to expel them from the organization. But the membership defeated these attempts, and the leadership was upheld by the majority of the organization.

The People's Council occupies a unique position here inasmuch as it is a mass organization of struggle. It has entered into the election campaign on an independent ticket, running workers on the basis of a revolutionary program chiefly embracing the demands of the unemployed. The platform includes all the points of the program of struggle contained in the new draft manual of the Unemployed Councils.

The leadership in the People's Council now welcomes the work of the Party within the organization. This is a case, where a mass organization, on a very broad basis, has been formed independent of the Party direction, but which recognizes, however, that the ideas originally came from the Party, applied by non-Party workers and farmers in this county. Much of the success of this organization is due to the foundation laid down by the propaganda work of the Party for the past few years. Its approach is based on the daily needs and struggles of the workers and it uses both the program of the Unemployed Councils and that of the United Farmers League.

In the face of this, it is necessary to point out that there still remains a huge amount of reformist ideology within the ranks of the People's Council, which will require tireless, well directed efforts to overcome. Some of the tendencies which must be eradicated are; chauvinism, opportunism of all shades, the fatal error of "exceptionalism", etc. This was reflected in the election campaign in the attitude of some of the members to fall into the error of voting for the "lesser evil".

All this means that the Party must work with more energy and determination than before. In this work it must carry on a wide campaign of education and training utilizing the best Party literature available—VH [Note: VH are the initials of my Party name which was used in Bellingham, Victor Haines.]

Call to Hunger Marchers to mobilize July 4, 1932, at the State Capitol; the first State Hunger March.

On to Olympia!

All unemployed workers, destitute farmers and progressive citizens with jobs hit the highway in cars, trucks, by train and on foot on the

FOURTH of JULY

Confront Gov. Roland Hartley at the State Capitol with the crying need for a

Special Session of the Legislature

at once to give relief to hungry city workers and bankrupt farmers

Thousands will be there---Spokane, Everett, Yakima, Tacoma, Grays Harbor and Seattle

Make it a real Independence Day Celebration

We'll Stay till Hartley Hears Us

Everybody on their way--50,000 Strong

Bring Blankets and Food for Overnight Stay

CALL ISSUED BY STATE EXECUTIVE COMMITTEE, UNITED PRODUCERS OF WASHINGTON,

M. M. London, Executive Secretary

ON TO THE CAPITOL!!

ALL WORKERS AND DESTITUTE FARMERS join the State hunger march on JULY 4th to demand that Governor Hartley call, at once, a special session of the legislature for:

1 - Immediate cash relief from the state at $15 a week for each man and $3 for each dependent, with no discrimination because of age, sex, color, nationality or political belief.

2 - Unemployment and social insurance at the expense of the state and employers.

3 - No forced labor. $4.50 a day for all relief work. $4.50 a day for all county and state work.

4 - No evictions. No turning off of light, water, gas.

5 - All state funds now used for military purposes, for military roads, national guard, etc., be turned over to the unemployed.

RENOUNCE the **MIS-LEADERSHIP**, and **PLACE** the **HUNGER MARCH** in **CONTROL** of the **RANK** and **FILE**

Assemble at Sylvester Park at 2:00 p. m. July 4th and join the parade to the Capitol.

United Front Rank & File Committee
Thurston County Branch

APPENDIX 4

Call to the Second State Hunger March on January 17, 1933.

ON TO OLYMPIA

ELECT 1000 DELEGATES TO PRESENT THE DEMANDS OF THE UNEMPLOYED AT OLYMPIA, JANUARY 17th, 1933

To all Workers, employed and unemployed, in the State of Washington:
To all organizations of the unemployed:
To all Trade Unions and Fraternal societies:

Brothers:

Hunger threatens thousands of men, women and children in the state of Washington. Relief for unemployed and part-time workers is not sufficient in a single county. In many places there is no relief at all. Even in Seattle, where the amount of relief is above the average for the state, child deaths are increasing. Unable to stand the cold weather because of poor food and clothing, six have died in one small neighborhood within the past two weeks. Thousands of homes are without light and water. Heartless evictions continue. Homes are seized for taxes and assessments. Mortgages are foreclosed.

Governor-elect Martin and the incoming state legislature received votes mainly on promise of relief to the unemployed. Past experience teaches that such promises are only on paper. It is up to the workers of the state to see that real relief is given. This means that we must send our own delegates to Olympia. To do this we must have unity of all workers, and all workers' organizations, based on a common program.

The National Hunger March, just over, brought tremendous pressure to bear on the Federal Government. Militant, united action in the state now stands a better chance than ever of forcing large sums from the Federal Government for state relief. Examples of what can be done are the millions of dollars sent by the Reconstruction Finance Corporation to Chicago and St. Louis as a result of the great UNITED FRONT DEMONSTRATIONS and HUNGER MARCHES in those two cities.

Militant Action Wins

This call for a march on Olympia is issued by a United Front Committee elected at the King County Hunger March, December 5th. This county hunger march teaches two great lessons: (1) Militant united action can win more relief. The demand for more food was granted and increased in several commissaries. (2) It is necessary to have the participation of every locality to get full results. In those parts of King County where the workers listened to misleaders who said, "It is not necessary or wise to take part in demonstrations," the food increase was not given.

Farmers and fishermen, whose conditions in many places are as bad as the conditions of the unemployed, are urged to join in the march. Organizations and groups should organize delegations and instruct these delegations as to what demands to present and as to what ways should be proposed for cooperation of the unemployed with the hard-pressed fishermen and farmers of the state.

A conference of all delegates will be held in Olympia Monday night, Jan. 16th, to decide upon the exact demands to be presented to the Legislature Tuesday morning. Neighborhood groups, organizations, and sectional conferences, called to support the state march, should all discuss the following demands and bring to the Olympia conference any necessary proposals for changes or additions:

1. Immediate emergency cash relief for food and winter clothing. A lump sum of $25 to each unemployed worker; $5 to each of his dependents.

2. Unemployment insurance at the expense of the state and employers. Minimum amount to be $10 a week and $2 additional for each dependent. This insurance to replace commissaries warrants, "relief work," or charity.

(over)

219

3. No evictions; no light, water, or gas shut-offs. No foreclosures, or seizure for taxes and assessments of the homes of unemployed and part-time workers and farmers.

4. Extensive program of public works (roads, dyking to prevent floods, State hospitals) to provide jobs at union wages. Such a program to replace present schemes of forced labor, and plans to force down still further the standard of living by hiring the unemployed worker for a bagful of groceries, and take other men's jobs in the bargain.

5. No discrimination against single workers, women, or youth.

WHAT TO DO!

Organizations, neighborhood groups of workers, mass meetings, should immediately elect delegates and give them credentials. As many delegates should be elected as can possibly be provided with transportation. Work must start at once in procuring trucks, cars, gas, food and banners for the trip. Letters from individuals and resolutions from organizations should be sent to Governor Martin demanding food and housing in Olympia for the marchers. (Martin takes office January 12th, and until then his address is Cheney, Wash.) Funds should be raised at once to finance the work of the State Hunger March Committee. Sent money, copies of credentials of delegates elected, copies of resolutions sent to Martin, all requests for information, and reports on the progress of preparations in your locality to State Hunger March Committee, J. F. McNEW, 814 East 104 Route 12, Seattle, Wash.

PROGRAM FOR MARCHERS

NORTHERN DELEGATION

Bellingham, Anacortes, Bryant, etc., leave by 7. A. M., Monday, January 16th. Welcome Demonstration in Mt. Vernon at 8 A. M., Everett at 10 A .M. Join Eastern Delegation in Seattle at 12 Noon.

EASTERN DELEGATION

Walla Walla, Spokane, etc., leave by 1 P. M. Sunday, January 15th. Stay overnight in Ellensburg. Wenatchee and Yakima join at Ellensburg. Plan to arrive in Seattle at 12 Noon, Monday, January 16th.

Welcome Demonstration in Seattle at 12 Noon for Northern and Eastern Delegations.

Welcome Demonstration in Tacoma at 3 P. M. for Northern, Eastern and Seattle Delegations.

SOUTHERN DELEGATION

Longview and Vancouver leave by 8 A. M. Join at Centralia at 1 P. M. for Demonstration.

WESTERN DELEGATION

Port Angeles leave at 8 A. M.   Grays Harbor leave at 1 P. M.

ALL DELEGATIONS REPORT IN OLYMPIA AT 418 E. FOURTH STREET AT 5 P. M.

(This call printed by voluntary labor of Unemployed Printers.)

APPENDIX 5

Vigilantes challenge January 17, 1933 Hunger Marchers.

5,000 TO MARCH ON OLYMPIA

To carry out their threats of terrorism and intimidations because of their demands NOT being met by the State Government, the Communist Leaders of the last "State Hunger March" of January are planning to return to Olympia on March 1 with a mob of over 5,000 and over-ride our city and county for five days.

The leaders of this "State Hunger March" are the same as those who lead the "Hunger March" on Washington, D. C. and to whom President Green, National Head of the American Federation of Labor, in plain language stated:

> "The A. F. L. is the representative of American workers, men and women, and we are unwilling to give consideration to a body dominated by Soviet leaders and communists. Your leaders do not want unemployed insurance. They thrive on misery, distress and hunger. Your leaders have mobilized you for one purpose, and that is for the overthrow of this Government. Your man Benjamin, is not a worker. He is an agent of Soviet Russia."

The leaders of the last Olympia "Hunger March" are paid Soviet agents. Jack Taybeck, who threatened the State Legislature from the Floor of the Chamber last January, while his mob of Hunger Marchers stood outside on the Capital steps singing the Russia Soviet Revolutionary song "International", is not an unemployed American worker. He is a paid Communist agitator who was recently arrested at Astoria, Oregon for inciting riots and and disorder there.

Today these revolutionary Communists from their Moscow controlled headquarters at 617½ University Street, Seattle, Washington are waging their war against our Government by taking advantage of the distress and unemployment of the American workers. State, County and City officials have been threatened; legislation is being affected, courts are being intimidated, jurors tampered with, the American flag is being desecrated, strikes are being fomented, mass riots and "Hunger Marches" instigated, sabotage committed and the laws of our nation and state are being violated by these Red Organized Bandits.

THEY CARE NOTHING FOR THE WELFARE OF THE AMERICAN WORKER !

All they seek is to create discontent around which strikes and riots can be agitated - and to turn these riots into civil war to overthrow the American Government and set up a Soviet Dictatorship controlled by Moscow with its aetheism, peonage and enslavement for their own personal self interest.

THEY HAVE CHALLENGED US - by setting up their RED Headquarters at 418-E Fourth Street in our own city ! !

NOW IS THE TIME WE AMERICAN CITIZENS OF THURSTON COUNTY MUST LET IT BE KNOWN IN NO UNCERTAIN TERMS THAT WE INTEND TO RUN OUR OWN AMERICAN AFFAIRS IN OUR OWN AMERICAN WAY WITHOUT DICTATION OR INTIMIDATION BY ANY FOREIGN COMMUNIST, CONTROLLED MOB OF AGITATORS, WHO DO NOT REPRESENT THE PRINCIPLES OF THE AMERICAN CITIZENSHIP.

EXECUTIVE COMMITTEE

AMERICAN VIGILANTES OF THURSTON COUNTY WASHINGTON

APPENDIX 6

A militant committee of the Unemployed Citizens' League issued this appeal which resulted in the occupation of the County-City Building for about three days and two nights continuously in February, 1933.

ALL DOWN TO THE COUNTY CITY BLDG. IMEDIATLY !!!

Twentey five hundred of Us Unemployed, have camped in the County City Bldg. since one o'clock yesterday. Demanding a hearing before the new County Wellfare Board. The Board refuses to meet with more than three of us. We DEMAND that they hear our Committee of twenty,

We are going to stick it out until they show up.

Shannon said yesterday that a family of four, will recieve from one to four dollars per week.

We are determined to raise this starvation rate. Thats way the County Board is afraid to meet us.

We need re-enforcements. Thousands must come to County City Bldg at once, to win our demands.

Just get on the Street Cars and come. Charge the fare to Mayor Dore.

KING CO, UNITED FRONT COMMITTEE OF ONE HUNDRED ELECTED AT CONFERENCE.

APPENDIX 7

Our letter appealing to the city of Olympia to accept our third Hunger march. It was very successful in March, 1933.

OPEN LETTER TO THE PEOPLE OF OLYMPIA AND THURSTON COUNTY:

Brothers:

The delegates elected to come to Olympia appeal to you for cooperation and support.

The demands of the Hunger March are for repeal of the vicious MacDonald bill, for emergency cash relief, for more adequate relief to all the destitue in the form of Unemployment Insurance. These are just, fair, reasonable.

The people coming to Olympia are elected delegates from labor and fraternal organizations. They come to exercise their constitutional right—their right to petition the state government for the aid to hungry men, women and children. Every part of the population will be represented. There will be exservicemen, unemployed, farmers, fishermen, indians and others. We ask especially that those of you with any spare room at home report to the headquarters of the march so that the women and children in the delegations may be properly cared for.

Wild rumors about riots must be stopped. Every hunger march delegate comes peacefully. There will be no disorder unless it is instigated by hoodlums or misguided officials. Every delegate is under pledge to keep even better discipline than the last march.

Our fight is the fight of all the workers and farmers of this State. Help us all you can.

Fraternally,
STATE UNITED FRONT COMMITTE OF ACTION

George Bradley, chairman.
R.P. Forrest, Secretary.

APPENDIX 8

Our Third Hunger March proposals to the Legislature.

OLYMPIANS

Many thousand ELECTED DELEGATES of the Working People of the entire State of Washington are marching in Protest Demonstration in Olympia today because:

1. The State Legislature has enacted the MacDonald Act which attempts to institute a system of PEONAGE and FORCED LABOR, and further attempts to enforce these conditions of SLAVERY by means of depriving the working people of the few Constitutional Rights supposedly guaranteed under the Constitution of the United States.
2. The People of the entire State of Washington are demanding CASH Relief, which is the only way to meet the "Emergency" existing in this State today.
3. The Jobless-Social Insurance Bill, which provides a permanent method of solving the Unemployment problem, has not been enacted into law, in spite of the fact that it was introduced into the Legislature on January 17, 1935, by representatives of duly elected delegates from all parts of the State, representing the Fishermen, Youth, Farmers, Ex-Servicemen, Indians, and Unemployed.

These CONDITIONS force every Man, Woman, and Child to make vigorous protest and to join each other in presenting their needs in the form of a UNITED FRONT DEMONSTRATION before the State Government of the State of Washington, located in Olympia.

THEREFORE, the People of the State of Washington today make the following demands:

1. The Immediate Repeal of the MacDonald Act.
2. The Granting of Emergency Cash Relief Immediately.
3. The Enactment of the Jobless-Social Insurance Bill.

The Marchers will come in well-ordered groups in caravans from as far North as Blaine and Sumas, the East as Spokane and Walla Walla, the South as Vancouver and Longview, the West as Illwaco, Grays Harbor, and Port Angeles. Large delegations from Bellingham, Anacortes, Yakima, Centralia, Chehalis, and Seattle will join the caravans along the line of march.

On every former occasion when the working people throughout the State of Washington came to Olympia, the greatest co-operation and solidarity has been demonstrated. And again this Solidarity and Co-operation will be demonstrated in spite of the "Hooligan" methods of a small group of self-stiled "Executive Committee of Vigilantes", who disregard facts in order to satisfy their own hatred toward the working people of this State.

GOVERNOR MARTIN has given his assurance to the Hunger Marchers that they will not be disturbed in any way. THEREFORE, Governor Martin will be held responsible for the well being of the entire delegation while in Olympia !

GREET THE HUNGER MARCHERS ! by joining in their Demand for adequate food and shelter at the expense of the State !

Fraternally,
STATE UNITED FRONT COMMITTEE OF ACTION

APPENDIX 9

The following document is an example of how at times the Party publicly criticized and embarassed its members who were leaders of mass organizations. It also shows how the Party sometimes attempted publicly to determine the course followed by these organizations. At the time, most of the leaders of the UCL were Communists.

Communist Party Statement on Bill Dobbins' Resignation as Chairman of the Unemployed Citizens' League

COMMUNIST PARTY, DISTRICT # 12

1915-FIRST AVE., SEATTLE, WASH.

March 28, 1934

TO THE MEMBERS OF THE UNEMPLOYED CITIZEN'S LEAGUE:

W. K. Dobbins has resigned as chairman of the Unemployed Citizen's League, Central Federation. This resignation is endorsed by the Communist Party. The Communist Party of which W. K. Dobbins is a member has requested him to make a statement clarifying his position and the reasons that his resignation is necessary for the growth of the Unemployed Citizen's League, and the development of mass struggles for relief.

Dobbins has refused to make such a statement. It is therefore necessary for the Communist Party itself to make clear its stand concerning this resignation and its proposals for improving the organizational structure of the Unemployed Citizen's League.

A year ago following the ousting of Pearl, Wells, Murray, Griffin, Smith, Hyde, from the leadership of the Unemployed Citizen's

League, members of the Communist Party were elected into the leadership of the organization and the program proposed by the Communist Party through its members, was accepted as the new program for the Unemployed Citizen's League.

This program was for militant struggle for cash relief, against forced labor, for union pay for all work, for Unemployment Insurance, for the Worker's Ordinance for city relief, against evictions and foreclosures. To put this program into effect, it was necessary to abandon the old habit of the U.C.L. leaders of making friendly deals with politicians, and instead to draw in the widest number of unemployed into the struggle for more relief.

Wherever the program has been pushed forward, (as in the forced labor strike) it has been proved to be correct. But on the whole, the Unemployed Citizen's League has failed to increase the standard of living of the unemployed. For example, single men receive 80¢ per week less in King County than in such counties as Thurston.

A top-heavy central apparatus has been maintained, which has served to stifle the independent action of the locals, City-wide demonstrations have been called frequently—prepared for only by leaflets and not by struggles around the voucher stations. As a result, these demonstrations have got little immediate results. The Worker's Ordinance for city relief has been allowed to die. Little has been done to push the Unemployment Insurance Bill. Above all, the locals have been encouraged to devote most of their time and energy on social affairs, dances, card parties, etc. While these are necessary for the life of any worker's organization, they can never replace the struggle for more relief and against discrimination. The social life must serve to draw more workers into the struggles.

The Communist Party holds itself responsible for this condition of the Unemployed Citizen's League, especially since it has members in every local whose duty it is to push forward the correct program. The Party holds itself especially responsible for having failed to take drastic steps to see that W. K. Dobbins put the program of the Unemployed Citizen's into life, that he break off from the old habits of the Unemployed Citizen's League leaders of maintaining friendly relations with the city officials (such as accepting money from Mayor Dore for rent). The most outstanding example of this collaboration with politicians was the procedure followed by Dobbins when 16 workers were arrested for organizing the defense of the home of Frank Frandsen, Rainier Valley worker. When the men were jailed, Dobbins instead of taking steps together with the I.L.D. for immediate working class defense, went directly to the prosecuting attorney to "spring" the defendants. With Lenihan and a court reporter, he went to the jail and as the defendants were brought one at a time into the room, told them it was ok to talk. Unskilled in court trickery many of these workers followed the advice of their "leader" Dobbins and made statements that were later used against them with great effectiveness by the vicious Lenihan. No one can doubt that this incident had a direct bearing upon the sentences of a year in Walla Walla for William Kominski, sentences of six months in the county jail for eight others.

Dobbins has been consistent in his opposition to the Voice of Action and its representation of the militant program of the unemployed. He has even attempted at times to prevent the Voice of Action from being mentioned on the floor of the Central Federation and has given no support to the financial drive and the building of the circulation of the paper.

The entire policy of Dobbins was clearly expressed at the C.W.A. mass meeting at the Labor Temple on March 16, where he refused even to mention the name of the Unemployed Citizen's League and refused to bring up the Unemployment Insurance Bill, and instead made a speech which in no way conflicted with that of Tom Smith, demagogic petty politician driven from the unemployed movement by the rank and file of the Unemployed Citizen's League. Both Dobbins and Smith presented no program of struggle, spoke only for the need of a new organization of the unemployed. This would have meant the death blow to the organization of which Dobbins was then chairman and of which he was duty bound to help build. This incident is a good example of the kind of mistake which has hampered the growth of the U.C.L. for a long time, namely the forming of a united front from the top with Smith, Griffin, and the like, instead of with the masses of workers on a clear cut program of struggle.

The Communist Party takes full responsibility for its failure to struggle with sufficient energy against this series of mistakes, against these wrong methods of work in the Unemployed Citizen's League. It is true these points were discussed many times with Dobbins and with other workers involved in the work of the Unemployed Citizen's League, both party members and non-party members, and definite efforts were made by the party to change the old character of the work of Dobbins and some other Communist Party members in the U.C.L. The Communist Party made every effort to correct Comrade Dobbins in his wrong policies, but after a long period of time, the Communist Party seeing that Comrade Dobbins has refused to make the necessary corrections in his work, agreed with him that he should resign and be removed from his leading position in unemployed work.

At this time when thousands of workers in Seattle are faced with starvation under Roosevelt's new relief plan, when the old U.C.L. leaders, Wells, Hyde, Boardway, etc. are again attempting to capitalize on the misery of the workers and to split their ranks: it is necessary for every member of the U.C.L. to take to heart the lessons to be drawn from Dobbin's resignation, and to turn the U.C.L. into a broad organization that will really fight for the interests of all the unemployed in Seattle.

To do this effectively, the Communist Party proposes:

1. That the U.C.L. immediately put through the program which it has carried on its minutes for a year,—for the formation of district councils.
2. That the locals call mass meetings of all fired C.W.A. workers who are being denied relief, and act and mobilize to get them back on the rolls.
3. That the district councils organize additional groups and locals to be delegated to the district councils.
4. That in West Seattle, mass meetings be called and groups formed with a militant program under any name the workers choose but with a definite effort to have these groups affiliate and send delegates to the Central Federation.
5. That the Worker's Ordinance be popularized and used as the basis for winning higher relief.
6. That workers on relief jobs be organized into job committees with membership in the Relief Worker's Protective Association where possible. These job committees to send delegates

to the Central Federation which in time must become the broad council representing and uniting thousands upon thousands of organized workers in Seattle.

The Communist Party calls upon its members to put every bit of energy behind such a program and urges all workers, Socialist, Communist, I.W.W. to unite shoulder to shoulder to build a fighting unemployed organization for the best interests of the working class of Seattle.

For the District Committee of the
Communist Party

/s/ Alan Max
Acting District Organizer

APPENDIX 10

I was a delegate to the second National Convention of the CIO, which met in San Francisco. As it adjourned, President John L. Lewis called an Executive Board meeting. C. W. Deal, President of the Inlandboatmen's Union, invited me to accompany him to that meeting where I took extensive notes and typed them as soon as the meeting was over. I got a distressing insight into what to expect of the CIO in the future. These are my notes.

CIO National Executive Board Meeting, October 14, 1939

Lewis chided the Vice Presidents for arriving late, remarking that he supposed the convention elected more of them so he would have to spend all his time waiting for them.

A telegram from Senator Wagner (Greetings) was read, ordered placed in the record.

Lewis arose deliberately and leisurely, stated he had two subjects he wanted to bring to the attention of the Board.

The first is about the organization drive. "I'm tired and out of patience with each organization which has not been paying its per capita tax." Organizations seem to be willing and able to do everything, except pay their obligation to the CIO. Chislers—those who have paid on only a part of their memberships—are the worse offenders, they are further behind in payments to the CIO. It seems that the nicer we are to them, the less money we get. They have offered every imaginable excuse. We won't listen to that any more. Some even have gone so far as to laugh about how they get by without paying their tax. The fun is now all over. Free riding is all over. The CURRENT TAX FOR OCTOBER MUST BE PAID AND PAID ON THE FULL MEMBERSHIP, AND SOMETHING MUST BE PAID EACH MONTH ON DELINQUENCIES.

Further, on the organizational question. Now is the time to hit the line, and "I mean hit it." That goes for all. In 1936 the campaign was directed and done by the central organization of the CIO. We captivated the imagination of the masses with daring, got a lot of newspaper publicity. But that ended with the Little Steel Strike.

Now we have 45 International Organizations. They are responsible for their own International Unions. All the Central organization can do is supplement and aid the Internationals. We cannot put on the same kind of drive as was done in 1936. At that time we captivated the imagination of the masses because the press was always talking about it. But after the Little Steel Strike the publicity from then on more than offset the favorable content of the stories previously. The drama is all out of the situation now. From now on out it is a question of hard steady work. We must have constant growth of all units. The Regional Directors and staff must augment and assist the International Organizations.

For a year and a half we have been devoting our time to administrative and routine matters. All have been taking things easy for a time. The Regional Directors have been doing too much letter writing, holding conferences with people who do not contribute to our job of organizing. We must now organize. Let's neglect office, clerical, legislative work if that is necessary to get some organization. Let's not fear being out of the office. I find that is true of myself as well as others. Frequently I am ready to leave the office for some real work when the stenographer comes in with an announcement to the effect that Senator Blank will be over in fifteen minutes, so I've been waiting fifteen minutes for Senator Blank. That means fifteen minutes lost to me, without contributing to the organization. All it does is make Senator Blank think he is more important than he really is. Hereafter, I'm going to meet Senator Blank when I want to, not on his bidding. So I say, if that is true with me, and it is, then it is just as true with all our staff, and I know we can all improve our work.

Administrative Changes:

I want to now announce certain organizational changes. The office of the West Coast Director is abolished. Harry Bridges is appointed Regional Director for California. Wm. Dalrymple is relieved of his assignment with the SWOC in California, and is transferred to Regional Director for the State of Oregon. Richard Francis will continue his work as Regional Director for the State of Washington. These three must synchronize their efforts so the whole coast will go forward. The West Coast is in splendid condition except that it does not have enough new members. The Convention has stimulated and enthused the millions of workers here. Now it is necessary that we show results from this enthusiasm. I might say that we are not going to organize the Movie industry now. That venture has petered out. And I'm not surprised. The liaison between industry with the AFL is too strong to overcome at this time. The really big field is agriculture in all three coast states of California, Oregon, and Washington. That field must be organized.

Alan Haywood is relieved of his duties as Regional Director in New York and becomes the Director of Organization with offices in Washington, D.C.

Mike Widman Jr., of Boston, is relieved of his duties to become Assistant to the Director of Organization, also in Washington, D.C.

Adolph Germer is relieved of his duties in Detroit to become Regional Director in New York.

The office of Director is abolished.

John Brophy becomes director of the Department of Industrial Unions, to act as President of this group, as well as constitute a liaison with the Central Office and serve as Assistant to the President.

I make these changes to speed up and centralize the organizational drive. I want the Executives of the International Unions to meet with and discuss with the Central Office their plans for organization. Let us know what they want us to do, and keep us informed as to what is going on, and to work out with us the matter of finances for keeping the drive going forward. There will be no limits in this except those imposed on us by failures of International Unions to pay their way on this road of organization.

Our big immediate future is in the Textile industry. There are more than one-and-a-half million to be organized there. Now is the time to do it. We propose to do just that. "The South can and will be organized." I get tired of those people who make excuses about the backwardness of the South. I say the South is awakening. That Feudal empire is stirring. And Congress will no doubt soon enact legislation abolishing the poll tax which affects nine states yet.

I realize there are specialized problems in connection with the drive in many industries, but these can and must be met and overcome.

Lewis on Construction Workers:

Now we are also pushing the drive of organizing the Construction Workers. That means building and all other forms of construction. This industry is only partially organized. Very conservatively speaking, more than seventy-five percent is unorganized. These conditions are due to the high fees which prohibit organization in the existing AFL unions. Then there is unemployment, and worse, that system of collusion between the AFL union heads with the Contractors which amounts to blackmail, etc., we are out to organize the unorganized, and remember that. I get tired of hearing those local officers and representatives of CIO say the time is not ripe, or that there is danger that this drive will weaken the local labor unity. Remember the AFL denied us a voice in the councils of labor. They haven't changed that attitude or policy. Any so-called unity on a local scale is deceptive. I say we cannot and will not allow any local deception like this to stop or impede our drive. Some are afraid to offend the AFL. I say "To hell with the AFL Building Trades."

"Joe Cannon, Regional Director, Philadelphia, stand up. The other day I read a newspaper story carrying a statement from your President of the Industrial Union Council in which he stated they were reserving judgment about the wisdom of the CIO drive to organize the Building Construction workers. I tell you now that when you get back to Philadelphia, you tell him what his responsibilities are, and if he doesn't learn from you, let me know, and I'll let him know just what they are."

In every community there are organizations of these United Construction Workers that can be built up. We may find that we will have to start out with contracts that will be based on what you can get now. Not all of them can be at the prevailing wage, and I don't care if it does displease the AFL. If Dan Tobin don't want to haul materials for our workers, then we will put our own men on the trucks and haul them ourselves. I know Dan Tobin, have known him for years. He is a likable fellow, and I could fraternize with him in social affairs, but that won't organize the unorganized. I know that a fighting militant organization can be built. That's what I want. I don't want a social fraternizing army. I want members.

Some have opposed our drive, right from our own ranks. That must come to an end. Remember the AFL has been the "Suttlers" of our advancing army. They got one million out of the drive in which we got three million.

On the Other Subject #2:

All know that I have not made any public statement having to do with public charges of Communism in our ranks.

I don't know any in our ranks, I haven't tried to find out. I have assumed there are some, due to the natural law of averages, and due to the fact that the employers have some in their plants. I haven't wanted to give any time to that subject. I have no knowledge of any Communists in executive capacity of CIO, and I haven't tried to find out.

I am not a Communist, any statement to the contrary notwithstanding. I know CIO is not controlled by Communists. I also know it is not going to be controlled by Communists.

I've been reading confessions by Communists, especially before the Dies Committee. I think they are confessing too much. I think they are being made by the Communist Party itself. I think the Communist Party is making a mistake by putting such confessions before the public. If they continue to take that medium, the Dies Committee, to present their views to the public, then they are going to hear from the President of the CIO. I want to avoid making any statement on the subject. What I'm saying now, I'm stating mildly.

Me thinks the lady doth protest too much, by sending these witnesses to testify. That technique won't fool a child.

I don't want our organization to waste time or energy in red-baiting. If I were a young Communist looking for a future in the labor movement, I would not look for that in the CIO. This is all I'm going to say.

I don't want Regional Directors, etc, to employ known communists. I do want them to give the benefit of doubt in all cases to persons accused of being communists. The fact that one is accused is not acceptable. I may be accused. And I know it is not true. I want everyone to understand this.

Communists have never had anything to say or do with decisions of the CIO. It is not true what is said in New York that they have control. I want this understood and they have no future.

I don't object to any man joining the Communist Party. I do object to anyone trying to impose that philosophy on the CIO. Remember this, when one is paid by the CIO he must serve the CIO all the time. Oil and water just will not mix. His loyalty just cannot be divided between two opposing philosophies.

Now you have the floor, who is first?

VAN BITNER: I certainly agree with all that has been said. The only real problem before us is to organize the unorganized. The Regional Directors must conform with the policies of the International Organizations. No Regional Director is going to interfere with our organizations. Our people haven't time to fool with other things than organizational matters, such as the League for Peace and Democracy, Lincoln Brigade, etc. Building CIO is the most important job. There are only twenty-four hours in a day, seven days in a week and three hundred sixty-five days in a year, and I find that is not enough. Some people think we should spend our time talking to the Chambers of Commerce, and other groups of businessmen. These people will never organize the workers, and it is a crime for us to waste time with them. We still have some CIO unions working like an old Business Agency Craft Union. Some are still disturbed because we won't accept AFL union cards to transfer members in the CIO. I say now we have nothing to do with the AFL, and we won't accept their membership cards for CIO cards.

On the Communist Party. No man should accept office in the CIO unless he is ready to devote his life to the CIO. We will have unity when the CIO is strong enough to accomplish it. We have got to get more members first. Then we can have the kind of unity which will do the workers some good.

We have found that some of our lodges have had to put a stop to taking up matters other than strictly affecting our union. We found that when John Jones came to the lodge meeting with a case of discrimination to settle, he had to wait throughout the whole meeting listening to everything else in the world being discussed, and at midnight the President of the lodge would announce that his case was postponed until the next meeting. John Jones would come to the next meeting and the same process would be repeated. We finally had to send out a letter to all lodges instructing them to take up Union matters first, then if there is time to take up other things that is permissible, but I don't believe there is time left for other things.

BROPHY: I was one of the first to enlist in this program of the CIO. I have given it the best I have. I enlisted for life. I knew that following the first drive there had to be a period of assimilation.. We have gone thru that now. We have laid fallow for some time so to speak. Naturally our first successes nationally brought sharp attacks on the leaders. We can expect more of them. I merely rise to state now before all of you that I've been the center of much of this attack, particularly as to duality of loyalty that I am devoted to the CIO, always have been and will continue to be. I accept the changes proposed and made by President Lewis. I am only too glad to play what part I can in this great movement. I am subject to your judgment. I know the goal of ten million can and will be attained and I for one will do my best in that work.

MURRAY: I rise to support President Lewis. The number one question is the Tax problem. We must stop this thumbing our way. I say here and now that the Steelworkers Organizing Committee will repay to the United Mine Workers of America the one-and-a- half million dollars which has been used to oganized the Steelworkers of America. We regard that as a loan, and an obligation, which must be repaid. Of course we launched our drive when Steel production was down to twenty-one percent in production. It is now rising. It is still very bad. But the first thing that must be done is to organize the remaining unorganized steel workers. So we are launching our drive on Bethlehem Steel Corporation just as soon as I can return to Pittsburgh and hold a conference of all the Regional Officers. We are at the same time, of course, putting on a drive in Republic. But Bethlehem is Labor's number one enemy.

On the Red Question; I've never been accused of being a red-baiter, and I have met all of the national leaders and some of the local leaders of the Communist Party right in my very own office. My creed is to organize the unorganized, and I say that no one should allow anything to stand in the way of the CIO. But today I'm troubled about it. The present drive of the Dies Committee is aimed to destroy CIO, not just the Communist Party. And the way some of these Communist Party members have been volunteering information to the Dies Committee leads me to believe there is a definite collusion, methodical, diabolical, and precisive. We must remember that the focal point indicates but one thing—a drive against the CIO. I won't quarrel with any man about the philosophy of the Communist Party, Marxism, either the good old unadulterated

Socialist variety or the modern streamlined Marxism of Lenin and the Communist International. But I am distressed today at their behavior.

Everything in Washington today indicates that the next session of Congress will include measures to control and curb certain agencies in the United States. Now, I am an immigrant, along with my good friend Mike Quill, and there are others among us here. I know that when Congress meets in January, I along with others of us are going to be forced to appear and testify before Congressional Committees as to what we know. So I say here and now that we have to build our organization without connection whatsoever with any outside source. Can't make any distinction among them, whether they are political parties, or social, religious, and fraternal groups. No other organization has been willing to organize the unorganized. Now we have assumed the responsibility to do just that. Now we have reached the place where no one can straddle this issue.

We've gone thru the period of adolescence. We will be subjected to the rigors of severe conflict. Some among us may lose their lives in the struggle to follow. I know that Eugene Grace of Bethlehem Steel will use everything he can to prevent the workers from winning the recognition coming from organization. And he is right now laying his plans to meet our new offensive. He is preparing to offer certain wage increases to his 78,000 unorganized workers. We know he can and must raise the rate to them, and we aim to have organization in this industry which will stand up from now on. The same goes for Girdler and Weir, who have for the past ten years been the mainspring behind the Republican Party in this Country. We've got to face these issues now.

CARNEY: Heartily concur with President Lewis, Van Bitner and Murray. I feel enthusiastic about the prospects to do the job when we return home. I know that we in New Jersey have made real progress since we licked Mayor Hague, and are ready to continue that at an even faster pace.

MERRILL: We promise to pay our back per capita tax. I want to say that I am not a Communist. In fact I'm getting tired of refuting the charge. So far our organization has been forbearing. In the future we will do two things. Where we find a Communist we will spank them, and if that is not sufficient, then we will lay the evidence before President Lewis and ask him to deal with it, and we know that he will.

LEWIS: Let's save time by not repeating each other. I'm interested now in plans for organizing the unorganized. Let's hear what some of you propose to do about such matters as warehouses, marine, and especially inland waterways.

HAYWOOD: Spoke briefly in reference to the excellent cooperation and friendly relationships among the several union heads with his regional office in New York. All agreed with him that the spirit of cooperation there was excellent and a model for the rest of the nation.

LEWIS: I suggest now that the new appointees take their necessary time to clean up their old assignments so when they start their new work they will not have a divided attention. The three new West Coast Directors must establish liaison relationships.

EMILE RIEVE: I never was bothered over the question of Communism. From the beginning I had the policy of not tolerating the injection of their theories into the CIO. We will go forward on this new drive to organize textile.

COULTER: Standard Oil is next to Bethlehem Steel as number one enemy of labor.

FLAXNER: I find everyone is avoiding discussing a problem which has disturbed us very much. I find in the first place that no one clearly identifies me and my work. They don't just understand the work of organizing the white collar workers who are employed by governmental agencies in State, County or Municipal. Now that brings up the problem that is being avoided, namely the organization of Industrial Union Councils. For example we have one in New York State, but not one for New York City. Now I maintain it is too much for the State Council to attempt to do what a City Industrial Union Council is set up for. And in this case we find that International Union Officers and others are too busy to do the little things in connection with contacting public officials which must be done if our organization is to have any chance to organize. In Chicago, there we have a situation where Mayor Kelly is in office. We ought to be making progress there, but we are not. And it arises out of the situation where we find there is no local organization able or willing to take up the fight in our behalf. I want to know what we are going to do about this. We will do the organizing for our organization, but we do need assistance which these Councils and only these Councils can render.

LEWIS: I will say right now that wherever you have that kind of difficulty where a Regional Director or any of our staff fail to give you that kind of assistance you speak of now, just let me know, and we will instruct them to cooperate with you.

BRIDGES: The new set-up on the West Coast will help our concentration. I want to call to your attention the fact that California is the key state in the West, and it is a thousand miles long and several hundred miles wide. It is big enough to put all the dinky little New England states inside it and have plenty of area left over.

I noticed that Carney of New Jersey started his report from the period when they established civil rights there in Jersey City, with the defeat of Hague. Here we have to fight and establish civil rights before we can hope to establish much organization. You have an example of that now in Madiera County where there are over one hundred and fifty workers in jail because they were spontaneously organizing to get a higher wage for their work.

I've followed the policy of sending organizers into those areas where I was willing to go myself. And there are plenty of areas here where a man's life is in danger when he goes there to organize. I don't think it is going to do much good to have our leaders killed off by vigilantes and Associated Farmers. We've got to crack this violation of civil rights first.

LEWIS: (Interrupting): Hasn't the Governor some power there?

BRIDGES: Yes he has, but he has not been able to use it yet.

LEWIS: Can't he do something, he says he is defending civil rights, why doesn't he do something about that?

BRIDGES: This is a ticklish question. We can do one of two things; ask the Governor to send in the troops, which he can't do until local authorities ask for them, or blast the Governor for not doing something.

LEWIS: Doesn't the Governor have authority to remove a sheriff for failure to uphold the law?

BRIDGES: Yes, he has that authority.

LEWIS: Then demand that he use that authority.

BRIDGES: Well, we might have to.

LEWIS: It seems to the chair that the Governor is obliged to protect the civil rights.

BRIDGES: (continuing): So far as the Movie Industry is concerned, that is the fifth in rank. We didn't expect to get many members for the CIO out of them, but we did try and I think we got the benefit of their political support and I think it will pay many dividends in the future. In the Northern states there too the organization drive must be accompanied with a political drive to establish civil rights. On Communism—I said my piece in three days where it did some good. On cooperation of Directors with International Unions, I've found that most of the trouble arises because the International Unions don't work with the Directors. [He then referred to some problems with the Construction Workers in San Francisco, the substance of which I missed.]

CURRAN: Promise to pay tax. Didn't know six months ago if we had a union. Do today. Are a half-million dollars in debt. But will overcome that. Ninty-fourth time deny I am a Communist.

JOHN L. LEWIS abruptly adjourned the meeting at this point.

APPENDIX 11

Memo-Conversation of Francis, Dennett and Brozovitch August 26, 1940.

Re: delegates from IWA Local 3–48. Brozovitch earlier brought in the office a report from 3–48, covering $9.00 for 300 members for the month of July; also the money covering this per capita tax plus two dollars affiliation fee. Francis contended this local had the right to three delegates, whereas Dennett said a twelve month period must be taken into consideration in allowing delegates from any local whose charter had been in effect, but which had not previously affiliated during the past year.

Dennett: The provisions of the constitution are outlined there in the Call, and you aren't going to get me to violate it.

Francis: I am familiar with the actions of the last convention. I am just carrying out the mandate of the last convention, which it is my duty to carry out. If I am at fault, let the convention correct it.

Dennett: I think we should have the opinion of the Executive Board on this.

Francis: My attitude is, the Executive Board has already accepted this, in compliance with the constitution.

Dennett: You are still not facing the facts, the basis of representation set forth in by the constitution.

Francis: I am abiding by the constitution.

Dennett: Under your interpretation, anybody and everybody could make an affiliation as of July, and have full representation at the convention.

Francis: Anybody whose credentials are contested would not be allowed to vote or take part in the discussion on the credentials . . . The Executive Board has already passed on it. If it is wrong, let the convention decide. (Shouting) Get this. I am instructing you to make out these credentials. If you don't, I will turn it over to the national office.

Dennett: You are demanding me to violate the constitution.

Francis: This is not my demand. It is the demand of the convention.

Dennett: What are you so excited about? I want the Executive Board's advice on it.

Francis: They have already acted on it.

Dennett: No, they haven't.

Francis: The Executive Board acted upon it at their last meeting. I tell you, it's up to the convention.

Dennett: I'm sorry Dick. Why is it that you don't want the Executive Board to pass on it.

Francis: They have passed on it at their last meeting. Any delegate involved will not be allowed to participate in the debate or vote. (Interruptions, shouting, etc.

Dennett: You are not going to scare me.

Francis: I'm just following the program of the organization.

Dennett: You are not trying to sell me on a program. You are just trying to stuff this down my throat.

Dennett: The program I follow is that which is in the constitution, which definitely calls for averaging throughout the year. That is what it calls for, and for my part I am going to submit this matter to the Executive Board.

Francis: Are you going to send those credentials down there?

Dennett: I am going to take it up with the Executive Board.

Francis: I am the President of this organization. You are just the Secretary. I'm supposed to see that these things are taken care of. Are you going to send those credentials?

Dennett: My answer is, it is going to the Executive Board.

Francis: Then you are not going to send the credentials down there?

Dennett: You are not going to put any words in my mouth. Why can't you be civil about it?

Francis: (Called Dennett obscene names). Be civil to you? You know what you have been trying to use this office for.

Dennett: I've been trying to use it for the benefit of the workers. And what have you been using yours for?

Francis: For the CIO.

(The conversation ended with Francis shouting and cursing, then leaving the office.)

[NOTE: The foregoing memo was taken down in shorthand and later transcribed by Dennett's secretary Dorothy Anne Patton.]

APPENDIX 12

When the Third Convention of the Washington State Industrial Union Council deadlocked over seating delegates, it adjourned without transacting any business or resolving any disagreements. I wrote the following letter to John L. Lewis in an effort to furnish him with the information necessary to understand what happened and why.

Washington State CIO Convention Report to John L. Lewis

September 24, 1940

JOHN L. LEWIS, PRESIDENT

Congress of Industrial Organizations
1106 Connecticut Avenue, Northwest
Washington, D.C.

Dear Brother Lewis:

In accordance with telegram, I am transmitting all the material available now on the Third Annual Convention of the Washington State Industrial Union Council. The rest of the material will be forwarded just as soon as the stenographers can complete transcribing the minutes.

The enclosed material covers:

1. Proceedings, First Day, Friday A.M., September 20, 1940 including opening address of President Francis, the only report he submitted to the Convention.
2. Report of Secretary listing fourteen recommendations, account of organizational growth, financial report, and memorandum on first order of business together with copy of Constitution of Council for ready reference by delegates as needed.

3. Forty-seven resolutions which had been submitted before the afternoon of the first day, as per the Convention Call.
4. The Convention Call.
5. The Convention Yearbook.
6. The detailed minutes of the State Council Executive Board meeting of May 25, 1940 which decided how the Convention Call should be issued.
7. The minutes of the State Council Executive Board meeting of August 31, 1940 which was called specifically to decide a question which had arisen between President Francis and Secretary Dennett over interpreting the Constitution on how many delegates a newly affiliated local was entitled to in contrast to a newly chartered local.

The delay in obtaining a complete record of the proceedings to forward to you is a source of great concern and regret. But this information will be ready very soon. I thought it advisable to forward the foregoing listed material without waiting for the rest, which covers the events of the attempted convention.

While other partisans in the present controversy may hasten to submit their version of the events of the Convention, I request sufficient time to examine the record, and speak from the record, which I believe contains all the essential information required on which to base a judgment. However, the basic issue throughout the entire struggle before this Convention focused on upholding the national policies of the CIO as articulated by yourself as President. You will see what my position was and is by the report. You will see in President Richard Francis' report no proposal endorsing your position, which has been his policy throughout the year.

Although I have several times during the past year reproached him for neglect to speak up in behalf of the policies you have publicly expressed, he has remained ominously silent until recently. Shortly before your visit to the Northwest, at which time I discussed two organizational and one political question with you, Richard Francis told me that if you got too far out of line the UMWA Executive Board would pull you back. We were discussing the position of the CIO on Roosevelt and the National Defense program.

Of significance is the fact that one Ed Benedict leased the fourth floor of the Kneeland Hotel in Olympia, our Convention City, for the duration of the Convention. Those rooms were used to house a bloc of delegates to vote for a third term for Roosevelt, at least they thought they could whip every such delegate into line. But I have been advised by one delegate so corralled, that the stuff that group attempted to put across on the convention was so raw he left the group and took another delegate with him. I am trying to again contact the delegate to request he send a statement direct to you.

Mr. Benedict also leased a banquet hall in the Crane Cafe in Olympia for the duration of the convention and held regular meetings (caucuses) of these delegates whom they intended should vote for the Roosevelt resolution (#64), and the National Defense resolutions (#18). Mr. Benedict was not a delegate to the Convention. However, he does hold the distinction of being the present state leader of the Socialist Party, is a member of the International Woodworkers of America, formerly secretary of the Northern Washington District Council of the IWA, but was turned out of office last year because he failed to build organization and attempted to excuse his dereliction by blaming the "reds".

A co-leader with Mr. Benedict was James J. Molthan, an attorney, reputedly having connection with the Dies committee, formerly on the CIO payroll here under Mr. Francis, listed as a Field Representative, actually doing some legal work, formerly attorney for the International Woodworkers of America, but discharged by them for cause, more recently claims to be the attorney for various locals of the International Woodworkers of America—those which have taken a prominent part locally opposing the policies of the International; and has been referred to as the legal counsel of the UMWA District #10.

These two were in frequent contact and held caucuses with various delegates in the Convention who bitterly fought the policies of the Secretary, and when it became evident that no matter how much maneuvering they did, or how many caucuses they held, the majority of delegates were opposed to any unqualified endorsement of either Roosevelt or the National Defense program, the group which I identify as a minority seemed to have to decided to prevent the holding of a convention. My concern is that Richard Francis,

President of this Council, and Regional Director, presumably responsible to you, was a party to that intrigue.

So far as I am concerned, and for that matter the majority of delegates and members in the CIO movement here; we do not propose to be stampeded into giving support to either Roosevelt or the National Defense program unless or until this meets with your approval. By that, we mean that we have confidence in your judgment and integrity, and believe that the action the minority here proposed would be against the CIO, against our best interests, and in fact is unsound. This is all for now. More later.

Fraternally yours,

(Signed) Eugene V. Dennett,
Secretary

[NOTE: Lewis never answered this letter.]

APPENDIX 13

The following statement absolves Lewis for any responsibility for the break-up of the Third Annual Convention of the Washington State CIO, although it is clearly established that it was his appointees who were responsible for that break-up, Adolph Germer, Wm. Dalrymple, and Regional Director Richard Francis. The appointment of J. C. Lewis to control the affairs of the Council effectively eliminated me and my following. Our signatures to this agreement were coerced from us because we had no alternative.

Agreement

To all CIO industrial unions, industrial union councils and local unions in the State of Washington Greetings:

Your delegation, representatives of international unions, national organizing committees, industrial union councils and industrial unions, in attendance at the Third Annual Convention of the CIO in Atlantic City, N.J., who were in disagreement with the state of affairs that developed in the recent convention of the Washington State Industrial Union Council, submits herewith a brief report in regard to the action of the Executive Board of the CIO and the fulfillment of that action in connection with this matter. It is not necessary in this report to review at any length or comment upon what happened in Olympia, Washington, September 20, 21, and 22. It is the purpose of this report rather to outline briefly to the affiliates of the Washington State Industrial Union Council, as well as to those who are eligible for affiliation, the present status and relate briefly the facts that were disclosed at the hearings before the subcommittee appointed by the Executive Board, which included the then Vice-President Philip Murray, Vice-President Reid Robinson, and Board Member George Addes.

It was developed during the hearing and in conversation with President John L. Lewis that he was in no way responsible for the action taken either in the convention at Olympia or by the Committee of Six subsequent to the adjournment of the convention; that he appointed a Committee as he fully believed upon the legal action of a legal convention and left it to the judgment entirely of the Committee as to their subsequent acts. This should dispel once and for all any rumors or whisperings or efforts of anyone to hide behind or excuse any action that they may have taken on the grounds that they were following the explicit instructions of President Lewis.

The CIO Third Annual Convention, in our opinion, did a magnificent job in every respect during the sessions of the Convention on behalf of the working people of this country. The CIO was confronted with many intricate and difficult situations and among those was the disposition of the difficulty to which we are directing this report, namely, the division, the strife and the bitterness engendered at and coming out of the Olympia convention to the complete detriment of the Labor movement and particularly of the CIO, and to the great advantage of the enemies of labor and the employers of all types in the Pacific Northwest.

The agreement that came out of the Executive Board deliberations provides that J. C. Lewis, former President of the Iowa State Federation of Labor, (no relation to John L. Lewis), and a member of the United Mine Workers of America, shall:

1) Proceed and take over the duties of the Committee of Six appointed by President Lewis; and
2) That he shall administer the affairs of the Washington State Industrial Union Council until a convention is held and duly accredited officials are elected by the accredited delegates at the convention, and
3) That he shall perform his duties and functions under the provisions of the current constitution of the Washington State Industrial Union Council and shall preside as Chairman of the convention; and
4) That his decisions in all matters during this period affecting the Council or its functions shall be final; and
5) He shall appoint a Credentials Committee which Committee when appointed shall represent the National Office of the CIO in the performance of its duties.

Mr. J. C. Lewis is in our opinion fully qualified in every respect to perform these various duties assigned to him by action of the Executive Board. He is we believe fair and impartial and wholly committed to the program of the CIO in extending and developing to the greatest possible extent the principles of industrial unionism.

It is the desire of the delegation to pass on to all affiliates and CIO unions in the State of Washington the admonition and advice of the Executive Board and our former President, John L. Lewis, and our newly elected President, Philip Murray, that the "bitterness and strife within our ranks must cease", and that the tongue, as President Murray aptly put it in his acceptance speech, "of the slander-monger must be stilled".

President Murray repeated and emphasized this admonition and it is the declared and determined policy of the CIO and of all the delegates in attendance at the Third Annual Convention to support to the fullest extent President Murray in this matter as well as in the great organizing of the CIO.

May we therefore in closing urge that all CIO unions join in supporting the administrator of the affairs of the Washington State Industrial Union Council until the completion of the convention and that we assist him in every way possible, and that we earnestly and sincerely apply ourselves to the job of making the Washington State Industrial Union Council the outstanding State Council in the great family of the CIO.

> (Signed)
> J. F. Jurich
> C. W. Deal
> A. E. Harding
> Paul Dale
> Eugene V. Dennett
> Karley Larsen
> Ted Dokter
> H. R. Bridges
> O. M. Orton
> Conrad Espe

[Dated November 22, 1940]

APPENDIX 14

This is the Party's official statement expelling me, my wife Harriette, and Claude Smith. This statement was distributed at the Bethlehem Steel plant gates by Party members without interference by the plant guards.

Notice of Expulsion

To All Sections, Clubs and Members of the
Northwest District Communist Party, U.S.A.:

This is to notify all Sections and Clubs of the expulsion from the Communist Party of Eugene V. Dennett, Harriet Dennett and Claude Smith.

In the case of Eugene Dennett and Harriet Dennett, the expulsion is based upon violation of the conditions of membership in the Communist Party as set forth in Article 9, Sections 1, 2 and 4 of the Constitution of the Communist Party, U.S.A., based upon the following facts established by the District Review Commission:

1. Admitted employment of Harriet Dennett by an agency of the F.B.I. and the submitting of regular reports to said agency over a long period of time, with the knowledge and consent, and direct participation of Eugene V. Dennett. This was established by his admission of personal contact with a known agent of the F.B.I. and his concealment from the Party of Harriet Dennett's activities and his own personal contact with the F.B.I.
2. Admitted personal and political relations by Eugene V. Dennett with known Trotskyites with established participation by Harriet Dennett.
3. An established record of anti-party, disruptive and provocative activity by Eugene Dennett on numerous occasions and by Harriet Dennett in several instances.

In the case of Claude Smith, the expulsion is based upon violation of the conditions of membership in the Communist Party as set forth in Article 9, Sections 1, 2 and 4 of the Constitution of the Communist Party, U.S.A., and based upon the following facts established by the District Review Commission.

1. Admitted participation in the preparation of the reports submitted by Harriet Dennett to the agency referred to above as well as sharing in the payment for these reports and concealment of these activities from the Party.

The District Review Commission wishes to call to the attention of the Party membership and its organizations the necessary conclusions from these facts. First, in this case as in many in the past, a negative, carping attitude toward the Party and its program has upon investigation disclosed enemies of the Party and the Working class.

The same thing must be said of toleration and association with Trotskyites who are simply fascists hiding behind "left" phrases. While such attitudes may be due to lack of understanding in new members, in the case of experienced long time members it can only be regarded as conscious assistance to fascism and to the agents of fascism. It must be noted also that the personal record of these people in marked by individualism, instability and extreme egotism.

The District Review Commission also wishes to point out that it is necessary to learn to distinguish between honest differences of opinion which we have to constantly resolve by discussion and majority decision and disruptive, dishonest attacks upon the program, activities and leadership of the Party, which is the earmark of the provocateur and agent of the enemy. Only by more resolutely defending and fighting for the program of the Party can we make this distinction clear. Only by becoming more alert to the smell of anti-Party poision can we root out these disrupters. Only by fighting for the unity of the Party and testing our cadre struggle can we creates guarantees that such elements will not remain long in the Party or be able to steal into its posts of leadership, and that the damage that they do will be reduced to a minimum.

Harriet Dennett is at present holding the position of President of the Seattle UOPWA Local Union #35. Eugene Dennett is a member of the Board of Control of the NEW WORLD and a member of the Steel Workers Union. Claude Smith is at present editor of the Washington State CIO News.

All Party members are warned against personal or political association with these expelled members and to give them no consideration or comfort in the excuses and protests they can be expected to make against the expulsion action which was ordered carried out by unanimous vote of the Northwest District Committee in executive session on October 6, 1947.

Signed:
> Henry Huff, District Chairman

> C. Van Lydegraf, District Org. Soc'y.

uopwa-#35   for the NORTHWEST DISTRICT COMMITTEE
                   COMMUNIST PARTY, U.S.A.

APPENDIX 15

GILLAND AFFIDAVIT Jan 29, 1954

. . . I met Eugene V. Dennett, three years ago while employed at Bethlehem-Pacific Coast Steel, Seattle, Washington. I had had several discussions with him during which he had accused me of being a company man and not being for the best interest of the union. Then on or about September, 1953 shortly after the company started an incentive plan Dennett approached me and asked me if I really wanted to become a good union man. I assured him that I was interested in the Union and wanted to do my best for the union. Dennett told me that he would give me a book that would familiarize me with how to become a good union member and that this book would save his time in explaining it to me. Three or four days later at the plant he gave me a book and told me to study and read it and said that if I could not understand it perhaps my wife could help me with it, because he knew she was a graduate of the University. The book was entitled "What is to be Done" by V. I. Lenin, published by the International Publishers, 381 Fourth Avenue, New York, copyright 1929. The Little Lenin Library Series. I am at this time writing my name Rolland L. Gilland, and the date January 29, 1954 on the back of the Book in question.

I discussed the matter of the book with Dennett several times after that and he told me that he knew that it would be difficult for me to understand that if there were difficult passages and I needed an interpreter he would help me to interpret it. He did urge me to keep reading the book and studying it so that I could be a good union member like the rest of the boys in the plant. Dennett became discouraged with me and didn't think that I was going to learn what was in the book and that I was working for the company and trying to get the union thrown out. He accused me of working to get the International Union in and putting the local leaders out of power so that the company would completely run us. On or about January 27, 1954 he said that he knew I would not become a union man and told me to bring the book back to him and he told me to read page 131 and understand it. He told me that if I did not understand it he would explain it to me. Repeatedly while we were standing by the locker he had told me to read page 131 and told me to bear it in mind as long as I was with the company. He told me to bring the book back to him the next day. I distinctly remember that it was page 131 that he referred to because he called it to my attention in a most forceful manner several times.

Before Dennett gave me the book he made me promise faithfully that I would not show the book to anyone or tell them that I had it. The only reason that I am now revealing that Dennett gave me the book is because after reading page 131, which he told me to read, I fear for my future jobs and for security of myself and for my family.

I have read the foregoing statement of two pages and know its contents to be true.

/s/ Rolland L. Gilland

SUBSCRIBED AND SWORN

/s/ Ruth Evans
NOTARY PUBLIC

SEAL

[Note: This statement was prepared under the supervision of Joe Kane, Attorney retained by the International.]

APPENDIX 16

Excerpts from United Steelworkers' Constitution

I was tried by Steelworkers Local Union 1208 on charges of violating these portions of the Steelworkers' constitution.

Article III, Section 4: No member shall be eligible for nomination or election or appointment to, or to hold any office, or position, or to serve on any Committee in the International Union or a Local Union or to serve as a delegate therefrom who is a member, consistent supporter, or who actively participates in the activities of the Communist Party, Ku Klux Klan, or of any Fascist, Totalitarian, or other subversive organization which opposes the democratic principles to which the United States and Canada and our Union are dedicated.

Article XII, Section 1, Any member may be penalized for committing any one or more of the following offenses:

(a) violation of any of the provisions of this Constitution, any collective bargaining agreement, or working rule of the Local Union;

(b) obtaining membership through fraudulent means or by misrepresentation.

(d) advocating or attempting to bring about the withdrawal from the International Union of any Local Union or any member or group of members;

(e) publishing or circulating among the membership false reports or misrepresentations;

(f) working in the interests of or accepting membership in any organization dual to the International Union;

(g) Slandering or wilfully wronging a member of the International Union;

(j) using the name of the Local Union or the International Union for soliciting funds, advertising, etc., of any kind without the consent of the appropriate body or officer of the International Union;

(l) deliberately interfering with any official of the International Union in the discharge of his duties.

APPENDIX 17

L.U. 1208 TRIAL BOARD REPORT

On March 21, 1954, L.U. 1208 Trial Board submitted the following report.

"We the committee of three members only, find the defendant, Eugene V. Dennett guilty of imposing his political views in the mind of Rolland L. Gilland, and not working with the Local and International Union in harmony.

"In all the best interests of the Local we make the following recommendations.

I. That Eugene V. Dennett not be expelled from Local Union 1208, but to be removed from office. The committee recommends that the above recommendation be voted on by each and every member of Local Union 1208 by secret ballot so that each man can express his own views.

II. That this vote be not sooner than (7) days or later than three (3) weeks after the committee's findings have been read to the members of the union.

III. That the briefs of the case be available to all members of Local 1208, and that the members be allowed to read these files up to the time of the vote.

IV. We recommend that the following be written in as a By-Laws: 'That in all future charges the charges will be first presented to the Chairman of the Local, and he will in turn be required to present this to the first meeting of the Executive Board thereafter, and that the Executive Board shall be required to study said charges as to the validity and as to evidence presented. And in the event they do decide the charges are valid they shall then conform with the existing rules regarding trials under both the Constitution and By-Laws.' "

INDEX

259